Canada's Undeclared War

Fighting Words
From The Literary Trenches

Kenneth McGoogan

Detselig Enterprises Ltd.
Calgary, Alberta

Canadian Cataloguing in Publication Data
McGoogan, Kenneth, 1947-
   Canada's undeclared war

   Includes index.
   ISBN 1-55059-032-4

   1. Canada—Civilization—1945- 2. Canada—Politics
and government—1963-1984. 3. Canada—Politics and
government—1984- 4. Authors, Canadian—Political
and social views. I. Title.
FC95.4.M32 1991   971.06   C91-091337-4
F1021.2.M32 1991

Detselig Enterprises Limited
P.O. Box G 399
Calgary, Alberta T3A 2G3

Detselig Enterprises Ltd. appreciates the financial assistance for its 1991
publishing program from
Canada Council
Alberta Foundation for the Arts

Printed in Canada   SAN 115-0324   ISBN 1-55059-032-4

To Sheena
and my parents

Acknowledgments

My warmest thanks to those at the *Calgary Herald* who gave this project their blessing, particularly publisher Kevin Peterson and managing editor Crosbie Cotton. Thanks, also, to *Herald* editors, past and present, who encouraged my forays and expeditions: Alan Rach, John Howse, Susan Scott, Reg Vickers, Gillian Steward and (especially) Mark Tremblay. Thanks to the editors at *Books In Canada* and *Quill & Quire* who helped along the way, and to those individuals who took a special interest: Jack McClelland, George Melnyk and Leslie Chapman. Thanks, finally, to those who sustained me—to Sheena, my wife, and our astonishing children, Carlin and Keriann.

CONTENTS

Pearl Harbor, Alberta

A Quebec separatist inspired this militantly Canadian book. Not long ago he won a governor-general's award for a collection of essays that exploded in my mind like carpet bombs. In *La Petite Noirceur* (The Small Darkness), author Jean Larose declared that Canada disgusted him. He urged his readers to turn the name of this country into "a synonym for placid stupidity." He sneered at Canadians as vulgar and primitive, as lacking in culture, and ridiculed the overtures of Canadian nationalists: "Now ... they want us to join them, to aid them against American cultural imperialism! When they have nothing but their stupid mediocrity to offer us."

To the slow-motion details of this attack I will return. Monsieur Larose's book stunned me—not just in its irrational vehemence, but also in its ignorance of Canadian culture. As a journalist, I've been writing about that culture and its makers for over a decade, and *La Petite Noirceur* drove me to my files. Sure enough, there I found documentary evidence of the cultural vitality I knew to exist.

But surprise! I also discovered that for 10 years, without realizing it, I'd been covering an undeclared war. That war is raging in the minds and hearts of Canadians and on many fronts: French-English, Canadian-American, native-white, East-West. The theatre of operations includes the whole world of books.

Since 1980, I've earned my living as Books Editor and Literary Columnist at the *Calgary Herald*. As such I've interviewed scores of Canadian authors, some of them several times, as they've whistle-stopped through town: Robertson Davies, Margaret Atwood, Timothy Findley, Alice Munro, Mordecai Richler. Name a Canadian writer and probably we've talked for the record—a record which has also included, on a freelance basis, magazines like *Books In Canada* and *Quill & Quire*.

I paid special attention, of course, to what was happening in my back yard; and so I witnessed the taking of Wild Rose Country—not just the emergence of dozens of writers, but the development of a dynamic publishing industry and the founding of such revolutionary institutions (yes!) as the Writers' Guild of Alberta and the Alberta Foundation for the Literary Arts. Toronto's journalistic establishment found these victories impossible to credit—and to this, too, I will return.

The world outside Canada came to Wild Rose Country with the Olympic Literary Arts Festival of 1988. It came with the visit of South African novelist Andre Brink, an anti-apartheid Afrikaner. When such events didn't come to Calgary, the *Herald* was exemplary in allowing me to go to them—at least as far as Toronto and Vancouver, Montreal and Quebec City. I reported on Canada's first International PEN Congress and covered the historic Quebec City *rencontre* dedicated to Jack Kerouac. At Toronto's International Festival of Authors, I interviewed Salman Rushdie soon after he published *The Satanic Verses*.

Canada's Undeclared War does not purport to be a work of literature. It's not a critical study that seeks to establish the wisdom of its author, nor even a collection of wise and witty columns—though there are opinion pieces here, revised and updated, as well as features, open letters, hard news stories and profiles.

Canada's Undeclared War is rather a book-length dispatch from the literary front lines. It's a late-breaking bulletin that draws on eye-witness, as-it-happened reportage, an extended telegram from the trenches about the country's shock troops and the battles they're fighting. It's an exploration of the politics of Canadian culture that has, I hope, both a documentary value and a coherent subtext, and that comes out shouting: "Hey! There *is* a Canada worth defending!"

But flash back to August of 1980 and my first books column for the *Calgary Herald*. I reviewed the column's history, then noted:

> Whatever its title, this column, without being exclusive or chauvinistic, has always been unabashedly Canadian. In June, 1975, Margaret Laurence was quoted here: "Good Canadian books can give us a whole other dimension which literature of any other country can't give us." Robert Fulford made an appearance in July, 1976: "If someone hasn't read books of his own culture, he's deprived, and that's the way it was for a very long time in this country."

Finally, I quoted my immediate predecessor, Kevin Peterson, now publisher of the *Herald*: "It is boosterism no doubt, but if I didn't believe in the value of Canadian literature, I wouldn't write this column."

I closed by declaring, "To all that, amen."

Fast-forward ten years and across my desk comes this missive from Sault Ste. Marie, Ontario. But my open letter of July 14, 1990 tells the tale....

1. Open Letter To A Quebec Separatist

To: *Monsieur* Jean Larose,
Author of *La Petite Noirceur*.

Mon cher Monsieur Larose:

Not long ago I received a letter from the Sault Ste. Marie Association for the Preservation of English-Language Rights (SAPELR). That organization isn't happy, Monsieur Larose, about your having won a governor-general's award for *La Petite Noirceur*. Indeed, the good folks at SAPELR want the G-G rescinded and the $10,000 prize money returned. "Ernest Zundel was tried for writing hate literature," the association president writes, "but now we have here in Canada a Quebec author who is honored by being given the highest literary award for promoting hatred of Canada."

I would have tossed this letter into the wastebasket, Monsieur Larose, but it quoted several lines from your book. Like this one: "We must be ashamed of being Canadian; we must faithfully retain our hatred of Canada." And these: "Everything that weakens and humiliates Canada ... must make us rejoice.... Abroad, we must make the case against Canada every chance we get.... It is up to us to see that the word 'Canada' (what a sickening conglomeration of syllables, don't you think?) becomes in all countries a synonym for placid stupidity."

We're quoting here from a book that won Canada's top award for French language non-fiction. You'll understand, Monsieur Larose, that as Books Editor here I felt compelled to obtain *La Petite Noirceur* and read it in its entirety.

The good news is that I found much to admire. Lively, imagistic, original, provocative—your book is all of these. I enjoyed watching the way you handle the French language and appreciated your occasional aphorisms. "The authority of knowledge is acquired with difficulty and over a long period," you observe. "The authority of ignorance is obtained at a single stroke, by an arbitrary decision that gives one's lived experience the force of a special statute." Bravo!

I also have to admit, Monsieur Larose, that I found much in your book to dispute. For example, what are we to make of your astonishing assertion that, after the election of the Parti Quebecois in 1976, the French press became "objectively critical" while the English-language media assumed an attitude of combat?

Do I really have to remind you of the way the Francophone media handled the fire-bombing of the headquarters of Alliance Quebec, and of the smear campaign segments of it mounted against the president of that Anglophone lobby group? To their credit, even many Quebecois journalists protested.

Our differences intensify as we approach the heart of the so-called language issue. I take your philosophical point that the language we speak determines much about us—who we are, the way we think and feel, the institutions we set up and even the way we debate. Though Australians aren't Ghanaians, nor Frenchman Haitians. And the Quiet Revolution won't be complete until working-class Francophones realize that their middle-class leaders are locking them into a unilingual ghetto while ensuring (quite understandably) that their own children speak impeccable English.

To you, fiercely committed to a unilingual Quebec, the province's language legislation (Bill 101) is necessary but insufficient. True, it gives Anglophones an opportunity to "play the persecuted." But the main problem is that it tempts Francophones to dispense with the essential, which is "to speak French with such force, such assurance and even such aggressiveness that the (province's linguistic) norm changes language." As if that norm hadn't already changed!

To me that same legislation is repressive, totalitarian and xenophobic, its hidden aim being to drive 600,000 Anglophones out of Montreal, which for almost two centuries (moi aussi, je me souviens) was a predominantly English city. But you've long since stopped listening to this argument. "The government elected in Quebec by the French-speaking majority," you write, "does not oppress the English minority; it is neither totalitarian nor racist nor anti-semitic." Perhaps you protest too much?

Still, so far you remain civil. What prompted the missive from Sault Ste. Marie, Monsieur Larose, is the final section of your book—that letter to a Quebecoise friend in New York? I draw your attention to the several pages that begin with your allusion to "the disgust that Canadians inspire" in you.

"Canada, what a bore!" you declare. "One has to wonder whether it's not out of disgust that the Quebecois made so much noise from 1960 to 1980, out of repugnance, their latin-Iroquois blood being unable to resign itself to Canadian equanimity, which is really a mediocrity tempered by prudence and moderated by the fear of making a mistake."

You continue: "What we absolutely cannot excuse in Canada is its total lack of genius. What's unpardonable in Canadians is that they resemble us at our worst. They send us back a caricature of Quebecois impotence, but without savour, and in English!"

You recognize one exception, pianist Glenn Gould, then turn to Canadian nationalism, with its talk of "cultural sovereignty" and preserving "the national identity." "Don't laugh, they're serious," you write. "All the big questions that the Quebecois have debated for years, they all came to the surface in the discourse of Canadian ministers or in the pages of the *Globe And Mail*, but like a flock of ghosts without flesh, grey-green, insipid, reduced to a few vulgar traits.

"Yes, vulgar is the word that best describes Canadians who have discovered, like religious novices, the highway the Quebecois have been travelling for 20 years, and that finished for them in a cul-de-sac (mainly because of Canadian impediments). Now that they're on the same road, but without a speck of the poetry that gave the Quebecois movement its beauty and almost its truth, they want us to join them, to aid them against American cultural imperialism! When they have nothing but their stupid mediocrity to offer us! Vulgar, yes, vulgar and primitive Canadians!

"Now we see the 'openness of spirit' in the name of which they stifled the sovereignty movement, these people who daily demonstrate their complete immaturity regarding this question. Big dumb Canada, that never wanted to understand Quebec, that reduced it to its own level, integrated it into its mediocrity, and that would like now to nourish its identity on all that we have produced in the way of beautiful texts and songs during our revolt against it."

There's more, Monsieur Larose, culminating in your admonition to nurture a hatred toward Canada, a hatred "which may even be incomprehensible to these red-faces white with anger." There's more, but you'll understand that I'm tired of translating it.

Much of the above, even in the original French, is to me offensive. But in English it's more offensive still, and in fairness I'd like to quote South African novelist and translator Andre Brink, who has expressed amazement at the extent to which different languages carry different "loads" of emotional content. "Afrikaans, like French," he wrote, "appears to offer a much higher resistance to overstatement; it is much more at ease with superlatives and emotions. In English, the threshold of overstatement is reached much more rapidly; 'valid' emotionalism in Afrikaans soon becomes unbearable in English."

I'd like to note, as well, that your style generally is forceful, uninhibited, no-holds-barred. "The argument of Leandre Bergeron is incoherent," you write, "like his dictionary; his own desire is unknown to him and his purpose badly articulated." The television show "Chez Denise," you declare, "is a degrading spectacle. Degrading for those who watch it, a disgrace for those who make it and who are contemptuous of those who watch it."

Then there's the question of context, of when you were writing: pre-Meech Lake. Your fear was that Quebec was about to be integrated into Canada, in which case, you felt, writers would have no choice but to leave. Bleak, Monsieur Larose. Bleak.

But I must insist that your attitudes and opinions are not typical of Quebecois. You not only hate Trudeau and Chretien, but you wonder about Bourassa and worry that the Parti Quebecois is soft. You're an extremist intellectual, Monsieur Larose, contemptuous of the values shared by most

Canadians, both French and English-speaking. The reason Canada Day is so boring, you declare, is that "it expresses the pride of the petit-bourgeois admiring the fence around his bungalow."

A good line. But you fail to appreciate its implications: that because it threatens economic dislocation, Quebec independence is a non-starter. You see, Monsieur Larose, most Canadians—and here I include Quebecois—don't give a damn about intellectuals or constitutional lawyers. But threaten their standard of living and you've got serious trouble. Threaten to take away their cars and their houses in the suburbs and you've got trouble that will make the *War Measures Act* look like a get-well card.

The facts of Canadian life, Monsieur Larose, are the same in French or English. We export resources: oil from Alberta, timber from British Columbia, wheat from Saskatchewan, hydroelectric power from Quebec. In return, we get an almost-American standard of living. And with that arrangement most Canadians are well-satisfied, thank you very much.

But I'm not writing to talk economics. I'm writing because Quebec independence is a non-starter, whether you like it or not, and that means we have to keep talking. You've made assertions that I regard as irrational, irresponsible and deliberately offensive, and here I underline the adverb. You're committed to Quebec independence, and if that means fostering ugliness between language groups, you're prepared to foster away.

I decline to play your game.

You, Monsieur Larose, may be unreachable. Certainly your superciliousness and passionate contempt for all things Canadian, documented above, suggest that even post-Meech you won't mellow. Still, to the larger "you" I have this to say: when it comes to Canadian culture, you're stuck in the '50s.

That bit about Expo '86? A series of photos of Canada making you sick? Very cute. But suppose I visited Place Bonaventure around Christmas, checked out the annual arts-and-crafts show, turned up some pink flamingoes hand-crafted by some old apple-grower from Pointe Calumet and then held them up to ridicule: Ha ha ha! This is Quebec culture!

You'd think I'd gone nuts.

Literary Canadians, Monsieur Larose, know the work of Roch Carrier, Marie-Claire Blais, Jacques Ferron, Nicole Brossard, Jacques Godbout, Madeleine Gagnon, Victor Levy-Beaulieu, Gaston Miron, Jovette Marchessault, Michel Tremblay, Louky Bersianik, Andre Major, Dany Laferriere, Robert Lepage, Yves Beauchemin—and so on.

Unfortunately, literary Quebecois can make no similar counter-claim. I think of the prominent Quebecoise journalist who, on radio a couple of years back, said: "Margaret Laurence? Er, who is Margaret Laurence?"

Certainly your own ignorance of Canadian culture is evident in every line you write about it. While you've been gazing at your navel, Monsieur Larose, say for the past 30 years, the literary culture of "English Canada" has come of age and outstripped that of Quebec.

Yes, I put it to you that the literary culture of "English Canada" is more mature than that of French Quebec—more accomplished, more sophisticated and far, far more diverse. I realize that this notion will strike you as ludicrous and outlandish, so smug and self-righteous have you become in your Quebecitude. But I invite you to see for yourself.

I'm calling you out, Monsieur Larose, you and your intellectual friends at *Liberte* magazine. Somehow you found the time and space to explore popular TV programs like "Chez Denise," each of you tackling one and writing about it? I hereby publicly challenge you to do the same with contemporary Canadian fiction writers who work in English. Time to put up or shut up.

To basics, then. You've heard of Mordecai Richler and Margaret Atwood? Well, in addition to them, three Canadian fiction writers have achieved international reputations: Robertson Davies, Mavis Gallant and Alice Munro. Along with these five, and citing one book each for starters, I refer you to Jack Hodgins (*The Invention Of The World*), Timothy Findley (*Famous Last Words*), Janette Turner Hospital (*Borderline*), Michael Ondaatje (*Coming Through Slaughter*), Rudy Wiebe (*The Temptations Of Big Bear*), Leon Rooke (*Fat Woman*) and George Bowering (*Burning Water*).

Then there's Robert Kroetsch, Jane Rule, Austin Clarke, Keath Fraser, W.P. Kinsella, Katherine Govier, Neil Bissoondath, Aritha van Herk,

Rohinton Mistry, W.O. Mitchell, Merna Summers, Matt Cohen, Joan Clark, Robert Harlow, Andreas Schroeder, Brian Fawcett, Trevor Ferguson, Jane Urquhart, William Gibson, Richard Wright, Paul Quarrington, David Adams Richards, Heather Robertson, David Helwig, Guy Vanderhaeghe, Sandra Birdsell, Roy MacGregor, minimum three books each. You want 40 names? Give me a call.

Oh, and let's not forget John Metcalf (*General Ludd*). His elitist denunciation of Canadian culture is almost as savage as your own, Monsieur Larose, only he's informed. And with Metcalf—oh, delicious irony—we're dealing with a bonafide Anglo-Saxon immigrant, the otherwise mythical "English Canadian."

As for the burghers of Sault Ste. Marie, Monsieur Larose, what can I say? Personally, I'm glad you won the governor-general's award. If we don't know what our declared enemies are saying, how can we refute them? Keep your $10,000, Monsieur Larose. It's the Canadian thing to do.

***

Part One

The Battle For Canada

An undeclared war is raging in Canada. In one battle zone we find Jean Larose, sneering at Canadians as "primitive" and "vulgar." In another, the free-trade deal has left the unbowed Canadian rightly worried about waking up some morning to find himself an American. In a third battle zone, native peoples are insisting, even to barricades and road-blocks, that white mainstream society stop talking and start listening. East versus West. Censorship versus freedom of expression.

If this country ends with a whimper, it will be because English-speaking Canadians do not understand that culture is politics. And that we have here a culture—a way of thinking and being, a country-wide set of values and preoccupations—worth defending. At the heart of that culture is Canadian literature—the only literature that tells us who we are and what it means to be Canadian. Nothing new in this except urgency.

But see Pierre Berton striding into the *Calgary Herald* cafeteria for the first time. He is six-foot-four, white-haired, and sports an expensive suit and his trademark bow-tie. The man is instantly recognizable and every head turns. December, 1982. Berton was in Calgary to talk about *Why We Act Like Canadians: A Personal Exploration Of Our National Character*. What he said then is equally true today—that history and geography have combined to make Canadians unique even if they don't know it.

Why We Act Like Canadians consists of six linked essays written as if they were letters to an American friend named Sam. Hokey, perhaps, but Berton said he tried to write the book straight and couldn't, and that he felt the letter form took "the curse of pomposity" off it. The man's message? We're not Americans. Unlike the United States, Canada didn't separate violently from England. Americans stand for life, liberty and the pursuit of happiness; we've opted for peace, order and good government. They're romantic, idealistic; we're pragmatic, literal-minded. Canada's ethnic mix is unique, and her geography is that of survival. "It's not what people think about," Berton said, "but what seeps into their unconscious."

Regions and even cities have distinct personalities, but such differences are superficial. Canadians invariably have more in common with each other than they do with people of other nationalities. Well, not invariably. But usually. So Berton argued. Not convinced? Consider the words "Meech

Lake," "free trade" and "Oka." Literate Canadians won't agree on what they mean. But, because they belong to the same community, the same culture, they understand their significance. Imagine running the same words past John Updike or Gore Vidal or Toni Morrison, the blank stares you'd get. Fine writers, different culture.

Then there's what Peter C. Newman calls our company-town mentality. Flash forward to November, 1985, when Newman turned up in a beaver hat to promote *Company Of Adventurers*, his blockbuster history of the Hudson's Bay Company. Canada's company-town mentality is the great legacy of the HBC, Newman told me. "When you live in a company town, you defer to authority. That's what a company town is all about. The emphasis is on collective survival over individual excellence. That's why we're different from Americans. Their frontier was very different. Instead of deferring to authority, they were challenging it—vigilantes, outlaws."

Newman, author of 14 books, among them *Renegade In Power* and *The Canadian Establishment*, was consciously revising Northrop Frye's idea of the garrison mentality. The only problem with Frye's notion, he said, is there were few real garrisons. Company towns dependent on the HBC, however, dotted Canada in the 17th, 18th and 19th centuries. Even today there are 120 HBC forts scattered around the country. The attitudes fostered in these company towns, such as respect for order and deference to a colonial authority, shaped the Canadian psyche—and still color our behavior.

The dust jacket of *Company Of Adventurers* shows a painting of the Nonsuch, which in 1678 brought the first group of European fur traders to Hudson's Bay. "That's our version of the Mayflower," Newman declared. In the decades after it arrived, explorers such as Samuel Hearne and John Rae performed incredible feats, journeying thousands of miles across a frozen hell of tundra for the HBC. "Never mind Davy Crockett," Newman said. "Why don't we celebrate these people? There should be novels and feature films on these guys. What's the matter with us?"

✳ ✳ ✳

I

First Battle Zone:
Those Damn Yankees

Two great themes have dominated Canadian history. One of these is Canada's relationship with its next-door neighbor, the world's last remaining superpower. In the mid-'80s that relationship was the focus of the Not-So-Great Free-Trade Debate, which culminated in the re-election of Brian Mulroney and his say-goodbye-to-Canada Tory government. Most people believe that the subsequent ratification of the free-trade deal with the United States marked a turning point for this country. Some say the battle's not over.

Peter C. Newman, back in Calgary in 1988, predicted that the next federal election will hinge, like the last one, on the issue of free trade. Canada and the United States have until 1995 to agree on what constitutes a subsidy, Newman told me. "We're talking about medicare, family allowances—all the government funds transferred to us. And so far there is no agreement." Newman said American culture "is the most successful export commodity in the world. And that's fine. More power to them. But Canadian culture tells us who we are and why we're here. You can't bargain away a culture."

Nor can we understand where we're going until we understand where we've been. Flash back to January, 1986. That's when the free-trade fight erupted in Alberta, at an Edmonton symposium sponsored by provincial writers' and publishers' groups. Publisher Mel Hurtig shone during the pivotal panel discussion. He argued passionately that free trade was the first step in a process that would lead inevitably to a customs union, then to a common market, and eventually to a political union with the United States. "The debate is not about free trade," he insisted, "but about the destiny of this country. It's not good enough to get our own industries taken off the table. What's at stake here is our ability as Canadians to decide our own future."

Jim Edwards, a Conservative Member of Parliament who was then parliamentary secretary to Communications Minister Marcel Masse, said Hurtig's "slippery-slope" argument didn't prove that trade liberalization would necessarily lead to political integration. The debate was healthy, he said, and would enable Canadians to come to terms with themselves and shuck off the uncertainty in the Canadian psyche.

And so the debate was joined.

The symposium explored American encroachment on Canada's film and publishing industries. Film-maker Al Stein said that 97 percent of the profits from film distribution go to non-Canadians, mostly Americans. This country's film-makers therefore do not have the means to take their films to the Canadian public. "The same people make, distribute and exhibit films," he said, "and there aren't very many of them, and they aren't from Canada."

Susan Crean, a Toronto-based author and culture critic representing The Writers' Union of Canada, reviewed the takeover of Canada's Prentice-Hall Publishers by the American conglomerate Gulf & Western. Crean explained that Canadian government policy called for Gulf & Western to sell its newly acquired branch plant to Canadians at fair market value. This would have increased, for the first time in 20 years, Canadian ownership in the profitable area of educational publishing. The conglomerate's refusal to comply—and subsequent threat to adopt "a scorched-earth policy"— brought Canadian authors and journalists into the free-trade debate....

2. The Face In The Mirror

The suggestion that Canada's "identity" could be threatened by free trade with the United States baffles many intelligent, well-informed Canadians. But let's look at the proposed pact from the perspective of the Canadian book world.

Nobody with any sense would try to define the "Canadian identity." Not without countless qualifiers. But no definition is necessary. As individuals we know who we are because every time we look in a mirror we see the same face. As Canadians, our collective identity is reflected in our cultural products: films, paintings, plays and, of course, books.

With books we're talking, obviously, about literary works by such writers as Margaret Atwood, Robertson Davies, Alice Munro and the late Margaret Laurence, as well as W.O. Mitchell, Aritha van Herk, Samuel Selvon and Rudy Wiebe. We're talking also about non-fiction works by people like Pierre Berton, Peter C. Newman, Andy Russell, Myrna Kostash and Grant MacEwan.

These books tell us who we are. But where do they come from? Not long ago the federal government released a study called *Vital Links: Canadian Cultural Industries*, which described Canada's book market as "abnormal." It's not only small (19 million Anglophones) and widely scattered, but dominated by foreign (mostly American) books.

In 1984, Canada's total book market was $1.3 billion. But titles published in Canada—80 percent of them by Canadian authors—accounted for only 25 percent. Canadian firms published 78 percent of all Canadian-authored titles. Yet foreign firms, which produced 22 percent of Canadian books, earned 61 percent of total revenues.

True, 79 percent of Canadian publishers are based in Ontario and Quebec. But in 1984 the remaining 21 percent included 25 Alberta publishers who brought out 90 books and generated revenues of more than $7 million.

Enough fine print. Canada's book publishing industry is culturally vital, foreign-dominated and faces unique distribution problems. Successful Canadian publishers are essential to the existence of Canadian books, which in turn are fundamental to our cultural development—and indeed our identity as Canadians.

Canadian governments have recognized this, and have developed programs to keep the publishing industry alive. Federally, the Canada

Council distributes roughly $5 million a year to support cultural objectives in book publishing. The department of communications, under its Book Publishing Development Program, doles out almost $10 million annually.

Then there's the postal subsidy, which is being phased out: $60 million of $225 million in subsidies is applied toward the mailing of books. That money helps keep book prices the same in Alberta as in Ontario.

Most provincial governments also support publishing to some extent, and in Alberta we have had the Alberta Foundation for the Literary Arts, with over $1 million a year from lottery funds. Such programs are needed to keep Canadian publishing alive, so we Canadians can read Canadian books and continually rediscover and redefine our collective identity.

So what's the problem with free trade? It doesn't specifically threaten publishing programs. We'll still read Canadian books. We'll still have health care, welfare, unemployment insurance and pensions. Right?

Well, most people agree that the free-trade debate is really a debate about Canada's future. So let's look down the road. It's the year 2,000 and the trade deal has long since gone into effect. A Calgary-based company that makes widgets is competing toe to toe with a Denver firm that does the same. The two are equally efficient, their products identical. They do the same amount of business. But suddenly, the Denver company announces that it's expanding and the local outfit has no hope of doing the same.

What's gone wrong? A quick look at the ledger tells the story. The Denver company pays $100,000 a year in taxes, while the Calgary outfit dishes out $200,000. It doesn't take a genius to realize that the local firm is going to protest: "Hey! We want a level playing field! We want to pay the same taxes as the Americans!"

How long is it going to take that widget company—and other companies in a similar situation—to force both federal and provincial governments to reduce business taxes? Obviously, when governments cut taxes, they have to cut spending. Are they going to reduce social programs? The education budget? Bet your UIC payments they will. First, however, they'll reduce spending on culture (Canada Council? the CBC?), because that will cost them fewer votes.

The Americans don't have to drag book-publishing onto the bargaining table. All they have to do is wait. When the going gets tough, we Canadians will disconnect the support systems ourselves.

Then, as fewer and fewer Canadian books are published, the Canadian reading public will no longer be able to see its own reflection. Imagine looking into a mirror and seeing somebody else's face. Pretty soon, you'd begin to think you were that somebody else. And then, in fact, you would be.

3. The American Way

The Great American Novel. That's what, in June of 1981, a 43-year-old advertising man based in Los Angeles sat down to write. "Shoot for the top," Duane Unkefer told me. "Why not?"

By November 1984, when Unkefer finished his book, he'd "lost everything." One gets the impression that his house and two cars were the least of it. But then Unkefer received a $150,000 advance for his book—one of the largest ever given for a first novel. Yes, *Gray Eagles* has "commercial success" written all over it.

On one level, the novel is a superb adventure story—a contemporary American cross between Alistair MacLean's *Guns Of Navarone* and Len Deighton's *Bomber*. Two German fighter pilots, Luftwaffe veterans, decide to recreate the Second World War in microcosm—in 1976, in the United States. They turn up six comrades, restore eight Messerschmitt 109s, turn themselves into a "staffel" and start strafing airfields in Arizona. Their goal is to provoke "a fair fight" with U.S. veterans flying reconstructed American fighter planes—old P-51 Mustangs.

Unkefer makes it all plausible. And if the stakes aren't as high as in most thrillers—the existence of the free world is never threatened—his book is still compellingly readable, hard to put down. The novel's only fully-drawn woman, Marta, is caught in a love-triangle between her husband (the staffel's mechanic) and one of the German pilots. This makes for enough kinky sex to satisfy the requirements of genre.

But *Gray Eagles* is most interesting for how it transcends genre. Some readers have hailed it as an anti-war novel, but this, I think, is a misreading. Challenged, Unkefer shrugs his shoulders, non-committal. Marta does give voice to an anti-war perspective, repeatedly urging the pilots to give up their mad schemes, which she says will only get them killed.

Trouble is, Marta is sexually "turned on" by these obsessive madmen, by their violence and firepower; and when, to prove it, her husband rapes her in the hangar, among the Messerschmitts, she enjoys it despite herself. Her actions repudiate her words.

Gray Eagles is neither pro- nor anti-war. But it is jubilantly pro-military. And this Unkefer reiterates: "Let's respect the military, God bless 'em—and be glad they're really good."

This brings us back to the author's original ambition, and to the best reason of all for reading this novel: for what it shows us—not only in itself, but as a spectacular success—about the United States. *Gray Eagles* is a celebration of macho. Even a half-wit hippy character, a throwback to the '60s, wants to hear it spoken aloud: "We have more, we have bigger, we have better."

Unkefer describes *Gray Eagles* as "patriotic." A non-American might use the word "nationalistic" and find the book scary—all the more because its author is personable, courageous, even inspiring. We have here an interpretation of the Second World War. The Americans won it single-handed, don't you know? Not because they had better pilots than the Germans (wonderfully impressive tough guys), but because they had more firepower, better hardware. More, better, bigger.

The British had a token role in victory—represented here by a gutsy but badly battered Spitfire pilot. As for Australians or Canadians, well, in this microcosm they don't exist. *Gray Eagles* shows us, with unusual clarity, far more than its author intended. It may not be a great novel. But it's unmistakably American.

4. If You Love This Country

So Canada and the United States signed a free-trade agreement that took effect in 1989. Countries make business deals all the time. Why the fuss? Anybody who wants an answer to that question should check out *If You Love This Country: Facts And Feelings On Free Trade.* It's assembled by Laurier LaPierre and published by McClelland & Stewart.

This 258-page paperback contains essays by 47 prominent Canadians—economists, industrialists, academics and authors. Among them are such luminaries as Margaret Atwood, Pierre Berton, Peter C. Newman, Alan Fotheringham, Bob White and Jack McClelland. Some of these pieces offer more passion than analysis and others are too strident to be useful. But the book contains at least two dozen informed, thoughtful and cogent essays that analyze the agreement and find it wanting.

Taken together, these pieces create, if not a painting, at least a mosaic of opposition whose features include the following arguments:

— Perhaps most surprisingly, the agreement will not significantly increase Canadian access to the American market. Roughly 70 percent of Canada's exports now enter the United States duty free, and fully 96 percent enter at a token duty of five percent or less. Canada's aim was to solve the problem of countervailing duties, which are retaliatory legal barriers used by U.S. firms to hamper foreign competitors. The vaunted "disputes mechanism" does not remove these barriers. It merely gives Canada the right to challenge, after Americans have imposed a counter-vailing duty, whether they have "faithfully and correctly applied" their own laws.

— Canada could get a better, more neutral system of settling trade disputes by working through GATT (General Agreement on Trades and Tariffs), an international organization largely responsible for reducing tariffs to current levels. Canada should be seeking global, not continental, cooperation. Diplomat George Ignatieff writes: "What we have here is continentalist and addressed primarily to American trading interests."

— The free-trade debate is not only about the agreement, but also about its consequences. It means accepting, eventually, the social standards of a country that has not yet introduced universal medicare, and whose social programs rank last among those of industrial countries.

— The U.S. economy will not continue to perform as it has during the past five years. Peter C. Newman, for example, bases his opposition to the agreement on the "avalanche-like decline" of the American economy. He predicts draconian measures ahead. This is the wrong time for Canada to move closer to the United States.

— The so-called exemption to the cultural industries is a disaster. The agreement narrowly defines culture for Canadians. It implicitly denies culture is a mindset that includes federally regulated banks, publicly funded universities, mandatory auto insurance, firearm regulations, environmental protection legislation and regional support programs.

Canada concedes in advance the validity of U.S. counter-attacks against cultural policies: "You Canadians are going to subsidize the distribution of Canadian films? Very well, we're going to slap a countervailing duty on grain products."

Rick Salutin argues that free-traders have revealed their real agenda in the area of culture: "Reaganism, absorption into the ways, and means, of the American marketplace." Free-traders want "a new kind of Canada, one which looks exactly like the United States."

— The chief proponents of this deal are large Canadian companies and even larger multinational corporations. But most jobs in this country are created by small companies (20 or fewer employees). Between 1978 and 1984, Mel Hurtig writes, small Canadian firms created 819,000 (over 93 percent of the total), while large Canadian firms actually reduced the number of jobs by 31,900.

— By allowing the United States unrestricted access to this country's oil and gas, Canada is giving up control over energy pricing and supply, which are integral to Canadian sovereignty. In this connection, Joseph A. Mercier, who ranches southwest of Calgary and is president of an energy company, has written what is probably the most courageous article in the book. He argues that Americans will buy Canadian oil and gas with or without an agreement, and that the National Energy Board is neutered by the treaty while its American counterpart remains untouched. "The voice of the oil industry is an American voice," he writes, "and it strongly supports the free trade agreement." For most of the oil patch, Mercier declares, "keeping Ontario hands off Alberta resources is the goal and free trade is the means to achieve it."

— The free trade agreement is not a politically neutral document. It's not solely about securing access to the American economy, but also about "deregulating" Canada, or diminishing the role of the state in Canadian life. It implies a laissez-faire view of society and will restrict our options in future.

There's more, much more—like this deservedly famous statement by Brian Mulroney, made in 1983: "Don't talk to me about free trade. That issue was decided in 1911. Free trade is a danger to Canadian sovereignty. You'll hear no more of it from me."

This book makes clear that, for opponents of the agreement, the question is this: "Are we going to keep alive the idea of Canada, which means living in and developing an independent country as a viable alternative to the United States in North America? Or are we going to succumb to 'manifest destiny' and start down the road to becoming Americans?"

* * *

II

Canada's Volunteer Army

Canada has an army of writers at war in the English language. They volunteered, as Mordecai Richler is fond of observing. They weren't drafted. And they're always at war because they're creating culture—order out of chaos, community out of estrangement. The non-fiction writers are at war on specific issues: free trade or abortion or the meaning of romance. The fiction writers are at war in the realm of moral values, because their characters make choices whose consequences reflect judgments.

I've been lucky enough to spend a decade in the trenches with Canada's writers, taking snapshots as they stormed barricades and over-ran fortifications. Some of my photos turned out well; others are blurred or badly exposed. I'd like to retake certain shots, try different angles, different settings. In some cases, I wish I'd been closer to my subject; in others that I'd kept my camera straps out of the way. Too late!

Non-fiction writers Pierre Berton, Peter C. Newman and Susan Crean have made brief appearances here, and others will do the same. But not in representative numbers. And there's a battalion of poets who will never forgive me because, in celebrating Canada's literary warriors, I've chosen to focus on fiction writers. An arbitrary decision, but I had to make some such. At least I know what I've done!

Fiction writers from Alberta I've treated separately in "Part II: The Taking Of Wild Rose Country," though many have fought in The Battle For Canada. Other outstanding authors are also absent—Robert Kroetsch, Michael Ondaatje, Jack Hodgins, Heather Robertson, Matt Cohen, Sandra Birdsell, Guy Vanderhaeghe, Constance Beresford-Howe, Graeme Gibson, Susan Swan, Keith Maillard, George Payerle, Carol Shields, Norman Levine, add your own names. Of those who *are* here, many deserve fuller treatment. This album is neither exhaustive nor balanced. It contains no studio portraits, just snapshots—photos of writers in action.

5. Mordecai Richler: Solomon Gursky Was Everywhere

In 1990, Mordecai Richler published Broadsides: Reviews And Opinions, *his fourth book of essays and ruminations. Richler also received international recognition for his 1989 novel,* Solomon Gursky Was Here, *which won the $20,000 Commonwealth Writers Prize as the year's best work of fiction. As well,* Solomon Gursky *won the 1990 QSPELL Prize from the Quebec Society for the Promotion of English-Language Literature, and made the shortlist for Great Britain's prestigious Booker Prize. Earlier in the year, the novel became the focus of a quintessentially Canadian controversy when judges omitted it from the three-book shortlist for the governor-general's award.*

For me, Solomon Gursky *was a superb work, a rowdy, roistering tour de force, Richler the Irreverent at the height of his powers—the literary event of the year. The biggest bad boy in Canadian literature had outdone himself. He'd taken his trademark juggling of time-lines (begun in* St. Urbain's Horseman) *as far as it could go, if only because the technique makes such demands on the reader.*

Solomon Gursky *opens in 1851, jumps to 1983, then bounces around between the early 1800s and the 1980s, with major focuses on 1906, 1917-19, the 1930s, the 1940s, 1956, 1968 and 1973. Here we find no unity of Time, of Place or even of Voice. The action moves from Montreal and the eastern townships of Quebec to London, Yellowknife, the Arctic barrens, the Saskatchewan prairies and the foothills of the Rockies. And certain major characters are dead before others are born.*

Richler holds this wildly diverse book together through the muted quest of one Moses Berger, who in 1983 is a failed writer, a self-described "degenerate drunk and cuckold." Moses is obsessed with finding out the whole truth about the Gurskys, an obscenely rich Montreal family headed by three brothers who made their fortune as prairie bootleggers during Prohibition.

One of the novel's surprises is an extended focus on the Franklin expedition, that uniquely Canadian obsession. Richler, who touched briefly on "Eskimos" and Arctic cannibalism in The Incomparable Atuk, *has always styled himself an internationalist and avoided Canadian themes. In* Solomon Gursky, *he treats even the Canadian West, drawing heavily, he acknowledges in a brief afterward, on the work of Calgary author James Gray. Is Richler mellowing? Not really. Just doing what his subject matter dictates—continuing to write what he knows, but remembering less and researching more.*

The usual sardonic asides are present. One begins, "Canada is not so much a country as a holding tank filled with the disgruntled progeny of defeated peoples." My own favorite alludes to a Quebec artist's suicide which "led in 1970 to a seminal essay by a Parti Quebecois metaphysician ... in which it was charged that the painter had been murdered by anglophone indifference, which would be the lot of all Quebecois artists, the white niggers of North America, until they were free to paint in their own language."

VANCOUVER—A white shirt and tie have replaced the open-necked blue shirt, and baggy brown corduroys the baggy blue ones he wore this afternoon. But the tweedy blue jacket is the same, and the disheveled, almost professorial aspect, and as Mordecai Richler fiddles with a recalcitrant microphone in front of 400 people at the Arts Club Theatre, I think again of how earlier he laughed guiltily, like a boy caught out in a prank, then peered over his reading glasses and declared: "I don't know what you're talking about."

I'd just reminded him of how, 15 years before, at the movie premiere of *The Apprenticeship Of Duddy Kravitz,* the wife of the late Samuel Bronfman congratulated him: "Well," she said, "you've come a long way for a St. Urbain Street boy." To which the author replied, alluding to the financial empire Bronfman had built from a family liquor business: "And you've come a long way for a bootlegger's wife."

If this is difficult and convoluted, so it should be: welcome to the world of Mordecai Richler, everybody's favorite Jewish anti-semite and Canadian anti-nationalist, master of the devastating put-down—maybe he has his reasons?—and famously loving father of five, a man whose contradictions and complexities are reflected most clearly in his celebrated fiction. Richler has just published his ninth novel, *Solomon Gursky Was Here*, and is on stage to give the Duthie Lecture at the Vancouver International Writers' Festival.

For the occasion the author has dusted off a speech made up of bits and pieces from various essays he has written over the years, mostly tracing his development as a writer, but with plenty of funny asides and more than a few barbs aimed at old favorite targets—can't have folks thinking he's mellowed. It's the same speech Richler has just delivered in Saskatoon to the Saskatchewan Writers' Guild, but how many party pieces can a serious writer be expected to have? Anyway, who cares? It's not as if he's playing to the same audience.

And few people are aware—it's nowhere, for example, in the inch-thick Richler file at the *Calgary Herald*—that the seminal novel for this not-always-nice Jewish boy was an anti-war classic written by a German: Erich Maria Remarque's *All Quiet On The Western Front*. Richler discovered the work by accident in 1944 at the age of 13, when he was home sick in bed, his room festooned with maps tracing the progress of the Allied campaign in Europe: "I never expected that a mere novel, a stranger's tale, could actually be so dangerous, creating such turbulence in my life, and obliging me to question so many received ideas."

Having learned that "Hitler burned books," Richler said, "I began to devour them. And through them, I grasped that I didn't live in the centre of the universe after all, but in a working class family in a country far from the centres of light: London, Paris and New York." At age 19, in second year at Sir George Williams University, now half of Concordia, Richler told a guidance counsellor that he wanted to become a writer. The man tested him, then suggested that he consider another line of work. "I thanked him and left for Paris."

Richler published his first novel, *The Acrobats*, while in his early 20s: "I've cleverly kept it out of print since." Then came *A Choice Of Enemies*, *Son Of A Smaller Hero*, and, in 1959, the novel "in which I found my voice"—*The Apprenticeship Of Duddy Kravitz*. By now Richler was living in England—he eventually stayed 20 years—and earning a living by writing screenplays, having begun in 1956 with *Room At The Top.* The rest, as they say, is history.

Before departing the Arts Club stage, Richler takes the usual shots at a straw man, in this case an obviously fictional friend named Harry who teaches creative writing at an obscure university in Nova Scotia. "We hear a lot about unjustly neglected writers," Richler says, "but perhaps not enough about those who are justly neglected." This leads neatly to his finale, a declaration of contempt for failed writers who wallow in self-pity: "We weren't drafted, we volunteered," he says. "And, even as I suspected in high school, you do set your own hours. You can go fishing when you feel like it. My father, a failed scrap dealer, worked a lot harder than I do and with far fewer satisfactions. On bad days, it's good to remember that."

Earlier, in the lobby lounge of the Hotel Vancouver, while knocking back two espressos and double scotches, Richler has been relaxed and forthcoming. Remember the furore in 1985 when, in an article on Wayne Gretzky in *The New York Times,* the author described Edmonton as "not so much a city as a jumble of a used-building lot?" He suggested that if Canada were a house, Vancouver would be the solarium-cum-playroom, Toronto the counting house, Montreal the salon and Edmonton the boiler room. "The uproar amazed me," Richler says. "I just never anticipated anything like that." The article also celebrated the civility of Westerners, he says, and noted that the West has been badly used by the East. "But I did describe Edmonton as I saw it," he admits—and paid for it by being on the wrong end of a torrent of abusive phone calls and letters.

Ask Richler about his children—they range in age from 21 to 31—and he lights up. Daniel, the oldest, will publish a first novel in the spring of 1991, and another son is in England, working on newspapers and magazines: "We're a dangerous family." Richler's wife, Florence, is travelling with the writer, though I don't meet her until later, and then it's briefly and in public: an attractive, gracious woman who retains a trace of the accent she picked up in England.

These days the author and his wife live, along with their youngest daughter, in a comfortable house on a lake in the Eastern Townships. They spend one month a year in England, and keep an apartment in downtown Montreal. Richler never regrets having returned to Montreal in 1972, though he is far from happy with the drift of language legislation. Twelve years ago, soon after the Parti Quebecois government introduced Bill 101, Richler wrote: "A bill to certify the supremacy of French here is one thing; but it is something else again to agree that the existence of a thriving English-speaking minority is a menace to the very survival of the French language and culture in Quebec." He also suggested that the Quebecois will be "held back by nationalism as they once were by a church-dominated school system."

The more recent Bill 178 is just more of the same. Having decided eons ago that ridicule is the best revenge, Richler notes: "It's a comic situation—grown men out there measuring letters on signs. You describe that outside the country, people burst out laughing. It's difficult to be angry, it's so ludicrous."

But keep prodding and what, if not anger, is this? "My language is forbidden to be seen in public places. The Supreme Court has said my rights were abrogated. And we've got a federal government doing nothing about it."

Solomon Gursky has been kicking around for years, Richler says. "I made several false starts. Then, three years ago, I moved to the country with my wife determined to stay until I finished." He'd set out "to put more demands" on himself, but the novel was also harder to write than others because he had to create so much from research. "Nineteenth-century London—those parts were difficult. I really had to imagine those characters, while at the same time putting my own spin on the material."

Richler has often said that he never knows what's going to happen when he sits down to write a novel, but the Franklin expedition? "That surprised me, too." Richler had visited Yellowknife for the first time in 1975, and returned four or five times. "I adored it. It was like travelling to a foreign country. I started reading about it, and found such rich material."

Another surprise that "just sort of happened and then grew" into a recurring image was the trickster raven. At one point in the novel, Moses, the author's surrogate, learns that although the raven stole the light of the world and scattered it throughout the skies, "his other appetites—lust, curiosity, and the unquenchable itch to meddle and provoke things, to play tricks on the world and its creatures—these remained unsatisfied." Richler the trickster raven? The old master grins, knocks back the last of his scotch, shoves his hands into the pockets of his sports jacket and is gone—gone with a sound like the beating of wings.

6. Robertson Davies: The Rear Guard Takes The Fort

In the fall of 1991, Robertson Davies will publish a novel called Unauthorized Translation. *It's billed as "a sweeping account of a Canadian family that ranges from Loyalists escaping the American Revolution through the generations to the present day." A conventional, multi-generational saga? With Davies, probably not. Nor will the novel be avant-garde.*

"I won't be bound by the latest models in writing fiction," he told me once, "many of which are restrictive and diminishing." It was 1988 and I was prodding him for a reaction to postmodernism. "The avant-garde is a lost cause," he said. "Militarily, its role is to go in and get killed." He leaned back, crossed his arms and smiled wickedly. "The rear guard comes and takes the fort." But that was the second time I interviewed him....

Celebrating Canada's introversion

"Canadians should wake up to the fact that the rest of the world is enormously interested in our literature," Robertson Davies declared in 1985. "I just got back from three weeks in Italy, where 20 universities are offering courses in Canadian literature. A year ago I was at a conference in Vienna, and centres of Canadian studies were there from 40 European universities—none from England.

"There are only two centres in England because they (the English) don't really care about us. But on the continent, they do. And we're very big in South America. It's time Canadians realized that we're making a place for ourselves in the world—not only in economics and politics, but as a literary force."

Davies, with more than 30 books and countless honors behind him, is one of Canada's most distinguished men of letters. He was in Calgary to promote two new books: *What's Bred In The Bone* and *The Papers Of Samuel Marchbanks*. But he happily discussed everything from how he develops his novels to the theories of analytical psychologist Carl Jung and the role of Canadian writers on the world stage.

Canada is an introverted country which lives next door to the most extroverted country in the world, Davies said. "Ours isn't a country you love; it's a country you worry about. We're a very northerly people, like Scandinavians or Russians, but we're not European—we're North American." Davies pointed to the influence on European literature of such writers as Henrik Ibsen, August Strindberg, Fyodor Dostoevsky, Leo Tolstoy and Ivan Turgenev. Canadian writers, he said, play a similar role in North America: "We're the northern conscience of the western world. It's not a role we assume; it's a role we have."

Not so long ago, Davies said, a bestselling novel would sell 5,000 copies in Canada. Now, in hard cover, it will sell "four or five times that." *What's Bred In The Bone* should exceed the 100,000 mark in this country, he said, including paperback sales. But to reach that figure "you've got to have a book that's not dead in six months."

Detractors claim that Davies is old-fashioned and didactic. But the novels of Joseph Conrad "are still read with enormous pleasure," he said—partly because they're written in "a mandarin English" which is classical, always grammatical. "The quickest way to make yourself old-fashioned is to try to be too contemporary," Davies said. As examples of novels which have aged badly he cited *What Makes Sammy Run* by Budd Schulberg and *Naked Lunch* by William Burroughs.

To the charge that his fiction is polemical, Davies said: "There's a prejudice in Canada against any novel which contains ideas." But such writers as Thomas Mann, Aldous Huxley and Graham Greene are "extremely polemical." In Canada, we have Rudy Wiebe's novels, which are both didactic "and very fine." Davies said he could "hardly think of a novelist of real quality" who doesn't explore ideas.

The avant-garde is a lost cause

With *The Lyre Of Orpheus*, the final volume in his "Cornish trilogy," novelist Robertson Davies laid to rest a ghost that had haunted him for 30 years. Davies told me that the trilogy, which includes *Rebel Angels* and *What's Bred In The Bone*, had its genesis in the real-life suicide during the 1950s of a close friend.

Once a brilliant fellow student at Upper Canada College, a private boys' school in Ontario, the man had "a very difficult career," Davies said. He ended his life as a monk, but only after he'd indulged in every imaginable depravity from "real rough-trade" homosexuality to drugs, booze, cheating and swindling.

Before killing himself, he poured his heart and soul into a novel which he thought "utterly magnificent," Davies said. He killed himself hoping that his death would draw attention to this work, which was unreadable —"it wasn't worth a damn"—and which he left to Davies.

Readers of *Rebel Angels* or *What's Bred In The Bone*, the first two novels in the trilogy, will have recognized the fictional John Parlabane, whose bastard son surfaces to provide comic relief in *The Lyre Of Orpheus*.

When considering a work of art, Davies said in a wide-ranging interview, people should look carefully at what goes into it: "It's not just the Sunday school stuff they think it is."

Davies, born in 1913 in Thamesville, Ontario, began writing at the age of 11. He attended Queen's University in Kingston, Ontario, and Balliol College, Oxford, where he took his degree in 1938. He joined the Old Vic theatre company, where he acted bit parts and taught theatre history. Back in Canada, he became literary editor of *Saturday Night* magazine, and later editor and publisher of *The Peterborough Examiner*.

While writing a weekly column under the name Samuel Marchbanks, Davies played an important role in the development of Canadian drama.

But neither his journalism nor his plays were as important as his fiction, which includes the acclaimed "Deptford Trilogy" (*Fifth Business, The Manticore* and *World Of Wonders*) published in the 1970s.

In 1986, with *What's Bred In The Bone*, Davies came within a whisker of winning Britain's prestigious Booker Prize. World-famous author Anthony Burgess has suggested that Davies deserves the Nobel Prize for literature.

The Lyre Of Orpheus, a review of which could easily fill several pages, is a complex, erudite and remarkably rich work. It teaches volumes about music, opera, stage craft, the Tarot, the Arthurian legends and what it means to be Canadian while exploring the inseparability of art and illusion, deception and ambiguity.

Besides the ghost of Parlabane, we find here Simon Darcourt, Maria Cornish, Clement Hollier and Penny Raven, entertaining old familiars haunting their usual academic habitats. And we meet such newcomers as Gunilla Dahl-Soot, a hard-drinking, lesbian doctor of music, and an insufferable student genius called Schnak.

The Cornish Foundation, run by Maria's husband Arthur Cornish, undertakes to support Schnak in finishing an opera by the Romantic German composer E.T.A Hoffman, and then to mount it: Arthur of Britain, or The Magnanimous Cuckold. As it turns out, contemporary life parallels the Arthurian legend, which serves as the book's controlling metaphor.

Late in the book, Davies has Darcourt quote the poet John Keats: "A man's life of any worth is a continual allegory." He elaborates by suggesting that "a man's life has a buried myth." This idea, rooted in Carl Jung's concept of the archetype, informs this latest novel, and indeed the whole "Cornish Trilogy."

Its development distinguishes Davies' work. But the author declined "to press too hard on it" because "people misapply this idea to everything and then are disappointed when it doesn't work."

Elsewhere in *The Lyre Of Orpheus*, the dead artist Francis Cornish, a pivotal figure in the trilogy, is described as having "dared to be of a time not his own." Davies, who has sometimes been criticized as old-fashioned, said he does not see himself as a literary Francis Cornish.

"But I won't be bound by the latest models in writing fiction, many of which are restrictive and diminishing. The avant-garde is a lost cause. Militarily, its role is to go in and get killed. The rear guard comes and takes the fort."

Davies noted that in his early novel *A Mixture Of Frailties,* he used ground-breaking contrapuntal effects. And in *The Manticore,* he employed Jungian analysis to explore, not the life of the analysand, but of the man's father—another original contribution.

In the "Cornish Trilogy," which on the surface is a middle-class Victorian three-decker, we find talking angels and a dead composer who speaks from Limbo. These are devices, Davies said, "from which Victorians would have shrunk." By giving voice to "creatures that don't exist in time," Davies adds dimension to his work, linking it with both past and future: "The idea is to explore the theme as widely as possible."

What's more, the myth of King Arthur and the Round Table plays a role in *The Lyre Of Orpheus* very like that of the wandering Greek in Joyce's classic novel *Ulysses*—surely as resolutely modern a work as has ever been written.

In this new novel, Davies has much to say about Canadians, the most worldly of whom shrink from "any imputation of high motives" and wear "greyness as a protective outer garment." At one point, Darcourt describes the life of Francis Cornish as a great adventure—"and a very Canadian sort of adventure."

Davies suggested that Canada could be a leader in the grand adventure of the next millennium, which will be an inward journey, not an outward one. "It will mark as great a turning point in the history of man as when language began."

Because Canada is an introverted nation, one uninhibited by a weighty intellectual past, "we can get on in this tremendous venture relatively unencumbered. But we'll do it by going in, not out."

7. Margaret Atwood: Who Does What To Whom?

Margaret Atwood is probably Canada's most famous fiction writer. Her last two novels, The Handmaid's Tale *and* Cat's Eye, *made the shortlist for Britain's prestigious Booker Prize.* The Handmaid's Tale, *which won Atwood her second governor-general's award, became a hit film in 1990 with a screenplay by Harold Pinter. Atwood herself has contracted to write the screenplay for* Cat's Eye, *which won several awards and prompted the Canadian Authors' Association to make her author of the year in 1989.*

Atwood has visited Calgary many times. The first time I interviewed her—over lunch at the Conservatory, all whispering waiters and white linen table-cloths—I brought a tape recorder so I could eat without scribbling notes. Atwood was then chair of the Writers' Union of Canada and I arrived with specific questions. She provided countless facts and figures, all from memory—an impressive performance.

When I arrived back at the office, buzzing and pleased with myself, I discovered that, though the little red light had been gleaming all the while, my tape recorder had picked up nothing. Zero. Once I'd digested this— colleagues say you could hear me groaning three floors away—I sat down and did what I could. The next time I ran into Atwood, fearing that she might have seen a clipping, I tried to explain, shame-faced as any guilty 10-year-old. She smiled that enigmatic smile. Probably had no idea what I was talking about.

Lunching with Peggy

Her enemies says she's a man-hater. But as I waited outside the restaurant for Margaret Atwood to arrive, I wondered. I'd met her five years before, at a party in Vancouver, and she'd seemed very nice.

"You hardly talked to her," a voice said. "What you know best, she knows better. She'll chew you up like an after-dinner mint."

"Her friends call her Peggy," I retorted. But here, before I could elaborate, in a long black cloak, flushed and beautiful, she stood.

If she hated me on sight, she hid it. "You look older," she said.

"Suffering will do that to you," I replied, or should have.

Together we entered the restaurant.

Atwood was in Calgary to promote her fourth novel, *Bodily Harm*. It's about a trendy Toronto journalist named Rennie Wilford who undergoes a partial mastectomy, splits from her live-in lover and flees to the West Indies, looking for fun in the sun. She's sucked into a political maelstrom, ends up in a dank prison cell and sees a woman friend beaten to death.

The book has received mixed reviews. Its author has been accused of self-indulgence, of "cluttering the text with clever one-liners and overwritten explanations of the obvious," and of shifting unnecessarily between first and third-person narration.

Bodily Harm has also been described as Atwood's "most satisfying novel yet," as a strong book sparkling with brilliant metaphors and images, and as a work that impresses "by the sheer virtuosity and skill" of its writing.

Myself, I think *Bodily Harm*, though flawed, is Atwood's best novel yet. It has a political dimension, I suggest as we eat, that's new to her work.

Politics, Atwood says, "is who does what to whom. All my novels have been political. This time it's more overt, that's all."

Bodily Harm is less contrived, I suggest, than *Life Before Man*. "Is *The Sound And The Fury* contrived?" she asks. "Don't you mean more accessible?"

And so it goes. I find myself reveling in the thrust and parry. "When you began the novel," I say, "what did you have? What did you start with?"

"What do you think?"

"The character Rennie," I say. "You've belonged to Amnesty International since the early '70s. You've taken some real cases from their newsletters, mixed and matched. How does that sound?"

"It sounds like me talking about Faulkner before I visited Oxford, Mississippi." She puts on a southern accent: "My deah, he didn't make up a thing." She points. "Theah's the fence Benji ran along?"

We both laugh, sip our wine. Not beautiful, exactly. Just very attractive.

To the charge that *Bodily Harm* contains "unnecessary" shifts in points of view, Atwood answers that the book has four time-lines. She demonstrates by laying out her cutlery on the table, the shifts help orient the reader in time.

To the claim that the novel is bleak, pessimistic, she replies that Canadians prefer to believe that the world outside is a rose garden, that cancer and torture don't exist except as projections of an author's inner reality.

We come to The Big Box. In *Bodily Harm*, Rennie picks it up and delivers it, machine-gun and all, thereby making credible her later arrest—except that virtually nobody, myself included—can believe Rennie is that naive.

But even here, and she makes it admirable, Atwood refuses to back down. Rennie thinks the box contains dope. She's drunk when she agrees to fetch it. Then there's her rural Ontario background: She's said she'll do it, and so she does it. "She's prepared for X and Y, but not for Z."

I'm not convinced. Atwood knows it. I know she knows it. She knows I know she knows it. And so again we laugh.

But we've been here an hour and a half. I'm astonished. Atwood says, "Time flies when you're having a good time."

I get her cloak: "Such refreshing immodesty."

"Wait!" It's that voice again. "What did you eat?"

Let's see. I had clam chowder, lamb chops and black forest cake. She had salad, roast beef—"In Calgary I feel I should have beef"—and custard pie. We each drank a glass of red wine, and I had coffee.

"So what's she like?"

Well, the epigraph to *Bodily Harm* is from John Berger: "A man's presence suggests what he is capable of doing to you or for you. By contrast, a woman's presence ... defines what can or cannot be done to her."

Margaret Atwood has a lot of presence.

"Yes, but what's she really like."

She's ironic about herself, about her image: "I've got clairvoyant blue eyes, you know."

"More!"

She laughed at my jokes.

"More! More! Tell us more!"

It must be nice to call her Peggy.

The Handmaid's Tale

Call it "a feminist *1984*" and Margaret Atwood won't argue. But she describes the novel as "a female *Clockwork Orange*." *The Handmaid's Tale* is "not science fiction in the usual sense," Atwood said. "It doesn't have spaceships or trips to Mars. But it is speculative fiction."

Like *Brave New World* by Aldous Huxley or *Woman On The Edge Of Time* by Marge Piercy, it belongs "to a long tradition of utopias—although in the 20th century, the vision is much bleaker and utopias have become dystopias."

While writing *The Handmaid's Tale*, Atwood was "very conscious" of this tradition, which began in the 16th century with Sir Thomas More's *Utopia* and includes Samuel Butler's classic *Erewhon*.

During the 1960s, when she was a graduate student at Harvard, Atwood studied the 19th century intensely "and a lot of utopias were written then."

Born in 1939, Atwood is widely regarded as the pre-eminent Canadian author of her generation. She has published fiction, criticism and poetry, and her works include *The Edible Woman*, Power Politics, *Surfacing, Survival, Lady Oracle, Life Before Man* and *Bodily Harm*.

Has her work become increasingly political?

Atwood resists the idea. She long ago defined politics as "who does what to whom"—that definition appears again in *The Handmaid's Tale*—and insists that all her works are political. "*Survival* was a very political book," she said in a telephone interview from Toronto. "But so was *Edible Woman*. It all depends on your focus."

"It isn't true that the novel is not a political form," she said. The genre "has gone through occasional periods of privatism, but it has also been used throughout the ages for social comment."

To an Irishman, even the supremely detached James Joyce was political, Atwood said. And British novelist D.H. Lawrence, the high priest of love, was "very class-oriented."

In Canada, Rudy Wiebe has explored the politics of Indians and Mennonites, and Mordecai Richler writes "very, very pointed social satire." The Quebec novel has always been politically engaged.

"The world is getting more explicitly political," Atwood said. "It's no longer possible for us to live only in our private lives. We can't exist in that exclusively personal world anymore."

Set in the near future, *The Handmaid's Tale* "is an extrapolation of present trends," she said. "It's set in the U.S. partly because I lived there for four years, but also because trends happen there first. Here in Canada, we don't see the structure. We're too cautious, too egalitarian."

The effects of pollution, for example, "are having an impact on the birth rate right now," Atwood said. "And it's going to lead to a situation such as the one I describe."

The Handmaid's Tale, however, is "as much about the past as about the present," she said. "There's nothing in it that hasn't actually happened somewhere. Polygamy? Check out the Mormon Church. Public hangings? They were standard in the 19th century."

Atwood got the idea for the novel in 1981. She spent one year "actively writing it" in three different places—West Berlin, Toronto and Alabama.

The book's title recalls *The Canterbury Tales* and so pays subtle homage to Geoffrey Chaucer. But it alludes mainly to the Bible, in which handmaids are described as bearing children for their mistresses.

Of the 12 tribes of Israel fathered by Jacob, Atwood said, eight came from children born to his wives, and four from those born to their handmaids. One of her novel's three epigraphs is taken from Genesis, where Rachel says to Jacob: "Behold my maid Bilhah, go in unto her; and she shall bear upon my knees, that I may also have children by her."

Atwood chose, as her first-person narrator, a new-age handmaid. This young woman has been re-educated, and her job, her sole function, is to bear a child for her "commander." To this end, she is stringently controlled and kept ignorant of the world around her.

"I wanted to work with a single person who was part of the society, and see how much I could tell through that person," Atwood said. "When you're unable to read, it's very hard to know what's going on."

"Let's have a theocracy!"

"If you were planning to take over the U.S.," Margaret Atwood said, "what line would you take? Would you say, 'Come on, gang, let's have Communism?' Would you say, 'Let's have a liberal democracy with two political parties?' They've got that already. My gang (in *The Handmaid's Tale*) says, 'Let's have a theocracy.'"

Atwood was explaining the logic of her futuristic sixth novel to a standing-room-only crowd of about 600 at the Central Library Theatre. "Nothing in my book is pure invention," she said, "or has been cooked up out of my fevered brain. The seeds of my scenario are not lacking."

Atwood made these remarks while answering questions after reading from her new novel for about 25 minutes. She said such trends as the declining birth rate, increasing pollution and creeping censorship make her bleak vision of the future entirely plausible.

In introducing Atwood, library director John Dutton said that the Toronto-based author's appearance was especially timely because it came during Freedom To Read Week in Canada. He noted that two of Atwood's earlier novels, *The Edible Woman* and *Surfacing*, have been challenged in past years by certain Ontario schools as unsuitable for young adults.

In response to a question about pornography, Atwood said that "the feminist movement is divided on the issue because it's a choice of evils." Pornography hurts women and children, she said, but "once you start burning books, it's hard to stop because they make such a big fire."

Atwood told the mostly female audience, which overflowed onto the stage and into the aisles, that she developed *Handmaid's Tale* from a series of mental pictures. "I'm an imagistic thinker," she said. "My first ideas always take the form of images."

Earlier, in an interview, Atwood said the first image with this book was one of "bodies hanging from a wall." White hoods covered the heads—the same color hoods as were used in Canada until public hangings were banned in the 19th century. And the wall was very like the one around Harvard University, where Atwood did graduate work: "It always seemed somewhat sinister."

A second image was that of "women walking along the street in pairs." They were wearing another kind of hood—like horses' blinders, or the bonnets in "those Old Dutch cleanser ads." Atwood proceeded by asking herself, "What's going on here?"

She'd been reading books on socio-biology, or pop-biology, "which I define as biology without a lot of numbers." And she'd encountered the idea that the essential form of human society was polygamy, with a few powerful males having a plurality of females, while males at the bottom had none—"sort of like walruses."

The work-in-progress became a magnet, attracting everything into its orbit. Atwood found herself collecting newspaper clippings on pollution and the falling birth rate. Gradually, she built up a mental image of the world she was writing about.

Still, she hesitated. "It wasn't a safe book to try. It could have been a total disaster, an artistic bomb." Atwood started writing another novel but found "it wasn't working." She returned to *The Handmaid's Tale*, even though she felt it was "a totally crazy thing to be doing."

The danger in writing a novel of ideas, Atwood said, "is that you can go off the track and forget you're writing a novel. Then you get a series of interpositions by the author, which get in the way of the characters."

Before she sat down to write, however, Atwood worked out the structure of her imaginary society "quite tightly—then I forgot about it." Characters unfold as you write them, she said. "I had the structure of the society firmly in mind. Then I let the character run loose."

The novel, narrated in the first person, ends with an epilogue set in the distant future. Some early reviewers have felt this detracted from the book. But Atwood noted that George Orwell's *1984* ends with a postscript indicating that the society depicted in the novel has ceased to exist. She decided to include a similar epilogue, she said, to take "the pessimistic edge" off an otherwise very bleak vision.

As well, she said, "I postulate a serious reader"—one who has questions about the book's imaginary world that her narrator is in no position to answer.

Atwood wouldn't differentiate this novel from her five previous ones. But with characteristic understatement, she noted, "I think that as a narrative, it stands up pretty well."

Cat's Eye took extra courage

Margaret Atwood waited 23 years to write *Cat's Eye*. Her earliest notes about this latest novel, she said, date back to 1964. "But I wasn't able to write the book then. I couldn't write it at 25, at 30, at 35 or even at 40."

Atwood said she last tried to write the novel in 1984, before turning to *The Handmaid's Tale*. But even then she wasn't psychologically or technically ready. "Some books you just have to wait for," she said. "Finally, I was able to do it."

Interviewed at her hotel in downtown Calgary, Atwood was relaxed and witty, warm and professional—an artist at ease with public attention.

Cat's Eye is radically different from *The Handmaid's Tale*. But Atwood takes exception to the notion, advanced in one review, that it's somehow "smaller" than her last novel. "That's like saying Faulkner is smaller than Tolstoy because he didn't write about epic battles."

The new work asks questions about feminism. "What happens to a woman," Atwood said, "whose traumatic experiences have been with other persons of the female gender, when then she hits feminism? That's what happens to my heroine."

Atwood said "the assumption that all women are supposed to feel sisterly is naive. But the fact that I'm able to say this without people calling me a gender traitor—that's new in the air." The book explores "how women relate to each other," Atwood said. "And you're not supposed to talk about that."

Publishing *Cat's Eye* required more courage than usual, she acknowledged. That's because in it Atwood reveals more of herself than ever before, and also "there is that risky feeling that you're saying things that might be wrongly construed as anti-women."

Atwood noted that readers of both sexes have applauded the book. The painter of the cover for the American edition, for example, a male Italian-American born in the Bronx, declared after reading it, "This is my childhood."

Cat's Eye is in a way "a ghost story," Atwood said. Painter Elaine Risley, the novel's central character, is haunted by a girlhood friend named Cordelia. "A false Cordelia appears in every chapter except the first and last," Atwood said. "Someone who might be Cordelia but isn't."

As a bildungsroman, a growing-up novel, *Cat's Eye* has prompted even more speculation than usual about its autobiographical antecedents. "I was one of those people who didn't want to know whether Wordsworth's daffodils were real," Atwood said. To seek real-life correspondences is to deny "the importance of imagination, inventiveness, skill with language—the essence of art."

✱ ✱ ✱

III

Second Battle Zone:
The Quebec Question

The second great theme of Canadian history is, of course, French-English relations. During the 1980s, it surfaced in the patriation debate, wound through Bills 101 and 178 and flowed out into Meech Lake. What? You don't remember the patriation debate? In the early '80s, it was touted as the greatest constitutional controversy since Confederation. People argued patriation at the office, in the cafeteria and on the bus.

Enter Peter Desbarats, a journalist and political commentator whose books include *The State Of Quebec* and *Rene: A Canadian In Search Of A Country*. Desbarats visited Calgary to talk about *Canada Lost/Canada Found*, an impassioned tract in which he offered not "a statement on specific constitutional reform but a polemic on the process and what it means to all of us."

According to Desbarats, Canada's history was a history of failure. The disappointment of CANDU, the immolation of the Arrow jet fighter: "We keep looking for technical explanations for our lack of success in many areas of enterprise. They have nothing to do with a failure of skill. All the failures reflect a failure of national will." The only way to reassert that national will, and so turn history around, Desbarats argued, was to bring home the constitution. This wouldn't solve our problems, but it would "give us confidence in our ability to deal with them."

One of the biggest stumbling blocks to patriation, Desbarats insisted, was Pierre Trudeau. The prime minister, he wrote, "has spent 15 years in Ottawa listening to western Canadians, some of them in his own party, and he gives no indication of having heard a word that they have said." On the other hand, Desbarats said in a downtown pub, "I wish Westerners could get past Trudeau's image somehow, and look at what patriation will do for the country rather than what it'll do for his historical image. I think it's tragic that the Tories couldn't join with the Liberals on this."

With the charter of rights if possible, without it if necessary, the constitution, Desbarats said, had to be patriated. To turn back "would be a much more serious failure than at Victoria in 1970. It would be noted outside the country, and felt by everyone in Canada. It would be a sign that we can't act coherently as a nation. Albertans would suffer as much as anybody. It would also mean that the next cycle of Quebec nationalism would start at 40 percent."

Patriation was going to be a response to the Quebec referendum of 1980, which in itself was an incomplete act. It "would be a sign that the rest of Canada recognizes the changes that have occurred in Quebec," Desbarats wrote, "and a symbol, for all Quebecers, of maturity in the rest of the country." It would also "be a symbol of our ability to change, to confront our failures, to recognize our divisions, and to accept new ways of looking at ourselves.... (it) would be a sign to the West that the nation retains the ability to reform its institutions."

Well, Trudeau brought the constitution home with a charter of rights. But he did it without Quebec's consent. And Canada's new age of self-confidence never dawned. Was Desbarats naive? No. He just never imagined that Trudeau's successor would be so foolish and prideful as to reopen the constitutional debate. In 1986, before Brian Mulroney brought the premiers to Meech Lake, even the late Rene Levesque was on the defensive....

8. Levesque Says The "S" Word

Quebec separatism isn't dead. It's alive and well and chain-smoking its way around Canada in the person of Rene Levesque. The ex-Quebec premier, three-quarters of the way through a month-long promotional tour for his book *Memoirs,* paused in Calgary long enough to become the ninth winner of the Bob Edwards Award.

In a witty, rambling and provocative speech at the 12th annual Bob Edwards Luncheon, Levesque poked fun at Calgary mayor Ralph Klein, former prime minister Pierre Trudeau and Ontario Premier David Peterson. But he also warned an audience of more than 500 people at the Palliser Hotel, and later an audience of 700 at the University of Calgary, that Quebec independence is not dead but hibernating.

There is political apathy everywhere now, "a low tide of disillusionment, a kind of 'fed-up-ed-ness,'" Levesque said. "But eventually the tide will come back. And in (that tide) will be the Quebec question."

Levesque said Quebec has gained a new self-confidence and French Canadians have entered the mainstream of the world. Thus, they no longer fear their future will be "the sad tale of a minority on its way to oblivion."

As Quebecers feel their new confidence and ability, however, they will want more autonomy. "The more Quebecers become self-confident through individual success and the momentum of development, there's going to be a need for more breathing space ... and, as time goes on, for more tools of decision-making."

Ribbing Klein has become a tradition of the awards luncheon, and Levesque maintained it: "If my book does really well, Mr. Mayor, could I rate a ticket to the Olympics?" Later, alluding to the notorious "creeps and bums" remark Klein made during Calgary's boom, Levesque told the mayor he no longer has to worry about Easterners arriving to rob banks: "They won't come now; it's not worth the trouble."

Levesque reserved his most caustic comments, as always, for Trudeau. He drew an especially hearty laugh with a reference to "this wonderful, bilingual, bicultural and harmonious country Trudeau has left us."

Jokingly, Levesque said his book was very like his speech: "It's rigorously organized. It begins at the climax and has no ending."

When the luncheon was over, dozens of people lined up to buy copies of *Memoirs* and have them autographed. As one reader put it, "It may not be a great book, but it is a historical document."

Levesque received the Bob Edwards Award—named after a maverick journalist celebrated for his satirical wit—for the "passionate advocacy of his beliefs."

9. The Forgotten Anglos

By the fall of 1989, Prime Minister Brian Mulroney and 10 premiers had signed the Meech Lake Accord, though some provincial legislatures had not yet ratified it. The previous December, the Supreme Court of Canada had ruled that Quebec's language laws were unconstitutional, that they infringed the rights of Anglophones. And Premier Robert Bourassa had thumbed his nose at the Court, invoking the constitution's not-withstanding clause and introducing Bill 178. Three English-speaking ministers resigned in protest. Quebecers went to the polls in September, 1989. The newly-created, English-rights Equality Party did even better than expected and won four seats—three mentioned below and one other. But the new realities facing Anglophone Quebecers were most clearly expressed, as always, in the world of letters.

MONTREAL—The question came from the floor at a spirited all-candidates meeting in Westmount riding, where the ruling liberals were facing a fierce challenge from the pro-bilingualism Equality Party: "If you were a bilingual Anglophone Quebecer, what would be the future for your children?"

Lawyer Richard Holden, one of four Equality candidates who even-tually won seats in the provincial election, responded by asking the largely Anglophone audience a question of his own: "How many of you have a close relative—a son or daughter, a brother or sister—who has left Quebec in the last few years?"

When 90 percent of those in the high school auditorium held up their hands, Holden said simply: "There's your answer." Strong stuff. But English-speaking Montrealers—roughly 600,000 of them in a city of 2.8 million—were upset and angry. And many of them intended to do some-thing about it.

Some people didn't want to hear this—like Premier Robert Bourassa, whose most recent language legislation, Bill 178, was expected to work like a magic wand. Presto! An English-speaking city the size of Calgary was supposed to disappear. Others were laughing up their sleeves, like Parti

Quebecois leader Jacques Parizeau, who wants to build a unilingual French Quebec, and prominent separatist Pierre Bourgault, who has stated flatly that the worst enemy of such an entity is "la minorite anglaise."

And then there were those Canadians—among them bilingual ex-Montrealers like myself—who were concerned from afar and baffled. But let's start with Alliance Quebec, an Anglophone lobby group that boasts 40,000 members. Dubbed "Compliance Quebec" by some outspoken Anglophones for its record of bending over backwards to appease the province's Francophone majority, the Alliance is entirely too visible for many Quebec nationalists.

Its office was fire-bombed in December of 1988, and the organization was still settling into a modest new office downtown. There Geoffrey Kelley, the Alliance's director of communications, produced figures. Between 1976 and 1981, Quebec suffered a net loss of 108,000 Anglophones. During the next five years, another 44,000 (net) left the province, leaving 760,000 Anglophones in a total population of 6.7 million. Kelley noted that certain groups were "over-represented" in the exodus: the young (20 to 44), the well-educated (college or university backgrounds) and, ironically, the bilingual.

That's where Anglophone anger was rooted—in the loss of friends and loved ones. Kelley, who opted consistently for the least aggressive position on any issue, noted that many Anglophones left, not because of repressive language legislation, but for economic reasons. Those who stayed, he said, worked hard to become bilingual, lining up in the dead of winter, for example, to get their children into French immersion classes. Until December of 1988, they believed they were gaining acceptance as part of Quebec society.

That's why so many of them felt so betrayed when Bourassa, who had promised to restore English-language signs banned by the previous Parti Quebecois government, used the famous "notwithstanding clause" to over-ride a Supreme Court ruling and bring in Bill 178. Three of his four Anglophone ministers resigned to protest this law, which says English can appear on indoor signs as long as French is clearly predominant, but not on outdoor ones. Presto! Invisible Anglos!

True, walking around downtown Montreal these days you can still see outdoor signs bearing offensive English apostrophes. One cries, "McDonald's!" Another shouts, "Wendy's!" But those U.S. franchises were exempted, you see, because the apostrophes don't really imply possession: they're part of a trademark.

Kelley insisted that the trouble is not racial but political, the problem, one of governments. "We're not anti-French," he stressed. "We're one of the most bilingual communities in the country." And he said that the best way for other Canadians to aid Quebec's English-speaking minority is to insist that Francophone rights be respected in their own provinces.

To understand what led to the creation of the Equality Party, then, and to Alliance Quebec's own suggestion that, as a last resort, Anglophones should spoil their ballots, one had to dig elsewhere.

Several months before, the editors of a French-language literary magazine called *Liberte*—where Jean Larose publishes regularly—had made an extraordinary gesture. They invited 16 Anglophone intellectuals—novelists and playwrights, philosophers and film-makers—to write about the language issue in Quebec. They then published these articles in French, translating where necessary, in the magazine's June issue.

From where the English stood, this obscure publication shone like a solitary beacon of light. After all, exclusivity has long been the rule in Quebec, where Francophone intellectuals are famous for talking only to each other and 99 out of 100 provincial civil servants have French as their mother tongue.

What's most striking about the June issue of *Liberte* is not the motif of anger in it but the multiplicity of Anglophone perspectives. Award-winning translator Sheila Fischman quotes a Francophone friend lamenting the decline of Montreal's cosmopolitanism: "My city has become a town." Film-maker Donald Winkler, born and raised in Winnipeg, describes how he thrives on switching back and forth between French and English, how he revels in the texture and tension of daily life in Montreal.

Carlos Ferrand, an "allophone" immigrant from Peru, argues that Anglophone Quebecers are just Yankee imperialists gone north. He confesses to a streak of vengeful glee at recent developments in Quebec. But Ferrand's outlook is decidedly idiosyncratic.

And anger is certainly the second most striking aspect of this issue of *Liberté*. Anger expressed, not in the windy, rhetorical and simplistic lexicon of politicians but, at least in spots, in the precise and logical or resonantly metaphorical language of intellectual discourse.

"What does the new sign law mean to us?" asks novelist Trevor Ferguson, whose latest book is *The Kinkajou*. "And more especially, what does the response of the Francophone community signal? In our darkest moments: that we will never be wanted or valued. And that the basis for that distrust is a deep-rooted animosity based on mythology, treachery, and lies."

Interviewed in a downtown brasserie, Ferguson elaborated. He was outraged, he said, not by the disappearance of English signs but by the heavy-handed abrogation of rights. And that the only opposition to Bill 178 on the French side came "from those who wanted it to be more extreme." English Montrealers have made extraordinary efforts to promote French, he said, and have been its foremost defenders out of province—"as long as our own language was not outlawed as some obscenity on the social landscape."

The Francophone response to Bill 178 left Anglophones feeling "not appreciated, not wanted and just not respected as part of this society," Ferguson said. "While Quebec Anglos have been insisting on the need to protect French in North America, Francophones have failed to realize that they are in power here. They're still acting as though they're defending themselves. They've won. Now is their time to be generous to the losers."

Ferguson said he would vote by spoiling his ballot—"I don't like one-issue parties," he said of Equality—but he will not leave Montreal. He cited "the new renaissance here" as a principal reason: the emergence of a new generation of Anglophone fiction writers, the recent formation of QSPELL (Quebec Society for the Promotion of English-Language Literature), and the arrival of several new bookstores (Ficciones, Lexus, a revamped Coles, a born-again W.H. Smith) to augment old reliables like Paragraphe and The Double Hook.

And Magnus Books? The store run by Stephen Nowell, who tried to organize a campaign of civil disobedience against Bill 178? "Well, there were bomb threats, acts of vandalism," Ferguson said. "People stopped going into the store. They didn't want to be there when something happened. So he had to close. His business had disappeared."

Back to *Liberte*. Henry Beissel, the playwright, poet and translator who directs Concordia University's creative writing program, described Quebec's language legislation as repressive and reactionary. "It tyrannizes the Anglophone minority; to Quebecois Francophones, it blocks free access to English; and it prepares the birth of a xenophobic state." At best, the province's draconian language laws will lead to "a maple syrup republic" catering to U.S. tourists, Beissel wrote. "At worst they reflect a fascist mentality ready to trample on fundamental human rights."

Beissel's personal history, which he outlined in an interview at Concordia, is instructive. Born in Germany in 1929, Beissel studied philosophy in England and then emigrated to Canada in 1951 to avoid living under the Prussian authoritarianism that had given rise to Hitler. In 1966, offered five different university jobs, Beissel chose Sir George Williams mainly so he could enjoy cosmopolitan Montreal.

By 1970, having become friends with many Francophone intellectuals, Beissel was appalled at the rising tide of nationalism: "I asked myself what would happen if a real mass manipulator turned up under these propitious conditions." In 1976, after the nationalistic Parti Quebecois came to power, Beissel remained at Concordia but moved out of Montreal and across the Quebec border into backwoods Ontario. "I felt suddenly disenfranchised," he said. "I didn't want to live in a society where my voice doesn't count."

Beissel is a strong advocate of a multi-cultural Canada, but he sees this as irreconcilable with the aspirations of Francophone Quebec. "The best thing might be for Quebec to separate," he said. The Quebecois can then build the nationalistic state so many of them seem to want, and the rest of Canada can become "a multi-ethnic society, kind of a model United Nations."

From a federalist perspective—and English Montreal is arguably the most federalist community in Canada—Beissel's analysis could get no darker. Graeme Decarie offered a more optimistic outlook. A Montreal native, Decarie is chairman of Concordia's history department. He was also vice-president of Alliance Quebec and a regular columnist for *The Gazette*. Decarie is the one who first suggested spoiling ballots as a way of protesting Bill 178. Alliance chairman Peter Blaikie then advanced it as a last resort at a well-publicized news conference. The reaction of Bourassa and prominent Liberals suggested that the notion touched a nerve.

English-speaking Quebecers "do have sufficient muscle" to make French Quebec listen, Decarie insisted in an interview. "A strong protest vote will scare the hell out of Bourassa." Decarie explained that only half a dozen Quebec ridings are predominantly Anglophone. "But in a close election, which this one is not," he said, "the English-speaking vote could make a difference in 50 or 60 ridings." (He exaggerated, but you get the drift.)

Decarie said also that French Quebec doesn't worry much about what English Canada thinks, but is extraordinarily anxious about its image in the United States. If Bourassa is repudiated by many Anglophone voters, Decarie said, he can't go south of the border and maintain that all is well in *la belle province*. As for the nationalist dream of creating a unilingual French society in a sea of English, Decarie dismissed it as gibberish. "English is the lingua franca of the world," he said. "The idea that you can turn your back on that is just head-in-the-sand stuff."

Decarie said the Francophone middle class has always been fluently bilingual, and keeps itself that way through a system of private schools. "Parizeau speaks better English than I do!" he said. "And 25 percent of the kids in my history classes are French. They're here to improve their English." The final phase of the Quiet Revolution won't come, Decarie said, until members of the Francophone working class wake up and realize that their middle-class leaders want them to remain unilingual to preserve their own privileges—privileges that come with being able to speak English.

Decarie said that for decades the French education system has taught pernicious myths about Quebec Anglophones, fostering the ludicrous notion that the English were all capitalist exploiters. In fact, most Quebec Anglophones have working-class backgrounds, Decarie said. "And we just don't feel guilty any more. We don't have any problem with the idea of protecting a distinct society, but we are not prepared to accept discrimination and something close to racism in an attempt to create a unilingual French Quebec."

Decarie was hoping that the percentage of Anglophones voting for the Liberal party, traditionally around 90 percent, would drop to 50 percent. In the preceding three elections, spoiled ballots totalled between one and two percent of the total. Decarie wanted to see five percent this time (and did), but said he would consider three a success. And the Montreal ridings in which the Equality Party candidates could win, he said, were D'Arcy McGee (87 percent Anglophone), N.D.G. (80 percent) and Westmount (72 percent).

That brings us full circle, back to the crowded high school auditorium. There, in response to the show of hands attesting to the Anglophone exodus, the Parti Quebecois candidate argued—to a chorus of boos and catcalls— that this emigration was simply part of a continental trend. William Cosgrove, the high-profile Liberal candidate who returned to Montreal to run after 16 years in the United States, said he didn't agree with Bill 178. He would fight for English rights from within the party—the same strategy employed by the three ministers who resigned over the language law.

Finally, the Green Party candidate who, throughout the evening, had made cogent observations on environmental issues, showed why he was not a mainstream contender. The language issue? The future of Anglophones in Quebec? His own son participates in events in both French and English, he said, "and he has a wonderful time. I wouldn't worry about it if I were you."

10. Meech Lake Blues

KINGSTON—The key moment came when Pierre Berton jumped to his feet and thundered at his fellow writers: "Let's use words that mean something! 'Distinct society!' Let's not pussy-foot around! If Meech Lake is lost, then Quebec really will be a distinct society!"

About 150 members of the 800-member Writers' Union of Canada were debating a resolution on the Meech Lake Accord at Queen's University. They were trying to decide whether to support the right of Quebecers to realize themselves within Canada as "a viable cultural entity" or "a distinct society."

Berton's passionate speech was instrumental in convincing the writers—all of whom have published at least one book—to adopt the stronger wording. The preamble to the resolution noted "the severe estrangement of the public of Francophone Quebec from the institutions of Canadian federalism" and TWUC's long commitment "to the plurality of cultural expression."

The passing of the resolution exploded the notion—advanced most forcefully by a certain "national newspaper"—that Canadian writers are not speaking out about the Meech Lake Accord the way they did about free trade.

Edmonton writer Myrna Kostash, in moving the resolution, said it would have been "grotesque" for the annual general meeting to end without once having addressed the current crisis: "Can you imagine writers in Czechoslovakia holding a series of meetings in Prague in December of 1989 without once referring to events around them?"

Novelist David Gurr gave a particularly powerful speech warning that political events have their own momentum: "This is a moment in history. The country is longing for people to stand up and say, 'For God's sake! Let's not throw it all away.'"

The emotional discussion triggered by what Kostash described as "a motherhood resolution" was the clearest expression of what was evident on every street-corner and at every informal party: the Meech Lake crisis was on everybody's mind.

Novelist Margaret Atwood argued outside the student residence in which writers stayed—"and I hope you report this"—that newspaper stories about statements she made in Quebec were almost willfully distorted. In explaining why so many Canadians are uneasy about the distinct-society clause, Atwood had suggested that the word "distinct" carries connotations of superiority. "We speak of 'a man of distinction' or of 'distinctive tastes,'" she said. "Distinct implies superior. If the accord merely meant 'different,' it should have said 'different.'"

Roch Carrier, one of French Canada's best-known writers, gave the annual Margaret Laurence lecture on the writer's life. His humorous, hour-long talk, which drew a standing ovation, was almost without political allusions. But he ended by describing his latest book, a children's novel called *Adventures In Canada*, in which a Quebecois boy travels all over the country in a flying canoe. He said he dropped the book off with his publisher with a note saying: "This is my manuscript about adventures in Canada. I hope you will publish it very quick."

Even the requisite humorous resolution took a Meech Lake turn as TWUC voted to send British Columbia poet Robin Skelton, a professed witch, to the House of Commons to perform an exorcism on "the evil spirits resident in that house." At last sighting, Skelton was seeking an Indian shaman to join him in performing the exorcism.

Besides a disputed baseball game, however, the Skelton initiative provided the weekend's only levity. With the Meech Lake crisis hanging over this southern Ontario city like a dark cloud, the annual general meeting was the most subdued in recent memory.

A resolution that in 1988 was defeated after an acrimonious debate was passed almost without a murmur, as TWUC voted to seek funding for racial minority writers to attend a three-day meeting to discuss concerns, set priorities and make recommendations. It appointed Lenore Keeshig-Tobias, an outspoken native writer, as union representative on the committee, which aimed to raise $71,500 to hold the meeting.

Montreal novelist Trevor Ferguson, who became union chair, said in an interview that minority writers would be one of TWUC's priorities. He tipped his hat to Marcel Masse for federal government plans to table a bill recognizing the importance of the artist.

And he spoke of the issue that had colored the weekend, and of writers' concerns about the political events unfolding in this country. "We are profoundly interested in Lac Meech," said Ferguson, who has written eloquently about the abrogation of English minority rights in Quebec. "And very concerned about the welfare of all our citizens."

***

IV

More Canadian Volunteers

11. Mavis Gallant: The View From Paris

Mavis Gallant, Canada's most celebrated expatriate writer, won a governor-general's award for her fifth collection of short stories, Home Truths. *During her 1981-82 sojourn in this country, Gallant received the Order of Canada and made her debut as a playwright with a Toronto hit called* What Is To Be Done? *In recent years Gallant has published* Paris Notebooks: Essays And Reviews *(1986) and two collections of stories:* Overhead In A Balloon *(1985) and* In Transit *(1986). She visited Canada again in 1988.*

Why she left Canada

WATERLOO—Paris-based author Mavis Gallant came home to Canada recently in more ways than one. Gallant, based in Europe for the past 40 years, returned both physically and spiritually to give the second annual Margaret Laurence memorial lecture to the Writers' Union of Canada.

Best-known for her short stories, Gallant talked movingly about her early days as an apprentice writer, revealing her previously secret reasons for leaving Canada. Until now, Gallant has been too embarrassed to reveal that while working during the 1940s for the now-defunct *Montreal Standard,* she was removed from two different beats.

She lost a regular column of radio criticism because "I'd parodied jingles and poked fun at commercials"—and a senior editor's golf partner had complained. Then she was taken off the movie beat after she gave a film a bad review and the movie theatre chain withdrew its advertising.

Those incidents made her question the wisdom of remaining in journalism and contributed to her decision to leave Canada. The celebrated Canadian author emphasized that she also ran into other kinds of censorship problems later as a professional fiction writer.

But, while painting an achingly beautiful "and probably idealized" portrait of being young in Montreal during the Second World War, she said that in many ways her years as a journalist were happy and extremely rewarding. At the *Standard*, Gallant learned how to "produce copy" and never to fear the blank page. The experience also "untied the knots of grammar and syntax" and taught her clarity and precision.

Early in her talk, Gallant explained that she wanted to focus on her "initiation and apprenticeship" as a writer because those were the only parts of writers' biographies that she ever found interesting. She wondered aloud whether a writer is born rather than made, "and if a vocation is not pre-language." As a young woman, Gallant was "absolutely terrified," she said, that she might have "a vocation and no talent."

Gallant has always said she published her first fiction in *The New Yorker*, where she still publishes regularly. But at the University of Waterloo, where the 675-member writers' union held its annual general meeting, she disclosed that in 1940 she published two short stories in a literary magazine called *Preview*.

Her lecture, laced with anecdotes and spiced with French words and phrases, drew a standing ovation from an audience of about 500. Earlier, during a quiet lunch, the author said that she'd torn up the original, more anecdotal version of her lecture "because I realized what I really wanted to say."

Gallant wrote the final version in longhand on the airplane and at her hotel room—yet prompted author Timothy Findley, in a brief statement of thanks, to remark with wonder and amazement on "the marvelous way" she uses language.

This extraordinary identity crisis

In 1950, when she was 28, Montreal-born Mavis Gallant quit her Canadian newspaper job and sailed to Europe. She has lived there, mostly in Paris, ever since, her two novels, several collections of stories and sundry articles earning her an international reputation. Abroad, Gallant is recognized, and has been for years, as Canada's finest expatriate writer.

At home, she has fared less well. Not until 1979, when she published *From The Fifteenth District,* did Gallant begin to receive the attention she deserves. Reviewers, myself among them, hailed the story collection with superlatives. I, for one, was astonished at Gallant's ability to get outside herself and into a foreign consciousness, and at the Chekhovian ease with which she compressed whole lives into a few pages.

These qualities had always been present in her work, of course, and had long been recognized outside Canada. Why, then, had Gallant been neglected at home? I think it's because she refused to compromise, and to indulge the Canadian taste for what she calls "domestic embellishment."

Take, for example, her view of "this extraordinary Canadian identity crisis," as she called it in an interview. "Sturm and drang nonsense, it seems to me. Posturing." She shook her head, baffled. "I've never suffered from any such thing, have you?"

In the introduction to her fifth book of short stories, *Home Truths,* Gallant elaborated: "I am constantly assured that Canadians no longer know what they are, or what to be Canadian should mean. It is as if a reassuring interpretation, a list of characteristics—the more rigid and confining the better—needed to be drawn up and offered for ratification."

Paradoxically, the book's 16 stories, the earliest of which was written in 1940, suggest a startling number of just such characteristics:

— "The children are more cautious than their parents; more Canadian."

— "The father was more reticent than the mother; perhaps more Canadian."

— "For all his early dash and promise he was as Canadian as his father, which is to say cautious and single-minded."

Cautious, reticent, single-minded. Ouch!

There's some solace, I suppose, in the fact that all of the stories in *Home Truths* take place before 1950. The first six are set in Canada, and five of them focus on children. This is Gallant's early work—remarkably accomplished and, in technique and attitude, curiously reminiscent of the young Marie-Claire Blais.

The middle four stories, which make up more than a third of the book, are subtler, more complicated. Here, treating adult Canadians in Europe, Gallant calls to mind Henry James—and bears the comparison.

The last six stories, which feature Gallant's alter-ego Linnet Muir as first-person narrator, are less Jamesian than Joycean. Written between 1977 and 1979, they provide a portrait of the artist as a fiercely independent young woman. The final story, "With A Capital T," finds Linnet working for a Montreal newspaper—and so brings us to the point when, in real life, Mavis Gallant left Canada.

She has returned, frequently, to visit, and says, "When I'm here, I never think about France." Will she ever come home to stay? "It's hard to say." Certainly not before she finishes here 800-page book on Alfred Dreyfus, the French-Jewish army captain wrongly court-marshalled in 1894—an affair which split French society down the middle.

And of course she has developed ties in France: "I can't move without causing considerable grief and stress, both to other people and me." On the other hand, Gallant said, "I would like to spend more time here in Canada, and write some contemporary fiction out of it. But return for good?" She shrugs, smiles—is that wistfully? "It's hard to say."

12. Alice Munro: Queen of the Short Story

In 1991, Alice Munro won a Canada Council Molson prize worth $50,000 for her outstanding life-time contribution to the cultural and intellectual life of Canada. Her seventh collection of short stories, the best-selling Friend Of My Youth, *was short-listed for the governor-general's award. Munro had won that award for the third time with her*

1986 book The Progress Of Love. *The Ontario-based writer grants few interviews—"they're so distracting"—but she did a limited publicity tour for that work.*

"People are always asking when I'm going to write a novel," Alice Munro said. "It's like they're asking whether I'm ever going to grow up. Or if I'm ever going to get my teeth straightened."

When she was a novice writer, Munro expected to graduate from short stories to the novel. "I felt inferior to writers who had written novels," she said over lunch. "But then I got past that, and reached the point where I didn't care."

Munro, born in 1931, is Canada's undisputed Queen of the Short Story. (Her only rival, expatriate Mavis Gallant, works in a variety of genres.) Since the late 1970s, Munro has regularly published fiction in the prestigious *New Yorker* magazine. She won her first governor-general's award for *Dance Of The Happy Shades* (her first book in 1968), her second 10 years later for *Who Do You Think You Are?*

Munro sets most of the stories in *The Progress Of Love* in small-town Ontario, where she was born and raised. The oldest child of working-class parents, she grew up in Wingham, Ontario. After two years at the University of Western Ontario on a scholarship, she married Jim Munro, moved to British Columbia and started having babies. (Her three daughters are now in their 20s and 30s.)

In 1972, the marriage broke up. By then Munro had published two acclaimed books. She moved to Toronto, taught at York University and was writer-in-residence at the University of Toronto. "I thought I'd go on living as a single parent," she said. But in 1974, when she published *Something I've Been Meaning To Tell You*, she heard from an old flame: cartographer Gerald Fremlin.

He was living in Clinton, Ontario—a town of 3,000 located about 160 kilometres west of Toronto, and only 30 from Wingham. In 1975, Munro joined Fremlin in Clinton, and there she has remained. "I didn't go back for any literary purpose," she said. "I thought I was through with small-town Ontario, and that I'd be writing about my years in Vancouver and Victoria—that background."

Munro draws on her surroundings for her fiction. The author keeps her private life to herself, but obviously could never have written *The Progress Of Love* if she weren't very much part of a small town.

Munro writes each morning from 7 to 10 or 10:30. She and her husband, who retired recently, "lead a fantastically physical life," she said. "We're walking all the time. In the winter, almost every afternoon, we go cross-country skiing."

Over the years, Munro's work has become more technically accomplished—and progressively darker: "I've come up against harder things." Each of her books has sold more than the previous one, Munro said. But *Lives Of Girls And Women* "may be the most enduring."

That work, published in 1971, resembles a novel made up of story-like chapters. But Munro regards it as a collection of linked stories. "It's perennially appealing because it's about childhood and adolescence," she said. "It has a charm that my other books don't have. It doesn't challenge people in any way they don't want to be challenged."

The Progress Of Love, on the other hand, features stories like "Lichen," which is "about a failed marriage—a failure of love," Munro said. "People think it's bleak. I think it's interesting." Then there's "Fits." It hinges on a murder-suicide, but is really about a man who has "married" a small town and discovers that he doesn't know it as well as he thought he did. It's one of the few stories *The New Yorker* rejected. "To me," Munro said, "it's the most interesting story in the book."

Joyce Carol Oates, reviewing *The Progress Of Love* in *The New York Times Book Review*, suggested that the whole collection might have been entitled *Fits*. Munro rejects the idea. She wanted to call the book *White Dump*, after yet another difficult story which explores adultery and its consequences. "But they talked me out of it."

These days, Munro is again thinking of Victoria as a setting for some fiction. "Right now I'm working on something that's probably the very worst length," she said. "About 60 pages. But I can't worry about that. I don't think about it."

13. Leonard Cohen: Magic Is Alive

Poet, fiction-writer and singer/songwriter Leonard Cohen was inducted into the Juno Awards Hall of Fame in Vancouver early in 1991. Cohen, whose 10 record albums have sold more than five million copies around the world, toured Europe in the summer of 1990 and played to sell-out crowds in 53 cities from Norway to Greece. Judy Collins, Diana Ross, Neil Diamond, Joan Baez, Joe Cocker and Jennifer Warnes have recorded his songs. Cohen's music video "I Am A Hotel," in which he stars as the resident spirit of a grand hotel, won several awards, among them a silver medal at the New York International Film and TV Festival.

Lovers of Cohen's poetry and prose—which includes the classic '60s novel Beautiful Losers—*are often ambivalent about the writer's success in music, feeling that it has distracted him. They may find solace in Cohen's promise, repeatedly renewed, to publish a book of memoirs any day now. A new selection of his poems and songs will appear in 1991.*

The strangest thing happened to Leonard Cohen in Calgary in 1984. He was sitting in an obscure little restaurant talking to an interviewer when a waitress slipped him a note. "Dearest Leonard," it began. Cohen stood up, went over to the waitress and asked her who had sent it. The woman was gone.

Not so strange? Hear me out.

First, flash back to the winter of 1966, when Cohen spent a couple of weeks in Edmonton. There he met two university girls and wrote a song about them—the well-known Sisters of Mercy.

Second, know that it was only by chance that Cohen happened, during his Calgary visit, to be anywhere near Flix, a modest (now defunct) eatery on Kensington Avenue. We'd had reservations at a fancy uptown restaurant. But, as Cohen put it later, wolfing down French fries, "That place would've killed us." We'd taken one look, exchanged a glance and ended up piling into my old station wagon and driving across the Bow River.

And here's the kicker. The note Cohen received was written by one of the original Sisters of Mercy—who now lives in Calgary and who somehow ended up in Flix at precisely the same time as Cohen.

After we left, Cohen, flabbergasted, showed me the note. The other Sister (Barbara), it said, is in San Francisco. "Must have been Lorraine," Cohen said. "What a coincidence! Why didn't she come over to the table? Maybe she didn't want to intrude. Delicacy! What incredible delicacy!"

Cohen was in town to promote his recently published *Book Of Mercy* and his forthcoming record album, *Various Positions*. Also to find out if he had an audience here for a concert tour he was putting together (he did).

But time for some context.

Born (in 1934) and raised in Montreal, Cohen still lives there part of the time. He has published two novels (*The Favorite Game* and *Beautiful Losers*), seven books of poetry and, now, one book of psalms.

Although his books have sold more than two million copies and are in translation around the world, Cohen has been "making a living out of music" since the mid-'60s. His songs include "Suzanne," "Chelsea Hotel," "Famous Blue Raincoat" and "Hey, That's No Way To Say Goodbye."

"Nobody should take it too seriously," Cohen said of the book he'd come to flog. "It might be useful to someone who needs to pray, who wants to enter into that landscape. If you find yourself in some kind of trouble, you might want to check it out. Otherwise, it can't have much significance."

Book Of Mercy consists of 50 contemporary psalms. It's an unorthodox work, beautifully written, rhythmic, very Old Testament Jewish, but shaded as well with Catholicism and Zen Buddhism.

Listen: "I lost my way, I forgot to call on your name. The raw heart beat against the world, the tears were for my lost victory. But you are here. You have always been here."

Or again: "Though I don't believe, I come to you now, and I lift my doubt to your mercy. Under the scorn of my own pride I open my mouth to ask you again: Make an end to these harsh preparations."

Cohen wrote this book because he had no choice: "Writing it was the only way to penetrate my predicament. I was silenced, crushed. I was in such a condition of impurity, I was so messed up that I felt a need to pray. All other references were annihilated."

Cohen finished *Book Of Mercy* in 1983. "It's over now. Those prayers were answered, though not in the way one might expect."

He gestured at the book. "This is the end of something. This equips me to go out again and mess it up thoroughly."

In 1980, after his last album came out, Cohen got a band together and did a 100-concert tour of Europe and Australia, playing to crowds of between 1,500 and 7,000. Cohen travels with a band—bass, drums, keyboard, another guitar and two back-up singers.

He likes life on the road, he said, and does at least five concerts a week. "It's gruesome, but the more gruesome it gets, the better I like it. Most guys have to give up their gangs when they're 13 or 14. I've been able to keep mine."

To Calgary, Cohen brought a small tape recorder and two sets of earphones. In Flix, while we talked, ate smoked meat sandwiches and drank more red wine than we should have, he played me half a dozen tracks from *Various Positions*.

No, his voice hasn't changed, unless maybe it's deepened a little. Cohen will never be known primarily as a singer. As a songwriter, though, he has few peers. "Here's to the few who forgive what you do," he intones on one song, "and the fewer who don't even care."

A couple of Cohen's previous albums were over-produced, the lyrics lost in an avalanche of sound. This time out, the mix sounds perfect. Religious imagery, which has always figured in Cohen's work, is everywhere. The idea behind the album title, he said, is that "you're walking around in a circle, looking at the same thing from different points of view, various positions."

Will any of these new songs etch themselves into memory the way some of Cohen's earlier tunes have done ("Let me see your beauty broken down, like you would do for one you love"). After a single listening, I honestly don't know.

How does the new album differ from earlier ones? Cohen laughed: "I don't think it does...."

Leonard Cohen wears nothing but black. He's five foot eight, slender. He smokes a lot.

These days he lives alone, mostly in Montreal. He grew up there in Westmount, a big house on a hill, but now he owns a modest old place in a neighborhood that's across town in every sense.

Cohen gets up at sunrise, works on one of eight or nine songs he has going at a time, then heads out to have breakfast in a nearby restaurant with friends.

Afterwards, he'll go to a gym or a pool, either work out with weights or swim a quarter mile. "I try to work out every day. It's one of the most important things a man can do."

Then, it depends where he is. Lately, Cohen has been staying in New York City, finishing his new album, and so he has been spending his afternoons in a recording studio. Evenings he visits his two sons, born in 1973 and '75, who live in New York with their mother. "Help them with their homework."

Cohen still spends time in California (he keeps a small flat in Los Angeles), studying Zen Buddhism with the "teacher" to whom he dedicated *Book Of Mercy*. "When you train in any tradition," he said, "you begin to see the similarities between traditions."

The tiny house Cohen bought on the Greek Island of Hydra in the early 60s? He still owns it, but hasn't been there in years. Friends care for the place.

What else? Cohen hasn't lost his sense of humor.

"Yes," he said, when prodded. "I'd like to write another novel."

"Great! Fantastic! When are you going to start?"

"Uh, tonight. I'll start tonight."

All right, one last question-and-answer. Has the quintessential ladies' man given up women?

"No. I just haven't set up house with anyone."

***

V

Third Battle Zone: Racism And Native Voice

The book beat often serves as an early warning system on social issues. That was the case with native issues, which surfaced in the world of books months before the summer of 1990, when Mohawk warriors barricaded the highway at Oka, Quebec....

14. Slug-fest Raises Tough Questions

It's the nastiest literary punch-up ever to erupt in Alberta. Heavy-weight fiction writers Rudy Wiebe and W.P. Kinsella have been battling it out toe-to-toe in print and on the airwaves for two months, and their slug-fest shows no signs of ending.

Wiebe has charged that Kinsella is irresponsible, and that in using real-life names and places in contemporary stories he is "ripping off" the Ermineskin Indians of Hobbema, Alberta. Kinsella, commercially success-ful, has retorted that Wiebe is "a petty little academic drone" motivated to attack by jealousy.

Here, certainly, we confront two different answers to the question, "How should a writer live his life?" Wiebe, whose seven novels include the acclaimed *Temptations Of Big Bear*, has spent most of his writing life as a tenured English professor at the University of Alberta. To him, fiction-writing is a vocation.

Kinsella, best-known for his novel *Shoeless Joe*, which became the hit movie *Field Of Dreams*, makes his living by his writing. When he finds a voice that sells, he uses it again and again: hence, four or five "baseball" books and, starting in 1977, six collections of "Indian" stories (only the latest of which has been attacked).

In one sense, then, this fight is a replay of the late-'70s battle between writer-academics from the University of Alberta, led by Wiebe, and John Patrick Gillese, the commercially oriented head of Alberta Culture's literary arts branch.

Why has the conflict erupted now? The Alberta-born Kinsella would argue that it's because he has only recently become visibly successful. But that keeps the fight personal. And the dispute's significance is that it raises the issue of writers of one culture writing about people of another—in this case, Canadian whites writing about native Indians.

Canadian writers have been debating this issue since 1988, when a co-operative Toronto publisher, The Women's Press, split up over whether to publish stories by white women about black women's experience. One faction cried: "Racism! You can't know what it's like!" The other responded, "Censorship! Back off!"

The latter faction, judging by a dozen telephone interviews, carried the day. Consider Toronto writer Marlene Nourbese Philip, for example, an ex-lawyer who leads a group that fights racism in the arts. She said that in the heat of The Women's Press debate "some people took positions they later realized were not quite correct."

Philip noted that Margaret Laurence's *The Tomorrow Tamer* contains superb stories about people from other cultures, and that her own group, Vision 21, is focusing not on individual writers but on the publishing industry: "All writers have problems getting published, but white writers have an edge." And, because they belong to "a power group," Philip said, white writers should carefully examine their motives before writing about marginalized peoples.

Several native writers reiterated this question of motive. Thomas King, who early in 1990 published an impressive first novel called *Medicine River*, said that if a writer is telling native stories simply because they sell, or because "Indians are the flavor of the month, then I think he should forget about it." King, who taught for a decade at the University of Lethbridge, stressed that he is against censorship—but would like white writers to be "more sensitive" when writing about native peoples.

Like King, who has edited one anthology of native writing and is preparing a second, Jeannette Armstrong takes a "non-confrontational" approach. Armstrong, author of the novel *Slash*, founded The En'owkin International School of Writing in Kelowna, British Columbia. She said that students in the creative writing program develop technical skills and explore "unique literary forms present in native literature."

Armstrong, one of the founders of Thetis Publishing, the only native-owned publishing house in Canada, believes that as white writers come to understand the issues—and realize that negative stereotypes can harm young Indians—they will agree that native stories should be told by natives.

This is where, in the heat of debate, tempers flare. Kinsella is on the record: "If minorities were doing an adequate job of (telling their own stories), they wouldn't need to complain. They don't have the skill or experience to tell their stories well."

Many would argue that good native writers are now emerging: King, Armstrong, Tomson Highway, Ruby Slipperjack, Beatrice Culleton, Maria Campbell, Beth Brant—the list goes on. And that this emergence is changing the context in which people read stories.

In a savage review of Kinsella's most recent book, *The Miss Hobbema Pageant,* Marilyn Buffalo MacDonald, a Cree woman from Hobbema, put it this way: "The author's attempts at satire fall flat because his jokes are outdated: what might have been funny in the early 1970s is inappropriate in 1989."

MacDonald argued that Kinsella has become rich "by pandering to an audience that thrives on reading racist and sexist accounts of Indians." Interviewed by telephone, she argued, less stridently, that "stereotyping a whole nation of people with one wide brush" is no longer acceptable. MacDonald was particularly incensed that one of Kinsella's characters, Blind Louis Coyote, bears the same name as "one of Hobbema's most beloved leaders," who died about a year ago.

Yet MacDonald, too, distinguished among white writers according to motive, and stopped short of arguing that they should not write about natives: "When they do they have to do their research. They have to start understanding the issues of protocol."

Lenore Keeshig-Tobias, a Toronto-based Ojibway author, elaborated. "There is a certain protocol in acquiring native stories," she said. "You cannot tell another person's story without asking permission." Keeshig-Tobias said that when native elders pick roots and herbs, "they go out and they ask—they talk to the plants and the trees and tell them why they are needed. And always they leave a tobacco offering."

Keeshig-Tobias, a founding member of the Committee to Re-establish the Trickster, a group committed to reclaiming the native voice in literature, sees native stories, myths and legends as natural resources that belong to particular peoples. "Stories reflect the deepest, most intimate perceptions of a culture," she said. "A lot of non-native, white, mainstream people don't understand the responsibility of the story-teller."

Whites who write about natives "should be prepared to live with us," Keeshig-Tobias said, "to live with our reality. And not just for three months on a reserve, researching a book." Maria Campbell, the Saskatoon-based author of *Half Breed*, took the same tack. "We have to start telling our own stories from our own perspective," she said. "And anything native people are prepared to share should be treated with respect." As for the fight between Wiebe and Kinsella, "that's the pot calling the kettle black."

Margo Kane, a Vancouver actress who writes one-woman shows, organized a meeting of native performers, writers and story-tellers called "Telling Our Own Story." She did this, she said, because in travelling the country she became increasingly aware that white writing contained a lot of "inaccuracies, biases and stereotypes" about natives. "We're talking about cultural autonomy," Kane said. "It's a sovereignty issue, one of self-determination, of ownership of our own history, our own story."

Non-native writers—among them Wiebe, Priddis-based Darlene Quaife (*Bone Bird*) and Calgary's Joan Crate (*Breathing Water*), who is actually part Indian—argue that nobody owns myths and legends; that as anybody can use stories out of the Old Testament or about Buddha, so anybody should be able to draw on native mythology. "These are myths about the whole land form that is Canada," Crate said. "They belong to the land as well as to the people. If we're going to understand the land—particularly now when the environment is in trouble—we have to understand those legends."

Kane doesn't buy this argument: "Quite frankly I'm tired of people trying to justify theft." Much material has been taken out of native communities, she said, "and doesn't even belong to the people any more. Others have claimed ownership." Furthermore, Kane is tired of writers using native characters to portray their own value systems: "Hey! We have our own voice. We have a vision all our own. We're tired of people imposing their value system, their way of telling stories—of using us to speak what they want to speak."

Wiebe, whose Indian novels and stories have all taken place in the past, stressed the need for a sense of responsibility when writing about native peoples. "Native people are saying, look, give us a chance to write our own stories. I think it's good. The time may now be here when they *should* be telling their stories."

Yet Wiebe rejected any notion of censorship, arguing simply that fiction writers have to be responsible—and so take the heat—for anything they write. Quaife made the case positively: "The imagination is the one territory that's still open and free. And empathy is the child of imagination. If I can't imagine what it's like to be you, then I don't have to care about you."

15. The Issue Is Access

Canadian publishers are being dragged into the increasingly public battle for a greater native presence in this country's literature. A panel discussion on Authentic Voice at the 1990 general meeting of the Writers' Guild of Alberta gave evidence of an emerging consensus among writers: the issue is not censorship versus appropriation but access to the reading public. And publishers control that access.

Panel member and native writer Jeannette Armstrong, author of the novel *Slash*, declared that Canadian natives aren't being heard "because of the nature of the publishing industry." The problem is that publishing is profit-motivated, she said, and aims most of its products at "the dominant culture." That culture prefers "a certain kind of reading" and has preconceived ideas about natives.

Thomas King, author of *Medicine River* and another member of the panel, observed that "individual readers read only what's available." The trouble with market-driven publishing, he said, is that it can accommodate only a limited number of native writers. King, who has edited two anthologies of native writing and is preparing a third, took issue with the argument that more native writers will publish books when they write better: "That's not a critical statement," he said. "That's a cultural statement."

The three-hour panel discussion, held in Calgary before about 200 of the guild's 850 members, was one of the highlights of the 10th annual meeting. It elicited all the old arguments in unusually cogent form. Panelists Joan Clark and Darlene Quaife, while acknowledging the need for respect and sensitivity, strongly defended the author's right to explore any subject. Clark, author of the acclaimed *Victory Of Geraldine Gull*, declared flatly: "I don't think anyone should tell us what we can or cannot write." Quaife, author of the award-winning *Bone Bird*, said that any push to restrict subject matter not only truncates literature but deals a blow to human empathy.

King and Armstrong insisted on the distinctiveness of native culture and vision while denying that anybody wants censorship. As King put it, "I can't see anyone saying you can write this but you can't write that." He went further, noting that American crime writer Tony Hillerman has been very successful in portraying the Navaho culture. "Others don't do the job as well," King said, alluding to writers who perpetuate negative myths and stereotypes. "To think that's okay, and that we'll just remain silent, is a little much. But don't mistake our criticism for censorship."

The emphases varied but all panel members—and most members of the audience—appeared to favor a greater native presence in Canadian literature. "The solution is better found," Clark said, "in affirmative action rather than warning off non-native writers."

Armstrong said sympathizers could lobby for more native materials in school libraries or support the En'owkin International School of Writing. King suggested fighting Tory government cuts to funding for native newspapers and magazines, which he said are vital outlets for beginning native writers.

And always the discussion circled back to publishing. "Censorship isn't the issue," Armstrong said. "Freedom of speech is there, no question about that. But I sense a defensiveness on the part of some writers, a refusal to look at the real issue. That issue is access to audience, the right to publish—that's something we do need to look at."

✳✳✳

VI

Still More Volunteers

16. Timothy Findley: Famous Last Wars

Late in 1990, Timothy Findley was working on an untitled novel he described as "the heart of Dachau set in Rosedale"—a monied Toronto neighborhood. And he and his partner William Whitehead were joking about a second book of Findley memoirs. "We're calling it Tales From My Anecdotage," he said. "The joke to me is that I'm never going to write it. Of course, I said that about Inside Memory, *too."*

Staring into the heart of Dachau

Timothy Findley cannot describe the photographs that changed his life forever. "I can't do it," he said. "Some things really can't be described. You can insert anything you want. The writer has to leave room for people to create their own images—in this case, the worst thing they can imagine."

Findley, best-known for such acclaimed novels as *The Wars, Famous Last Words* and *The Telling Of Lies*, was talking about his first non-fiction book, *Inside Memory: Pages From A Writer's Workbook*.

In it, toward the end, Findley tells the story of how, as an actor in his 20s, he and a woman friend visited Ivan Moffat, a hugely successful screen writer and film director. Moffat lived in a glorious house high above the lights of Hollywood.

Left alone to browse, Findley discovered a book of official-looking photographs and realized that he was "staring into the heart of Dachau," one of the most horrific Nazi concentration camps of the Second World War. Moffat had been the first official army photographer through the gates.

It cannot be told, Findley writes, "what it meant to see those photographs that night. Such images, in all their appalling intimacy, had not yet entered the public domain. The pictures we had seen—the ones the public saw—the ones they showed at Nuremburg—were bad enough. But these in Ivan Moffat's books were beyond all comprehension."

Findley experienced an epiphany that night: "I did not know how to say it then, but the vision of Dachau in Ivan Moffat's photographs told me that I was just like everyone else. We are all a collective hiding place for monsters."

This theme of identification with all of human kind pervades *Inside Memory*, as it does the best of Findley's fiction. It also explains why, since the death of Findley's close friend Margaret Laurence, Canada's writerly "tribe" looks to this author—not for leadership but for inspiration, for heart.

Don't misunderstand. *Inside Memory* has its dark and moving moments, its elegies to Laurence and Marian Engel and Ken Adachi. But it shines, too, with light and laughter and, indeed, hilarity.

Findley said his publisher, Stanley Colbert, inspired the book by suggesting that he write an autobiography. The author opposed that idea adamantly—"it would have been awful, just so boring"—but his companion of almost 30 years, documentary writer William Whitehead, had organized the novelist's archives.

He talked Findley into investigating them for three days at the National Archives in Ottawa. The author discovered that his workbooks, which dated from as far back as the 1960s, contained some delightful material, all about others, that he'd completely forgotten. And put him in mind of more.

In a wonderful preface to *Inside Memory*, Findley argues that our memories consist mostly of other people and not ourselves. "I am my Aunt Marg, for instance, telling me not to lean into the cemetery over the fence at Foxbar Road. I am not me leaning over the fence, I am her voice— because that is what I remember."

Here, through Findley's memories of his early days as an actor, we meet such theatre greats as Thornton Wilder, Ruth Gordon and Vivien Leigh. We also come to know Stone Orchard, the Ontario farm where Findley and Whitehead have lived since the 1960s.

The author organized the book not chronologically but thematically. He built six of 11 long chapters around his novels: *The Last Of The Crazy People*, *The Butterfly Plague*, *The Wars*, *Famous Last Words*, *Not Wanted On The Voyage* and *The Telling Of Lies*.

Even so we encounter few long dark nights of the creative soul— though Findley said there were many, and that's precisely what he wanted to avoid. Instead, we get anecdotes about Findley's research—spending a night out in a pen with his dogs, sloshing around in the mud in driving rain to get a feel for war, or being surprised on an apparently deserted beach in his underwear, his face in the sand, his bum in the air, while trying to get a cat's eye view of the world.

A verbal snapshot of the inebriated would-be novelist chasing manuscript pages down New York's Madison Avenue, reflections on Salman Rushdie, the saga of the removal of a major character from *Famous Last Words*—*Inside Memory* is a writer's potpourri. A reader's delight.

Here literature comes first

Three quarters of the way through Timothy Findley's *Famous Last Words*, a minor character shoots a jettisoned fuel tank out of the sky, igniting a gasoline fire that sweeps through a crowd of panic-stricken dignitaries, the Duke and Duchess of Windsor among them, while overhead a Spitfire airplane quotes the Bible in smoke: "Mene mene tekel upharsin ... Thou art weighed in the balance and found wanting."

Suddenly, as I read this, I thought of George Bowering's *Burning Water* which won the 1980 governor-general's award for fiction, and click! Of course! Findley was one of the competition judges. I could see what Findley must have liked about Bowering's novel:

— Its "anti-realist" aspect. (Captain George Vancouver's two ships suddenly lift free of a West Coast river, sail up over the mountains and settle gently, after a cross-Canada flight, in Hudson's Bay.)

— Its insistence that literature comes first, real life second. ("Without a story-teller," Bowering wrote, "George Vancouver is just another dead sailor.")

— Its deliberate mixing of historical and imaginary truth. (Bowering's Vancouver is shot to death on his way home to England, while in "reality" he died peacefully three years after his arrival.)

Sure enough, when I asked Findley about *Burning Water*, he spoke of Bowering's daring. Then he said: "Lots of people get terrific ideas. But he had a talent great enough to keep pace with his daring, and to make something marvelous out of his idea. That novel is a major contribution to Canadian literature."

Of Findley and *Famous Last Words*, the same could be said, with only slightly less chance of starting an argument. This, the author's fourth novel, belongs to the "hyper-realist" strain in Canadian literature, which surfaced in Leonard Cohen's *Beautiful Losers* (1966). The work is nothing if not controversial.

"Frivolous," one prominent reviewer called Bowering's book. And another described Findley's latest work as "pretentious." In my view, these criticisms are reactionary.

But let's get particular.

The idea of placing the principal narrator of *Famous Last Words* in one of the great hotels of Europe (the Grand Elysium in the Austrian Alps) at the close of the Second World War, and of having him etch—not write, but etch—his story into the walls of his suite, is a brilliant one. It's brilliant simply because in "real life" it's unthinkable.

To choose as that principal narrator a character, Hugh Selwyn Mauberley, who never existed outside a poem by Ezra Pound, but who did exist there, is a stroke of genius. In this world, the choice declares, literature comes first, life second.

Finally, Findley has his way with history, as Bowering and Cohen and Michael Ondaatje have done before him. He mixes imagined characters, Mauberley chief among them, with such historical personages as the Duke and Duchess of Windsor, and intertwines wildly fictitious events, such as the Spitfire Bazaar mentioned above, with real ones, like the years-long residency of the Windsors in the Bahamas.

"Literature has to be literary," Findley insisted, "just as theatre has to be theatrical. I'm fed up with going to the theatre and seeing people I see on the street every day. I want a heightened version of those people. I want to walk away from the theatre with an altered view of reality."

Yes, *Famous Last Words* is an ambitious novel. Its subject is no less than the rise of international fascism through the 1920s, '30s and '40s. In Findley's novel, a powerful cabal nick-named Penelope engineers that rise. The cabal aims to take over all of Europe, deposing Hitler and Mussolini and installing the Duke and Duchess of Windsor as puppet king and queen of England.

Findley invites us to view his subject, not through the supposedly clear window of psychological realism, but through a kaleidoscope that mixes fact and fantasy. The novel tumbles past in technicolor fragments—characters (Ezra Pound, von Ribbentrop, Lana Turner, Charles Lindbergh), settings (China, Italy, Spain, France, England, Portugal), years (1910, 1945, 1936, 1942, 1938). This is craft!

And I haven't even mentioned the wonderfully resonant way Findley has framed his tale. Two army officers, one obsessed with the horror of Dachau, the other enamored of culture in all its manifestations, debate the merits of the etched testament while in the next room Mauberley's dead body lies putrefying.

I could go on. I could talk about the brilliance of particular scenes—for example, one in which the Duke confronts past, present and future selves in a mirror. I could argue that *Famous Last Words* represents a considerable advance over Findley's already impressive third novel, *The Wars*, which won a 1977 governor-general's award. I could quote Findley tracing the new book's arduous evolution, from a teleplay about the Canadian establishment set in the Bahamas, through three major rewrites to the product before us.

But I've gone on long enough. 1981 was a terrific year for Canadian fiction, and *Famous Last Words* was the best novel of the year.

The Telling Of Lies

Timothy Findley's *The Telling Of Lies* began as a joke, developed in mysterious ways and turned into an iceberg. He described this evolution in Calgary after reading from the novel to an enthusiastic audience of more than 100 at the University of Calgary. Findley, whose acclaimed novels include *The Wars*, *Famous Last Words* and *Not Wanted On The Voyage*, was nearing the end of a five-week, cross-Canada promotional tour.

The author always waits to eat until after a reading. In a student bar, over spaghetti and wine, he said he conceived *The Telling Of Lies* on a beach in Maine. Since 1936, when he was six, Findley has spent almost every summer there at the Atlantic House Hotel: four stories, lots of windows and white peeling clapboard walls.

In 1983, he was standing in the water looking back across the beach when in his mind's eye he saw a series of cross-fading scenes. He watched the empty beach at morning gradually fill up through the afternoon and then empty again, until at last, in a deck chair, one figure remained: that of a dead body.

"I loved it," he said. "A murder had been committed in the middle of a crowd on the beach." Findley described this vision to friends. Before long, he said, "we were talking about this mystery that 'Findley' was going to write one day. We thought we were joking."

Gradually, the dead body became that of Calder Maddox, a pharmaceuticals king. And the person to tell the story—and to play detective—arrived in Vanessa van Horne, a fictionalized version of a real-life octogenarian Findley had known since childhood.

The iceberg was a complete surprise. It turned up as Findley was walking his narrator along the beach. At first he threw down his pen, resisting the idea of letting it into the book: "This was really too much."

But Findley has been writing fiction for 30 years, and experience has taught him to explore his impulses. He decided to let the iceberg stay—an iceberg off the coast of Maine in mid-summer—but "to refuse to lie about it."

He decided, rather, to make it as symbolic as possible, and so gave it the shape of the American Capitol Building in Washington, D.C. "I admit it's funny," he said. "But there's an iceberg in this book, as well as in the bay."

The iceberg, he explained, "is the classic image of what a lie is about. Up here, on the surface, everything is pure, everything is sunlight; but down here, below the surface, is what it's really all about. And usually we have no idea about what's going on down here."

Indeed, *The Telling Of Lies* could easily have been called, simply, Iceberg. On the surface, the novel is a murder mystery. Down below, *The Telling Of Lies* is a powerful statement about politics in general and Canadian-American relations in particular.

The novel is fueled "by some anger, if not rage," Findley said. The author is angry, for example, about drug experiments the CIA conducted at the Allen Memorial Hospital in Montreal, using unsuspecting Canadians as guinea pigs.

And he's angry about the way Canadian politicians allowed this to happen. Speaking of a minor character in the novel, a Canadian government official who is more obsequious than Uriah Heep, Findley rubbed his hands together fawningly: "That's why Nigel is Nigel, and doing this all the time."

Findley's most nationalistic novel? "I haven't thought about it in those terms," he said, "but that's undoubtedly true."

The war was just endlessly there

Canadians are still living with the results of the Second World War, novelist Timothy Findley said in 1989. "That war is still with us, defining who we are and what we're about."

Findley, who won a 1977 governor-general's award for his novel *The Wars*, was host of a six-part CBC-Radio documentary called *Lost Innocence: The Children Of World War Two*.

In a telephone interview he said that the series looks at the war through the eyes of children and teenagers whose lives were shaped by it, but whose stories are rarely told in conventional history books.

Findley, who was nine when Canada declared war on September 10, 1939, shares his own memories of the period in the second episode, "War At A Distance."

He remembers that his father tuned in to the war months before it began. "The radio was never off," he said. "We had to listen. The war was just endlessly there."

Findley vividly recalls his "feeling of being abandoned" when his father joined the air force, and also the upheaval that followed. "I remember looking up and seeing my father coming down the hall dressed in uniform for the first time—my terrible sense of betrayal and shock. Because to me that meant he was going to die."

Findley's father survived the war. But the author also remembers when the phone call came telling his father that he was going to Europe: "I ran into the room and he was jumping up and down on the bed like a child, yelling, 'I'm going! I'm going!'

"And I remember absolutely hating my father at that moment, because he was rejoicing in the fact that he was getting away from us."

Since the war, Findley said, most Canadians have been living "very materialistic, self-centred lives: nobody has had to deal with questions of survival."

But the next 10 years will "not be magical, wondrous days," he warned. *Lost Innocence* has something to teach. "We need to learn how to survive again—and in the company of other people."

17. Janette Turner Hospital: An Aussie Perspective

Janette Turner Hospital is among the most exciting writers to surface in Canada in the past decade. In 1982, she won the $50,000 Seal First Novel Award with The Ivory Swing, *a sensuous, evocative novel that focused on a Canadian couple sojourning in southern India. The following year she published* The Tiger In The Tiger Pit, *which revolved around an estranged New England family gathered for a 50th-wedding anniversary. Both books were published internationally and nominated in Great Britain for the Booker Prize.*

In 1985, Hospital published Borderline, *a novel that revealed both the breadth of her talent and the extent of her ambition. The author's willingness to take risks was evident in her choice of narrator. He was a minor character not present at any of the story's turning points, who sat in his room after the fact and recreated events as best he could. This approach put the novel on the borderline between psychological realism—the conventional novel—and the postmodernism of* Famous Last Words *and* Burning Water.

In 1989, Hospital published Charades, *a New Physics novel. In the spring of 1991, she gave the world* Isobars, *a second collection of stories, and in the summer she hopes to complete her fifth novel, title undecided (possibly* The Last Magician In Australia). *That's five novels not counting* A Very Proper Death, *a mystery she published in 1990 under the pseudonym Alex Juniper. A literary reputation, even one flowering in four English-speaking countries, "will bring you lots of prestige," Hospital told me, "but no money to speak of. If I could whip off a mystery in 10 weeks of each year, I could live by my work and have a lot of time left to do my serious writing."*

The last time I interviewed Hospital in person, in the summer of 1990, she spoke of commuting between Canada and Australia. "Maybe the solution is to spend half a year in each country," she said, laughing. "Skip out on Canadian winters altogether and get two summers." Now it's happening. In the fall of 1991, Hospital will spend nine weeks as writer-in-residence at the University of Queensland, her alma mater. And in 1992, she will become an adjunct professor of English at La Trobe University in Melbourne, and begin spending the first half of each year Down Under.

KINGSTON—Janette Turner Hospital is still reeling from a two-month sojourn in India. "The most astounding change," she says of the country she first visited in 1978, "is television. There are 750 million people in India and 80 percent of them have access to television. Television has given them a window on the world. Twelve years ago I was a zoo animal. I couldn't go out without feeling like a pied piper. This time people barely noticed me."

Hospital drew on her initial visit to India for *The Ivory Swing*, a first novel which won the $50,000 Seal Award in 1982 and launched her career with fanfare. "I'm perpetually grateful for that early nurturing," she said over lunch. "It enabled me to stop scrabbling around for teaching jobs and concentrate on my work."

Since publishing *The Ivory Swing*, the Australia-born Hospital has emerged as a prolific and exciting fiction writer—a Down-Under answer to Margaret Atwood. She has produced three acclaimed novels—*The Tiger In The Tiger Pit* (1983), *Borderline* (1985) and *Charades* (1989)—and a book of stories called *Dislocations* (1986). She has made the shortlist for Australia's two major fiction awards, and twice made the long-list for England's prestigious Booker Prize. She won the Fiction Award of the Fellowship of Australian Writers, and was named one of Canada's 10 best fiction writers under 45.

Born in 1942, Hospital shows no signs of slowing her pace. She is working long hours on a novel tentatively entitled *The Last Magician In Australia*, hoping, she said, "to get the bulk of the first draft done before I leave for Australia in August" of 1990. She was going to attend the Australia launch of *Isobars*, her second collection of short stories.

Isobars? "They're those lines on a weather map that join places of equal pressure," Hospital reminded me. "The stories are a nomad's stories, points linked by the pressure of memory. Three-quarters are set totally in Australia, while the others link Canada and Australia."

Hospital and her husband, Cliff, left Australia in 1967 and lived in Boston for four years. In 1971, Cliff became a professor in the department of comparative religion at Queen's University, and the Hospitals—they have a son and a daughter at university—have lived in Kingston ever since. (Hospital has visited India during her husband's sabbaticals.)

In 1986, the Hospitals moved 10 kilometres east of the city, and now their back yard rolls away through a forest of trees to the St. Lawrence River. It's amidst this peaceful greenery, in a second-floor studio with a bay window, that Hospital does most of her writing. For the past three years, however, she has spent four months in each of Australia and Boston (she was writer-in-residence at the Massachusetts Institute of Technology).

All this moving around "makes you extremely conscious of how perceptions of reality are governed by cultural constructs," Hospital said. "I'm becoming more and more skeptical of the nature of perception. People can be very dogmatic about something, but then you cross a border and you find them just as dogmatic, but on the opposite side. Travelling around the world makes you more conscious of these disjunctions."

Hospital traces her fascination with the theme of dislocation and displacement to her childhood. Her parents were Christian fundamentalists, she said, stressing that they were warm and loving and supportive while "living in New Testament time and imminently expecting the Second Coming."

At age five, when she entered the hedonistic, resolutely working-class world of school, Hospital found she "had to function as two people. Neither world could understand the other. That was my early training for being a writer," she said, "mediating discrepant views of reality. I've been doing it since age five."

In recent years, though in Boston the author becomes "a vehement Canadian nationalist," Hospital has found Australia figuring more prominently in her fiction. "I don't feel I choose my subject matter," she said. "It chooses me." She mentioned several Canadian expatriate writers—Mordecai Richler, Norman Levine, Mavis Gallant—who returned to Canada, at least in subject matter. "You can't predict life's curve," she said, "but there seems to be a mid-life thing that happens."

For Hospital, that "thing" involves exploring her Australian roots. The result is that she feels divided, her writing acclaimed in Australia, England and the United States and ignored in her adoptive country of almost 20 years.

"I don't think Canada is to blame," she said. "It's so involved right now in establishing the identity of its scattered parts against the U.S. This is totally understandable and can't be avoided. But there's no tradition of tropical writing here, and most of my nurturing is coming from Australia and England.

"Canada is just not interested in an Australian voice examining what it feels like to be an Australian in Canada. For me this is the big problem with writing here. You tend to want to be where the ethos is nourishing your writing, responding to it."

This country's obsessive insecurity "hits me oddly," Hospital said. "Canada is so absolutely different from Australia or the U.S. that sometimes I feel like shaking Canadians by the shoulders and saying, 'Good Heavens! Wake up!'"

18. George Bowering: The Fighting Anti-Realist

Vancouver author George Bowering has published almost 50 books, among them works of poetry, fiction, short stories and essays. In his 1990 novel Harry's Fragments, *a take-off on the spy thriller, Bowering continued his exploration of genre fiction, which is highlighted by the anti-western* Caprice.

As For Me And My Horse

If the world of Canadian letters were a classroom, Vancouver writer George Bowering would be the kid who sits at the back with his feet up on the desk, looking out the window and making wisecracks. Behind the banter and bravado of this studied pose, however, hides one of Canada's most accomplished writers.

Born in 1935, Bowering has twice won a governor-general's award for literature, most recently for his 1980 novel *Burning Water*. His 1987 novel, *Caprice*, is reminiscent of that earlier work and even features a couple of familiar-sounding Indians. Yet it differs from *Burning Water* in significant ways.

The eponymous heroine is larger-than-life, for example, a mythical figure—yet she never does anything magical. This time around Bowering has resisted the temptation (one can imagine the agonized writhing) to thumb his nose at psychological realism by introducing, say, horses that suddenly soar into the air. Some readers will miss the hyperbole of the earlier approach, the unruly excessiveness. Yet Bowering is wise to opt for greater self-control. *Caprice* insists on its own reality, but more subtly than *Burning Water* did, and so it will alarm and alienate fewer readers.

Caprice is set mostly in British Columbia in the 1890s. It's replete with good guys and bad guys, cowboys and Indians, and a central figure obsessed with tracking down a killer and bringing him to justice. It's an old-fashioned western—except that the hombres have ethnic identities and the Indians debate metaphysical questions. Oh, yes, and the would-be avenger is a gorgeous, red-headed, French-Canadian woman who is six feet tall, carries a European bullwhip, makes poetry when she isn't suffering from writer's block, and has a schoolteacher-boyfriend who plays baseball, can't understand her quest and wants her to settle down.

We have here an entertainment with a polemical subtext—not an old-fashioned western but a postmodern one. In drawing attention to the conventions of genre, Bowering reasserts the aesthetic that informed *Burning Water*: "You're reading a story, amigo, and don't you forget it."

The plot of *Caprice* is starkly conventional. A ruthless American gunslinger named Frank Spencer kills a French-Canadian wrangler who calls himself Pete Foster—shoots him in the back over a couple of bottles of whiskey. Foster, otherwise known as Pierre, dies with his sister's name on his lips: Caprice.

This we learn in an early flashback, the narrative having opened with Caprice's arrival in the West to embark on her quest. She rides a beautiful Arabian horse named Cabayo, and pursues Spencer from Canada to the Mexican border and back again. But most of the novel takes place in British Columbia, in Kamloops and the nearby Okanagon Valley (where Bowering was born and raised).

Here we meet Strange Loop Groulx, Spencer's French-Canadian sidekick and necessary foil; Everyday Luigi, an Austro-Italian linguist who works as a handyman for the local Chinese community and gets his bottom jaw shot off after performing an act of gallantry; and Roy Smith, Caprice's boyfriend, whose confidence in his own grace and power is such that "in front of one of his classes he was not afraid to flip a pencil end over end and catch it pointed the right way."

Other characters include an overweight Mountie named Constable Burt; Gert the Whore, who has—you guessed it—a heart of gold; an obsessive photographer named Archie Minjus; and Arpad Kesselring, a visiting Austro-Hungarian journalist who romanticizes the West to further his own career.

Then there are the first Indian and the second Indian, whose counterparts we met in *Burning Water,* and who provide a running commentary on the action. They play a larger role here than in the earlier work, where they yielded frequently to a first-person narrator. They're like the talkative soldiers in Timothy Findley's *Famous Last Words* or the angels in Robertson Davies' *What's Bred In The Bone* (though Bowering would shudder at that idea).

Their conversations are absurd, wildly unrealistic, deliberately fantastical—and often funny. One Indian asks the other if he has ever considered where they come from. "If you mean in a metaphysical sense," comes the reply, "I suppose the Great Spirit sent us here to suffer inferior hunting and landscape, so that we would be filled with a hankering for the Happy Hunting Ground."

Later, the first Indian notes: "The western man of action believes that his actions are saving his country, as he calls it, from the decay of its early promise that set in when life became easy enough back east for people to make their living without getting dirty."

This motif, West in relation to East, runs through the novel—and not only in the Indians' dialogue. The omniscient, third-person narrator contributes epigrams and some brilliant passages, most notably a lament that begins, "By the 1890s the west had started to shrink."

In *Caprice,* Bowering distinguishes fancy from imagination, rejects motivated characters in the name of fate and invites his readers to collusion: "We can look back to what they (the characters) looked forward to." For this author, old familiar ploys.

Occasionally, too, Bowering is corny: "The two riders approached fast, their horses wild-eyed. One of the horses was brown-and-white. The other was white-and-brown." And his oft-repeated insistence on "now, or rather then," together with its variations, is an annoying affectation: "He hoped that he could forget (his anger) for two hours on the field this afternoon, or rather that one."

But these are peccadilloes.

Bowering will no doubt be chastised by the critical establishment as an irreverent smart-aleck. Yet he will have the last laugh. With *Caprice*, he has demonstrated yet again that he's one of Canada's most original writers.

Speaking of Burning Water....

"From its conception in pioneer journalism the Canadian short story inherited in turn its most characteristic feature: a realism so intimate and natural that what it describes is often mistaken for real life." So says editor Wayne Grady in his preface to *The Penguin Book Of Canadian Short Stories*.

Indeed, realism is the hallmark, not just of the Canadian short story, but of Canadian fiction, period. West Coast writer George Bowering says Canada has always reserved its awards "for authors who seek to reproduce in words the lives of real Canadians in real Canadian settings."

Bowering blames Canada's "good old puritanism" for this. "In most countries of the technological world the writer of postmodern fiction is no longer in the avant-garde, but is rather the prime product for export. In Japan, the United States, Europe, Latin America, the writer who wants to produce something that the sophisticated reading audience will agree to call the real, creates rather than recreating; he makes a post-Auschwitz world out of fable, collage, travesty, tall-tale, visual hi-jinx—in short, out of contemporary versions of the literary means common to prose before Zola & James invented modern realism."

Bowering, who in 1969 won a governor-general's award for poetry, is in the vanguard of a movement to supplant realism in Canadian fiction, to replace it with what he calls "anti-realist, post-modern or language-centred fiction."

"Movement" is perhaps too strong a word. But certainly Leonard Cohen, Michael Ondaatje, Leon Rooke and Jack Hodgins have all produced works that one could describe as anti-realist or postmodern.

In any case, Bowering was in Calgary to promote *Burning Water*, his first full-length novel since 1967. I talked with him about that book and about "anti-realist" fiction in general. But let's look at the latter through the former. On one level *Burning Water* is about Captain George Vancouver, who in the early 1790s led two 99-foot sloops on a four-year search for the legendary Northwest Passage, mapping 10,000 miles of the Pacific Coast in the process.

Bowering frames Vancouver's story in a conventional manner, setting up a present-day, third-person narrator named George who proceeds to tell the captain's tale, cutting occasionally to his own life and travails in Vancouver, Trieste and Costa Rica. The "anti-realist" aspect of the novel is most evident in its content.

At one point, Vancouver's two ships, the Chatham and the Discovery, lift free of a river on the West Coast and sail up "through the rocky air above the first peaks of the Coast Range." They touch down again, after a comfortable cross-Canada flight, in the "slightly rippled" waters of Hudson's Bay.

Bowering's Vancouver has a homosexual love affair with a Spaniard, Captain Don Juan Bodega y Quadra. He claims friendship with the British soldier James Wolfe, although in truth he was only two years old when Wolfe died on the Plains of Abraham. Finally, our hero is shot to death by botanist, doctor and chief antagonist Archibald Menzies before he reaches England, when in "reality" Vancouver died peacefully three years after his arrival.

Yes, Bowering is deliberately making a hash of history. Anti-realist fiction, he says, "invites disbelief as opposed to suspending it." In so doing, it draws attention to the fact that fiction is created, not out of memories or reveries, but out of language. "The real is in the text itself. It doesn't lie behind the text."

Bowering says "history is fiction anyway"—that everything we know about George Vancouver has come to us through words on a page. "The

George Vancouver in my book is not the George Vancouver in anybody else's book," he says. Different Vancouvers exist in different books—in Menzies' journal, in Peter Pond's journal, in Vancouver's own journal. "I've got another one. And I hope my George Vancouver will get a fair trial."

The assumption of the realists, Bowering says, is "that we're products of our history, and all we have to do is tell the story. The truth is, we're not the products but the creators of history." Or, as Bowering put it in the preface to his novel, "Without a storyteller, George Vancouver is just another dead sailor."

The anti-realist writer invites the reader, not to stand looking at carefully motivated characters through a one-way mirror, but to involve himself with what's happening on the page, to participate in an act of creation.

Writing in the *Canadian Fiction Magazine*, Bowering described an imagined reviewer picking up a language-centred novel, sniffing it and saying, "This must have been fun to write, but it is frivolous." At least one prominent reviewer has responded to *Burning Water* in just that fashion. Myself, I enjoyed the book immensely, found it witty and refreshing. More, I consider it an act of courage. And one thing I hope I've made clear: *Burning Water* is anything but frivolous.

***

VII

Fourth Battle Zone:
Freedom Of Expression

"Towards the end of her life," the late Hugh MacLennan declared angrily, "Margaret Laurence had to go to war with self-righteous idiots who wanted to ban her books. Perhaps without that she would still be here." The year was 1987. The place, Kingston, Ontario. MacLennan, five-time winner of the governor-general's award for literature, was delivering the inaugural Margaret Laurence Memorial Address at the annual general meeting of the Writers' Union of Canada.

Laurence, whose best-loved novels were *The Diviners* and *The Stone Angel*, had died the previous year of cancer. During the final months of her life, MacLennan telephoned her every couple of weeks. "She was calm and accepting," he said. "She knew she had done her work." But her war with book banners, he told a hushed audience of more than 200, had taken a terrible toll.

That MacLennan chose to discuss book-banning in his address was no whim. Censorship may not be the issue when considering native voice. But the freedom to read is under continual attack in this country. Examples abound. In late 1990, to cite a recent one, Margaret Buffie's novel *Who Is Frances Rain?* was banned from the school library and classrooms of Queenswood Public School in Orleans, Ontario. Buffie's novel had won the Young Adult Canadian Book Award in 1987 and the following year was runner-up for the Canadian Library Association Book of the Year for Children Award, but what do those people know? Never mind that *Books In Canada* described the novel as "a sensitive and realistic treatment of the problems and tensions facing modern families." The words "hell" and "bastard" appear in that book! Can you imagine what reading those words could do to your children? The mind boggles.

Over the years a shocking number of books have been challenged by people seeking to have them banned from Canadian high schools, libraries and bookstores. Books by authors like John Steinbeck, William Faulkner, W.O. Mitchell, Alice Munro, J.D. Salinger, Truman Capote, Aldous Huxley and, yes, Margaret Laurence. These attempts at censorship spring frequently from principals or school trustees responding to pressure. Those advocating banning often hold strong religious convictions—shades of the Ayatollah Khomeini!—and object to certain passages as offending Judeo-Christian values.

In an Ontario challenge to Laurence's *The Diviners* in 1978, for example, one line deemed offensive was, "No, I'm crying for God's sake." That same year, Mitchell's *Who Has Seen The Wind* was challenged in several places, including Saint John, New Brunswick, where the words "god damn" were cited. In 1981, Salinger's *Catcher In The Rye*, recognized around the world as a classic, was attacked for containing "obscene language and profanity," and removed from school reading lists in two Ontario counties.

But ignorant would-be book-banners are only half the problem. Canadian laws have turned 5,000 Canada Customs officers into instant literary experts. Over the years these genius-judges have detained books by James Joyce, Marcel Proust, William Faulkner, Norman Mailer and Salman Rushdie. Customs officers routinely search three quarters of shipments going to bookstores that serve gay communities—to Glad Day in Toronto, l'Androgyne in Montreal and Little Sisters in Vancouver—and delay them for weeks or months.

Magazines and newspapers, as well as books, have come under attack. In 1984, for example, Calgary's municipal government set up a task force to find ways of curbing the sales of pornographic books, magazines and films. This resulted from pressure by the Calgary Coalition Against Pornography, which represented about 30 city and provincial social action groups. The task force held public meetings to define "pornography" and explore whether the city had the constitutional clout to enact a bylaw. But "pornography" is notoriously difficult to define and, fortunately, the task force came to naught.

Hate literature has complicated the censorship problem. Remember *The Hoax Of The 20th Century*? It argues that the Holocaust never happened. The League for Human Rights of B'Nai B'Rith Canada labelled the work "hate literature" and wanted it banned. The University of Calgary library successfully fought a ruling that saw two copies of the book removed from its shelves. But that the library had to fight at all is worrisome. Yes, the book is disgusting. But a law providing for its removal from libraries is not the answer—not if you value democracy.

Freedom of expression makes democracy possible. To bring in censorship of any kind is to threaten that freedom, because laws have a way of being misused. Would-be censors forget that unless people can compare conflicting perspectives and ideas, they develop opinions out of prejudice, bigotry, ignorance and worse. The only "free" ideas are those freely chosen.

Here we see the importance of organizations like the Writers' Union of Canada (TWUC). In late 1990, the union, the International PEN Canadian Centre and the Canadian Committee Against Customs Censorship attracted a standing-room only crowd of 450 to a reading from titles that Canadian customs officials have banned in the past 75 years. And that meeting at which Hugh MacLennan spoke? It happened while the federal government was considering Bill C-57, which Pierre Berton, the union's incoming chair, called the "censorship bill." The proposed legislation sparked an intense hour-long debate—imagine a crowded amphitheatre, much shouting and waving of arms—that reflected the usual divisions over ways of combating sexual exploitation and violence against women and children.

Both are already illegal under the criminal code, Berton said, "and we don't need censorship laws" to fight them. "I don't see how any writers' organization worth its salt can countenance any form of censorship." Novelist and essayist Jane Rule, whose books have been seized at the border by Customs officers, drew applause with a passionate denunciation of the bill. "We cannot ask the government to legislate our morality for us—and you're fools if you ask them to do it." Rule quoted the late Marian Engel: "If you go after de Sade, you will get Margaret Laurence every time."

Non-fiction writer Susan Crean suggested dealing with pornography and violence against women not by amending the criminal code but through systems of classification. In the end, TWUC voted overwhelmingly to condemn Bill C-57, and also passed a resolution asking the government to curtail the powers granted Canada Customs officers to seize and destroy books, periodicals and other materials which have not been deemed illegal.

Writers have not yet won that last battle. Bill C-57, the censorship bill, eventually died a quiet death. But did I mention Salman Rushdie?

19. The Satanic Verses

Never has a book evoked such hysteria.

One day scholars will devote careers to the controversy that erupted over *The Satanic Verses* by Salman Rushdie.

Here and now visibility is poor, the forest obscured by inconvenient trees, the air thick with the fog of knee-jerk reactions and easy misconceptions.

Take the editorial that argued in another newspaper, and rightly, for freedom of expression. In passing, it suggested that Rushdie's novel "is obviously a carefully-crafted attack on Islamic fundamentalism."

But *The Satanic Verses* is no such thing. It's a towering work of art. And I'm not saying this in reaction. Months before Iran's Ayatollah Khomeini abused the work to attract the attention of Islamic fundamentalists, I described the novel as "a stylistic tour-de-force that mixes myth and reality in ways reminiscent of James Joyce."

Let me back up.

In the fall of 1988, when I was preparing to attend the International Festival of Authors in Toronto, I particularly looked forward to interviewing Saul Bellow, Jerzy Kosinski and D.M. Thomas. I'd heard of British writer Salman Rushdie, and knew he'd won the Booker Prize for his novel *Midnight's Children* (1981), but (blush) I'd never read anything he'd written.

A couple of weeks before the festival I began reading *The Satanic Verses*. Its magnificence staggered me. Halfway through the book I realized I was in the presence of a contemporary master. By the time I finished, the Toronto festival had been transformed. Now I was going to interview Salman Rushdie, and everybody else—including Nobel-prize winner Saul Bellow—was secondary.

I told anybody who'd listen that *The Satanic Verses* was the best novel I'd read in a decade, and that Rushdie was one of the greatest writers of his generation—and mine! The man was not yet 42! And he'd written a masterpiece!

The day before I arrived in Toronto, Rushdie's book was banned in India. This made me furious. Oh, I knew this twist would make for a more "newsworthy" story. But it distorted our interview. Now I had to get Rushdie to respond to aberrational political events, and how often does one get to spend 40 minutes with one of the great writers of one's own generation? I wanted to talk about *The Satanic Verses* and how Rushdie created it, not some crackpot reaction to the book.

Before the banning, it had never occurred to me that Muslims would find the book offensive. As Rushdie noted during our interview, and I duly reported, the novel "is at least partially comic: It's a book about migration, metamorphosis, London, Bombay, coming to terms with death, learning how to love—all sorts of things politicians are not interested in." And only 70 of its 547 pages relate in any way to Islam.

Politically speaking, what struck me about *The Satanic Verses*, and this too I wrote, was its "devastating portrait of Margaret Thatcher's England." Rushdie abhors Thatcher's neo-conservative revolution. During our interview, he spoke bitterly about "the trick of Thatcherism"—how the Iron Lady remained in power by pitting those who had jobs against those who had none.

The Satanic Verses offers a savage indictment of Thatcherism, yet—and this, too, comes at me out of the fog—the government of England acted rapidly and decisively to circle wagons around the threatened author. Compare this with the shameful dithering of our own government. Believe me, I never thought I'd say it, but it looks as if jolly old England still has a few things to teach the rest of us about principled behavior.

Other commentators have noted that Khomeini does not speak for all Muslims, but this bears stressing. Most Christians would not want to be identified with Jimmy Swaggart, say, much less with some ignorant zealot who had just stepped out of the Middle Ages.

And what do we make of those bookstore chains, Coles and Woodward's, that followed the lead of even bigger American bookstore chains, caving in to irrational threats and pulling *The Satanic Verses* from shelves?

But in fairness, I think we have to remember that a bookstore chain is not an old-fashioned, owner-run bookstore. Employees can't be called into a room and given an opportunity to weigh pros and cons. Above all, I have trouble with the idea of forcing bookstore clerks, many of whom are working for minimum wage, into the front lines in the never-ending battle for freedom of expression.

This experience underlines the importance of having small, independent bookstores. Maybe, instead of condemning bookstore chains for not being something they never pretended to be, and for erring on the side of caution, we should make a point of patronizing independent bookstores.

Finally, say a prayer for Salman Rushdie. At least one international expert on assassinations, a security consultant, has said that the author is "a dead man, no matter what Khomeini says now." That's because someone, somewhere, some time, is going to get him.

We're talking here about one of the greatest writers of a generation. What a comment on mankind.

20. The Fuddy-Duddy Reads First

Call me old-fashioned, but I like to read the books I write about. Fuddy-duddy that I am, I've even done the odd bit of original research before getting up on my soapbox.

That's why I'm left almost speechless when newspaper colleagues, donning the ever-popular mantle of the anti-elitist, proudly proclaim their total ignorance of books they then proceed to vilify and denounce, justifying their actions by saying, hey, everybody else is doing it.

I'm not talking just about Salman Rushdie's *Satanic Verses*, which has been dismissed as "an anti-Islamic, anti-religious tract" by columnists who have no intention of reading it. I'm talking also about *John Dollar*, the novel by Rushdie's wife, Marianne Wiggins.

We've been informed in this newspaper, by those who haven't read a word of the author's four books, that Wiggins has published "a novel mocking her religion with a skill and dedication equal to that of her husband."

"Gee," I thought when I read this, "my old journalism profs would have jumped on that as hearsay, and maybe thrown in a lecture on question-begging. Guess I'm out of touch."

Still, you can't teach an old newspaperman new attitudes. And would you believe that when *John Dollar* turned up, I took the darn thing home and read it? Not only that, but I even read numerous reviews and articles about its author. Crazy, eh?

Anyway, Wiggins's latest novel was inspired, in part, by William Golding's *Lord Of The Flies*. Set mostly in Burma immediately after the First World War, it moves inexorably toward a grim revelation after several school girls are marooned on an island.

The book explores patriarchal attitudes, British colonialism and, in ways reminiscent of Joseph Conrad's *Heart Of Darkness*, spiritual disintegration. It's relentless, harrowing and beautifully written, although it's marred by an affectation: wide margins filled with headings, sub-headings and occasional notes.

Now, Wiggins has, in fact, described herself as "an opponent of religion." In a *London Times* interview, she said that with *John Dollar*, "I wanted to show how powerful it (religion) is and how it needs to be questioned. It is always this close to evil, as are all of these things which are structured to keep society tamped down."

The first consideration here is context. Wiggins was born (in Pennsylvania, 1947) into a Protestant fundamentalist sect founded by her grandfather. Furthermore, she was discussing *John Dollar* while Islamic fundamentalists were banning and burning a novel her husband had dedicated to her.

In brief, that's the religion Wiggins opposes: intolerant fanaticism of any faith or creed that spawns death threats against citizens of other countries—threats which leading Muslim spokesmen have also condemned.

John Dollar, like *Heart Of Darkness*, is not for everybody. But it's a serious work of literature that raises serious metaphysical and political questions. To dismiss it as "mocking" without having read it is cheap and irresponsible.

❋ ❋ ❋

VIII

Canadian Volunteers Keep Coming

21. Robert Harlow: Unsung Bomber Pilot

In the spring of 1990, when West Coast real estate was at its peak, Robert Harlow sold a townhouse in suburban Vancouver and moved to Mayne Island, British Columbia. There he bought a house on a hill, mortgage-free, and he says, "On a good day, you can look out and see all the way down to the San Juan Islands." Harlow recently completed a war novel—"I did five or six drafts"—called Flying Blind, *a sequel to his acclaimed growing-up novel* The Saxophone Winter. *Advance readers have hailed it as his best book yet, and Harlow hopes to see it appear in 1992. Early this year, he spent six weeks in Costa Rica, researching "a kind of thriller" set there. He calls it* Longford's Address.

Building a culture

VANCOUVER—The free-trade battle may be over for many, but for Canadian novelist Robert Harlow it's just beginning. "The worst thing that can happen to a real free-trader is to come up against a strong culture," Harlow told 200 people gathered to celebrate his achievements. "But if we lose what we've made in the past 20 years, we'll be back at square one."

Harlow, author of seven novels, was speaking at the closing-day brunch of the second annual Vancouver International Writers' Festival. After apologizing for speaking seriously on "one of the most beautiful days of my life," Harlow said that building a culture during the 1950s and '60s was "like trying to build a platform 10 feet in the air while standing on it.

"When I tell people horror stories about trying to get published in the '50s, they simply don't believe me." The turning point, he said, was the birth of the Canada Council program of block grants for Canadian publishers.

Harlow, whose novels include *Scann, Paul Nolan, Making Arrangements* and *The Saxophone Winter,* had recently turned 65 and retired from teaching at the University of British Columbia. He'd been there since 1966, when he left CBC Radio to head the first separate creative writing department in Canada.

At CBC, he'd been the first director of radio in the West, and with Robert Weaver, launched the literary program "Anthology." Before that, he'd been the first Canadian to attend the famous Iowa Writers' Workshop.

Author Robin Mathews, hired by Harlow in the '50s to work at the CBC, told those assembled that the novelist was "recklessly caring" about people and ideas and had "the marvelous gift" of being able to release the creativity of others without feeling threatened.

Novelist George Payerle, one of many of Harlow's ex-students at the brunch, said that "in the beginning Harlow was like a literary father to me, but as I got older and he got younger, we became friends."

Harlow, born in Prince Rupert and raised in Prince George, flew Lancaster bombers during the Second World War. "When I got home I discovered that they'd pay me $60 a month to go to UBC," he said. That sounded much better than his alternatives—"being a lumberjack, driving a truck or working on the railway."

Harlow, who has been called the most important under-recognized novelist in Canada, is certainly one of the finest western Canadian novelists of his generation. His 1972 novel, *Scann,* is widely recognized by writers as a technical tour de force, and has been published in the New Canadian Library series.

In 1988, Harlow published *The Saxophone Winter,* his warmest work. It's a remarkably detailed portrait of growing up in backwoods British Columbia just before the Second World War.

The maleness of the male

Robert Harlow pours himself another glass of wine, then launches into a wonderful, rambling anecdote set in Costa Rica, all about running into a blockade while trying to visit fellow writer William Deverell, and suddenly I'm back in the faculty club at the University of British Columbia. It's 1975 again and Harlow is regaling me over lunch with tales of his days as a bomber pilot, interspersed with observations on the "new" South American novelists and suggestions about how to improve my own work-in-progress.

For 11 years, ending in 1977, Harlow was head of UBC's department of creative writing. During most of that time, he taught a graduate-student workshop in novel writing. Scores of writers and would-be writers have taken that workshop, and have had their understanding of fiction immeasurably broadened and deepened, and often completely transformed, by the man I've brought home to dinner. I'm one of them.

Objective, then, I can't pretend to be—not when it comes to Bob Harlow, who was in Calgary to promote his fifth novel, *Paul Nolan*. My bias declared, however, I have no qualms about reporting that *Paul Nolan* has been eliciting raves across the country, with one reviewer, writing in *Maclean's*, comparing the novel to Malcolm Lowry's *Under The Volcano*, and suggesting that the visceral power of Harlow's prose is "worthy of D.H. Lawrence himself."

"Not bad company," Harlow admits.

In his third novel, *Scann* (1972), a little-known Canadian classic, Harlow demonstrated his mastery of compression, the fictional technique of generating energy by collapsing time, and condensing the events of many years into a much shorter period—in that case, an Easter weekend.

This time out, Harlow's novel spans five days—five days and roughly 45 years in the life of Paul Nolan, 49, archetypal macho man. Nolan has Got It Made. He owns a lucrative personnel consulting business and drives a Jaguar. He has a magnificent home in West Vancouver, complete with a swimming pool and a view of the harbor. He has a charming wife—they've been married 27 years—and three children, now young adults.

Alas, poor Paul, he also has an eye for the ladies. "Paul's inability to grow up sexually is his undoing," Harlow notes. "He's unable to deny himself anything." Paul helps himself to two whores, for example, while in the next room, shocked, his accountant son waits. Or again, he tries to seduce his best friend's sister hours after attending a funeral for her mother. Finally, he has intercourse on the lawn by the pool with his younger son's girlfriend while in the house his wife goes about her domestic duties.

Sound familiar? One woman told Harlow, "I could name 40 guys just like this s.o.b." Another allegedly keeps the book by her bed so she can enjoy turning her back and saying, "Not tonight, I've got a headache." A male friend of Harlow's exclaimed, "My, God, Bob! You've sold us all down the river!"

Harlow shrugs, laughs.

But I haven't begun to convey the textural richness of this work. For 25 years, Paul Nolan has been corresponding with a boyhood friend named Matthew—a diplomat cum philosopher with whom he argues metaphysics. During the novel, these two, reunited, discover that a shared childhood trauma—mother/son incest—has shaped both their lives.

As well, in flashback, we sojourn with Paul in a little town in Spain. Here, we're treated to a beautiful Spanish funeral that contrasts with the decidedly ugly North American rite which has brought Matthew home. Also, not incidentally, we learn of Paul's first infidelity, flagged as the beginning of his sorry end. "Yes, you are guilty," his wife says, shoving him toward the door, "yes, you are a cheater; yes you are sick. Get out!"

This novel is studded with off-the-cuff insight, imbued with unassuming wisdom. Of his own generation, Paul notes in passing "that their upward mobility was only apparent, part of a general thrust given by a six-year world conflict to a sparse post-war generation, so that certifiable defectives, middle-aged, were now general managers, cabinet ministers, instant real estate millionaires...."

And Vancouver! Its sights and sounds, its ambiance—oh, the tick-tocking horror of rush hour on Lion's Gate Bridge—have never been better captured. But enough.

Harlow finished *Paul Nolan* in 1978 and couldn't get it published. Five years later, he says: "People just weren't ready to deal with the maleness of the male. Now they are."

For the rest, Harlow recently finished a screenplay about drug-running. And he's fine-tuning yet another novel: *Felice: A Travelogue*. It's told from a woman's point of view, it's set in Poland—and more, though I ply him with wine, he will not divulge.

Boy in winter

During the mid-'70s, when he was head of the creative writing department at the University of British Columbia and I was a know-it-all graduate student, Robert Harlow taught me more about the novel than I was able to admit.

My bias confessed, my debt acknowledged, I'm happy to declare that Harlow's seventh novel, *The Saxophone Winter*, has leap-frogged into a tie for first place in my private ranking of his books. The author's third novel, *Scann*, is still the one I admire most. A writer's novel, it's a technical tour de force, a casebook study of advanced novelistics. But *The Saxophone Winter* has heart. Technically self-effacing, it's a reader's novel—the warmest, most human work Harlow has written.

Harlow, who was born in Prince Rupert (in 1923) and raised in Prince George, sets this deceptively low-key coming-of-age novel in the fictional B.C. town of Long River (population 4,000) during the winter of 1938-39.

The Saxophone Winter focuses on Christopher Waterton, a sensitive 14-year-old who dreams of playing the saxophone and sets out to make his dream a reality. Christopher provides the novel's eyes and ears, though the narrative perspective, the authorial voice, is completely mature.

The novel opens slowly, as we watch Christopher fall in love (for the first time) with a 13-year-old girl named Emily. The light-hearted novel of puppy love soon darkens, however, as Christopher finds himself at odds, not only with his parents, but also with his best friend, Fielder.

During the winter, merely by living day to day, Christopher comes up against hypocrisy and broken dreams, terminal illness and the many faces of adult sexuality. He battles the Philistine mentality of the town: "I got out (of school) at grade four myself," the mayor says, "and I haven't done bad at all." He discovers the unfairness of the world: "So, if he or Fielder or Smith quit school the law would be enforced. Doucette and May could quit and nothing was done."

And he learns about human resistance to change: "...what had been happening between (Christopher and Fielder) since Christmas was some kind of struggle. Not on his part, but on Fielder's, to keep things as they'd been since they'd first met."

See what I mean about deceptively low key?

Harlow has always been a master of compression. Here, he has squeezed a lifetime of experience and, yes, wisdom, into a single winter—and that winter, finally, into a few well-chosen days.

While evoking the emotional landscape of adolescence, Harlow finds space to write authoritatively on everything from jazz to ski-jumping, incidentally creating a whole town. Talk about texture and richness of context. We're never allowed to forget that, while Christopher is growing up in backwoods British Columbia, the Second World War is looming—and about to change the world forever.

This resolutely unfashionable novel gives evidence of remarkable attention to detail and astonishing patience. But what's most stunning of all is that, while staring retirement in the face, Harlow has been able to project himself so completely, so convincingly, into the mind and heart of a 14-year-old boy.

At the very least, Harlow has again demonstrated that he is one of the finest western Canadian novelists of his generation. The rest awaits the judgment of posterity.

22. Paul Quarrington: Let The Kid Have His Moment

When his writer-in-residency at the Orillia Public Library ended in the fall of 1990, novelist Paul Quarrington returned to Toronto. Early in 1991, he was adapting Whale Music *for the screen and anticipating the release of the movie* Perfectly Normal, *for which he wrote the final draft of the filmscript. He was also doing "a couple of musical projects," one of which was an operetta for Toronto's Young People's Theatre to mark the 200th anniversary of Mozart's death. Quarrington was still juggling assorted book projects and jogging regularly, and said that lately he'd been reading a lot of medieval poetry.*

ORILLIA, Ontario—Novelist Paul Quarrington stood on the front porch of the Stephen Leacock House. Making a visor with his hands, he shielded his eyes and tried to peer through a dark window. "The alcove is right there," he said. "You can see it. That's the wall he scribbled on."

Quarrington, winner of the 1989 governor-general's award for fiction, and also of the 1987 Leacock Award for Humor, had been describing a childhood incident that inspired him to become a writer.

His parents, Toronto-based psychologists, had a summer cottage on Lake Couchiching, which stretches north of Orillia. One summer—"I must have been eight or nine"—Quarrington and his parents visited Leacock House, where humorist Stephen Leacock (*Sunshine Sketches Of A Little Town*) had lived for many years.

"He had a phone booth, a kind of alcove," Quarrington said, "and a little stool he'd sit on. But what impressed me was that when he wanted to write down a phone number, he'd just scratch it on the wall. I was very impressed with that. I thought a writer must be a good thing to be if you could get away with scribbling on a wall."

Quarrington, born in 1953, has become a prolific scribbler. During the past 13 years, he has produced six books: *The Service* (1978), *Home Game* (1983), *The Life Of Hope* (1985), *King Leary* (1987), *Whale Music* (1989) and *Logan In Overtime* (1990).

Having won the national awards cited above, and been named one of Canada's best writers under 45, Quarrington is a rising star in Canada's literary firmament.

The author, his wife (Dorothy) and infant daughter (Carson, named after Carson McCullers) moved to Orillia (100 kilometres north of Toronto) in September of 1989, when Quarrington accepted a year's appointment as writer-in-residence at the local library.

They rented a comfortable old red-brick house, in the driveway of which Quarrington—an avid angler—kept a sailboat he bought with the $10,000 that comes with the governor-general's award: "I named it Gigi."

But here's the comic writer on himself: "Paul Quarrington was born in Don Mills, Ontario. (Skier) Steve Podborski always cites his birthplace as Don Mills, Ontario, thereby making it sound like a quaint town nestled in the mountains. This is fine by me, even though Don Mills is really suburban Toronto."

The writer continues: "Paul Quarrington comes from a musical family. His brother Joel is a famous double-bass player (if such a thing is possible) and his brother Tony is a guitarist and songwriter. Paul himself plays the guitar, bass and piano. This no doubt seems rather impressive. You would not be as impressed if you could actually hear him play these instruments."

A decade ago, Quarrington was a member of the duet Quarrington/Worthy, whose single "Baby & the Blues" was a hit during the week of January 12: "Just the one week." For five years the author was also a member, along with brother Tony, of Joe Hall and the Continental Drift, a five-piece band that never did make the charts.

Meanwhile, Quarrington logged two years at the University of Toronto, studying English. But here's one final bit: "Having decided to pursue a career as a novelist, Paul Quarrington, for reasons not clear to anyone (especially him), wrote largely about the world of sport. *Home Game* is about baseball. *King Leary* follows the exploits of an old-time hockey boy. *The Life Of Hope* has something to do with fishing. Many times the author was asked, "Paul Quarrington, why don't you write about the world of music—a world there's a chance you might know something about?" The syntax was questionable, the point valid.

The result was the acclaimed *Whale Music*, whose rock 'n' roll superstar hero bears more than a passing resemblance to the idiosyncratic Brian Wilson of the Beach Boys. The novel, deliberately cartoonish, is a triumph of voice that makes us laugh when the only alternative would be to cry—an accomplishment sufficient unto the governor-general's award.

Over lunch in a restaurant not far from Leacock House, Quarrington shrugged off the controversy that erupted after Mordecai Richler's novel *Solomon Gursky Was Here* failed to make the three-book short list. "I was upset on his behalf," Quarrington said. "But three of us (the finalists) took the heat on that. In the end, if I were Richler, I'd say, 'Let the kid have his moment.'"

In Orilla, Quarrington was a regular at a local gym, where he swam, ran and worked out in the weight room. Then, three days a week, he headed to the library, where he made himself available to anyone with an Orillia library card.

Would-be writers, he said, "come in three varieties. I scare a lot of them away by telling them it's a lot of work. Others are immensely ambitious and bring in huge manuscripts, but they don't want to listen to you. The last thing they want to hear is ways to do it all over again."

Finally, he said, there are those "who come seeking criticism, even if they've written a huge manuscript. They're few and far between—but I've found a couple."

With several "fantasy sports novels" to his credit, Quarrington sees affinities between his own fiction and that of Alberta expatriate W.P. Kinsella (*Shoeless Joe*). "Of course, he's older," Quarrington says with a grin. "But he's the only contemporary writer I know who has publicly expressed admiration for Richard Brautigan (*Trout Fishing In America, In Watermelon Sugar, The Abortion*).

"I like that phantasmagoric stuff too—Brautigan and (Kurt) Vonnegut. Just apply that to an old-fashioned sports novel—*The Southpaw, Bang The Drum Slowly*—and you have sports fantasy."

These days, and typically, Quarrington has a variety of projects at different stages. An ornate playhouse in the backyard of the red-brick house gave him an idea for a "Stephen-King-like" novel. "What if the playhouse was bigger and even more complex," he said, "and neighborhood kids had been playing in it for years. Then the original family moves away for some reason, and a couple moves in and stops kids from playing in it. This makes the spirits who live in the playhouse angry, and they start behaving like 10-year-olds, see?"

Before he turns to that novel, however, he'll probably finish a novel about a writer of dime-store westerns, a cross between Ned Buntline and Zane Grey. It involves refabricating the Old West, Quarrington says, "but I wouldn't mind writing a big, fat book."

Quarrington is also working on "a shorter or regular-length piece" whose working title is *Dolly And The Monsters*. He tells the story from a woman's point of view—"I decided to take the bull by the horns"—and mixes baseball, *Beowulf*, a contest-crazy husband and a trip to Florida. "That one's going really well."

For the rest, Quarrington is "doing a lot of screenplays." He and a screenwriter friend, Richard Lewis, have drafted a movie version of *King Leary*, "and I just signed to do another one of *Whale Music*."

Finally there's the book of limericks he's editing for the Leacock Heritage Festival. From this he has learned two things. First, that Orillia doesn't inspire a great variety of rhymes: "I've seen a lot of thrill ya and kill ya." Second, and to put it bluntly, "I don't really like limericks."

23. William Gibson: King Of Cyberpunk

Vancouver writer William Gibson published The Difference Engine *in the spring of 1991. He has begun working on a novel,* Virtual Light, *set in the near future. "It's close to a contemporary novel," he said, "not a total sci-fi thing like I was doing in* Neuromancer." *Gibson is also collaborating on a multi-media project—"that's the only way to describe it"—for the Seville World Fair in 1992.*

VANCOUVER—Science fiction writer William Gibson crossed his long legs at the ankles, clasped his hands behind his neck and shook his head emphatically. "I don't want to go back to Cyberspace," he declared. "That cycle is closed."

Gibson, considered the most important SF writer to emerge in the 1980s, was discussing his work—four acclaimed books starting with *Neuromancer* (1984)—in the living room of the Kitsilano home he shares with his wife and two children.

Touted as the King of the Cyberpunk movement, Gibson said: "From the beginning I maintained there was no such thing. 'Cyberpunk' is just a label. At the logo-level it's a snappy neologism. All these essays about Cyberpunk as a literary movement seem to me spurious. They made me suspicious of literary history in general." Gibson, whose work is set in a gritty near-future of conglomerates and world-wide computer networks, said he regards Cyberspace as "a metaphor for the media world we already live in."

Readers have linked him "with outlaw hackers and computer vandals, but I never had anything to do with that," he said. "I'm barely computer literate. I wrote my first three books on a manual typewriter. When I wrote *Neuromancer*, I didn't know there were disk drives. I didn't know what a modem was. I just listened to what computer enthusiasts were saying, and to the language of computer ads, and deconstructed it the way I was trained to do."

Gibson, who took a B.A. in English from the University of British Columbia, is far more comfortable discussing literature—favorite writers include novelists Kurt Vonnegut, John LeCarre, Don DeLillo and William Burroughs—than software, floppy disks or hard drives.

A long-time fan of Thomas Pynchon, Gibson confessed to being disappointment with the 1990 novel *Vineland*: "It's like a man has run 60 miles to bring news of a battle only to find that the results have been faxed in." Gibson also thought it curious that "all the evil was external to the hip culture: the bad guys were all narcs or Nixonian monsters. I lived through that period. It wasn't all just happy freaks. What about the psychos on acid?"

Born in Virginia in 1948—his speech still shows traces of the American south—Gibson moved to Canada in the late 1960s. "Those were the years of the Vietnam War," he said, "but I was never drafted. I'd lived in San Francisco. But to a kid from the backwoods of Virginia, Toronto was wildly cosmopolitan. Also very easy going compared with some American cities. Not the same level of weirdness and violence."

In the early 1970s, Gibson and his wife moved from Toronto to Vancouver—"she wanted to finish her B.A."—and soon he was studying English at UBC. In 1977, while taking a science fiction course, Gibson was permitted to write a short story instead of a critical term paper. He sold the 12-page manuscript, called *Fragments Of A Hologram Rose*, to an

American literary magazine for $28. "I thought, 'this is ridiculous,'" he said. "I'd agonized over every word. And I didn't write another story for two years."

In 1979, Gibson produced a yarn called "Johnny Mnemonic" and sold it to *Omni* magazine. "They paid me enough money ($850)," he joked, "that I couldn't afford to stop." In truth, an editor at Ace Books, which was publishing a line of first novels, spotted the *Omni* story and suggested he write a novel.

"I cannibalized 'Johnny Mnemonic' and another story ("Burning Chrome") and built stuff around that," Gibson said. "For a couple of years I ground away in terror. I just didn't think it would fly. The whole thing was written in fear and trembling."

The finished book, *Neuromancer*, won all three top science fiction awards—Nebula, Hugo, Philip K. Dick—and by 1990 was in its 14th printing. Set in a hard-edged future where information is power, it tells the story of an ace computer cowboy who plugs into Cyberspace—a matrix in which blocks of information have visible form—and attempts a massive heist.

Gibson said that, in retrospect, "*Neuromancer* seems to me structurally crude. It's a Hollywood caper plot—very, very linear. I did that deliberately, of course. I wanted a tractor to pull through the narrative. But what I like about *Count Zero* (his second novel) is that there is a level in which the text discusses the creation of the text."

Gibson is less satisfied with his most recent Cyberspace novel, *Mona Lisa Overdrive* (1988), which features several intertwined story lines. "I have a sense of the material being stretched too tight," he said. "Probably because I was trying to close the cycle (which includes the anthology *Burning Chrome*)."

That closed cycle has attracted the attention of Hollywood movie producers, who have taken options on *Neuromancer* and three stories from *Burning Chrome*: "Johnny Mnemonic," "New Rose Hotel" and the title story. Gibson, well aware that such options have a way of never being exercised, remained guardedly optimistic about seeing these works on the silver screen. He has also written a film script for a third sequel to the box-office hit *Alien*, "but I don't think there's anything happening with that."

Gibson's literary background has made him impatient with "prominent science fiction writers who, when they get among their peers, proudly explain that what they're doing is the only literature there is, and all the rest is just artsy-fartsy nonsense. These people brag that they've never read James Joyce and never will—which is one of the terrible things about SF culture."

On the other hand, Gibson said, "I've never written anything that wasn't science fiction at some level. The reader comes to 'genre-SF' expecting to read about the future. But the best SF is really an impressionistic take on contemporary reality. The trick is to come up with a pose of authenticity. The genre has always been kind of scarce on realistic specificity. What I did was try to create an object-specific world, to show what brand of jeans people wore, what kind of cars they drove.

"In ways, the tools developed within the science-fiction ghetto are the only tools capable of analyzing contemporary reality, of treating the impact of technology, because SF deals in whole systems. Think about the impact of television. And what is Nintendo doing to our children? We're living in such a weird, accelerated time right now."

Gibson has just completed a long novel on which he collaborated with Bruce Sterling, whose four SF books include *The Artificial Kid* and *Crystal Express*. It's called *The Difference Engine* and focuses on Charles Babbage, a Victorian (1792-1871) known for trying and failing to build a mechanical computational device—a precursor to the computer. The novel offers "an alternate history in which he does build it," Gibson said. "We've taken the trauma of the industrial revolution and cranked it up to screaming. The book deals with artificial intelligence, tries to get to the roots of industrial society. It's a cycle in its own right."

Initially, the two writers collaborated by modem, Gibson said. "But we were spending more money on telephone time than it cost to Federal-Express disks across the country." And so they went the courier route, each rewriting the other on disk. The key to the collaboration, Gibson said, "is that we trust one another stylistically: I know he's not going to drop the ball."

Collaborations have long been part of science fiction, Gibson agreed— "but not for the best of reasons: two people can hack-write faster than one." Having gained some acceptance from mainstream critics, Gibson wondered whether the new, collaborative work "will be treated seriously by the legitimate literary world. I mean, can you imagine? Margaret Atwood and ... and who? It just wouldn't happen."

As for what's next, "I'm deliberately not thinking about it," Gibson said. "The part of me that does that stuff is not functioning these days. But one thing I do know. I don't want to go back to Cyberspace."

***

IX

Fifth Battle Zone:
Canon Fodder

In the fall of 1980, I hailed John Metcalf's novel *General Ludd* as "a prodigious work of imagination, a satirical tour de force whose aim is to revolutionize the way we look at what's happening in Canada today—to language, to literacy, to our ability to think." I described it as teeming with life and riddled with humor, as "a savage (and frequently hilarious) indictment of new communications technology and its effects." The elitism I ignored.

By 1987, I had a better fix on Metcalf. Reviewing *The Bumper Book*, in which the author suggested that most newspaper book reviewers would be better employed driving trucks, I wrote: "Metcalf's assumption, widely shared, is that the primary function of a newspaper book reviewer is to serve the literary community. Trouble is, that community isn't paying his salary. The newspaper is. And the newspaper is a business. It's not an academic journal. It's not a trade magazine. It survives by meeting the multifarious needs of its audience. In Canada, with perhaps a single exception, that audience consists of a miscellaneous assortment of people who happen to live in and around the same city.

"Every story in a mass-market newspaper is expected, if not to interest, at least to be accessible to every reader. Ergo, a mass-market newspaper is not, and never will be, a forum for sophisticated literary debate. That's not the fault of those in the front lines of the battle for literacy, weathering a daily barrage of deadlines, ringing telephones, fights over space and questions about why, of the 110,000 books published in English each year, a particular work has not been reviewed. Great Britain, France and the United States have populations large enough to support a few newspapers where journalists can conduct the kind of discourse Metcalf so passionately desires. Canada does not."

There was more. Some of it figures in what follows. I've let the piece stand, though now I regret taking that cheap shot at Louis Dudek. A poet I'm not.

24. Who's In, Who's Out And Other Skirmishes

Not long ago, writing in *The New York Times Book Review*, ex-Canadian Bharati Mukherjee argued convincingly that immigration is the opposite of expatriation. By refusing to play the game of immigration, she suggested, psychological expatriates "certify to the world, and especially to their hosts, the purity of their pain and their moral superiority to the world around them. In some obscure way they earn the right to be permanent scolds, soaking up comfort and privilege and nursing real grievances until privilege and grievance become habits of mind."

Mukherjee was writing about ex-colonial, once-third-world authors, but her remarks put me in mind of John Metcalf, that uncrowned king of Canada's psychological expatriates. Metcalf arrived in this country in 1962 at age 24, though in ways that matter he never really left his native Great Britain. Soon he was flailing away at literary Canada in satirical stories and novels, and when those failed to transform the embarrassing backwater in which he found himself, Metcalf turned to collections of essays, writing *Kicking Against The Pricks* (1982) and editing *The Bumper Book* (1987).

Carry On Bumping (ECW Press) is the third in this series of frontal assaults on CanLit and CanLitCrit, and once again Metcalf aims his most savage body blows at book reviewers, regionalism and the Canada Council. The good news is that, for the most part, *Carry On* eschews the vindictive pettiness that marred *Pricks*, and the one pseudonymous piece here, unlike the scurrilous hatchet job in *Bumper*, rises above personal attack to make a general point. Both earlier anthologies had their moments, but *Carry On Bumping* is the best of the three, with much to recommend it and even more to make the blood boil.

If this volume has a central debate, its focus is the Canadian Literary Canon: Who's in it, who's not. In three brief, imaginary dialogues, science fiction writer Linda Leith offers a cogent, jargon-free condemnation of academic exclusivity. And Vancouver writer George McWhirter contributes a grammatically problematic but pithy formulation of one position: "If Canada cannot be seen, like nobody has ever seen it before, but must always be an addition to acceptable representations, the joint is in trouble."

The meat of the argument, however, is found in two elaborately polite, back-to-back essays by English professors—Walter Pache of Germany and Toronto's William Keith, author of *Canadian Literature In English* (1985). In analyzing Keith's book, Pache asks: "Should Canadian literature be exposed to the rigorous criteria of analysis and evaluation that are applicable on an international scale, or can it claim a more lenient consideration on the grounds that it has a special function as a vehicle of explaining the nation to itself—a function that can also be met by works that are second- or third-rate by literary standards."

Keith replies that Canadian literature can hold its own in international company, and draws a distinction between literary history and criticism. Those studying the drama of the English Renaissance need to know not only the works of Shakespeare, Jonson, Marlowe and Webster, but also such relatively obscure texts as *Ralph Roister Doister* and *Gammer Gurton's Needle*. These last are important historically because they made "more artistically successful work possible." Keith also suggests that Pache "cannot really believe that, if literary history has been pronounced obsolete in Europe, Canadians are at liberty to dissent from this judgment."

Great fun, what? Further afield, we find Marco P. LoVerso arguing that Margaret Atwood's novels are really moral fables, each with a controlling metaphor, a split protagonist who achieves a new vision and a welter of symbolic secondary characters. Lawrence Mathews takes effective issue with postmodernist reviewers, and one of his observations could serve only too well as a description of this whole business of literary polemics: "Of course what we're talking about is not revolution but market share. (Pick a name) wants people to pay more attention to the poets whose work he likes.... He just wants a larger slice of the pie for himself and his literary friends."

Vancouver writer Brian Fawcett contributes an idiosyncratic and bracingly irreverent article which is probably unfair to author Eric McCormack but raises interesting questions. Fawcett distinguishes the privileged postmodernists of North America from their South American heroes, charging "that their lack of any detectable interest in questions related to authority hides an extremely reactionary (if covert) ideological stance, a demand (or wish) that the present structure of privilege and rewards be allowed to exist unexamined."

Heady stuff.

But scattered among these essays we find the bizarre musings of antiquarian bookseller William Hoffer, who delights above all in taking cheap shots at the Canada Council. (No, I've never received a grant.) A flippant anti-regionalist fantasy by Montrealer Hugh Hood betrays the insularity of a Central Canadian who has lived too long in a single urban centre. And Ray Smith, who has written some unforgettable fiction, disappears into a rambling, incoherent and self-indulgent monologue that touches on semiotics, structuralism and inter-subjectivity. (As editor, Metcalf made his biggest mistake in putting this arcane lucubration near the front of the book.)

Then there's an article by poet Louis Dudek, who castigates Canadian book reviewers as "incompetent and unqualified for the critical task." He goes on to create a straw man, give him my name and mis-use a review of *The Bumper Book* in which I wrote that Metcalf "doesn't understand what a Canadian newspaper is or how it works. If he did, he'd think twice before undermining the credibility of his staunchest allies in a world obviously foreign to him, and in which he himself wouldn't survive two weeks."

Still, Dudek's superciliousness surprised me—though not as much as his suggestion that, when I described the mass-market newspaper as a business, I was denying that it has an important role to play in elevating standards, or that a newspaper with a good book section can reap rewards in heaven and become "famous across the land." Like most book review editors, I have often made these arguments and others besides. Surely Dudek knows this? Why was he deliberately misrepresenting me? I dug out my review of *The Bumper Book* and there, near the end, found my explanation: "I'm puzzled," I'd written, "as to why Louis Dudek is so well-represented with so much mediocre poetry."

Hey, that's how it is.

Metcalf himself has produced one of the most readable essays in this anthology, and it's easily the most offensive. Where to begin? Metcalf asserts that "because the Canadian literary world is wholly subsidized by the State it is impossible to write imaginatively or critically without being conscious of being Canadian, without being self-consciously Canadian, without being conscious of the pervasive social and political desire for 'Canadianness'." Nonsense. Scores of Canadian writers have no such problem, and those who do address specifically Canadian concerns are often saying something uniquely relevant to those of us who live here.

Metcalf argues that "Canadian nationalism is the motivation behind the subsidy (funnelled mainly through the Canada Council) and it has failed to produce an audience." Hogwash. The first Canadian print run on Margaret Atwood's last novel was 50,000 copies—though Metcalf chooses to ignore such figures. The Canada Council—from which Metcalf himself has frequently benefited—has made a spectacular difference in Canada in just three decades. I say give it a century.

Another of Metcalf's favorite targets is regionalism, which "actively promotes mediocrity." Metcalf sneers at provincial writers' guilds and "subsidized regional presses dedicated to promoting and preserving the literature and 'culture' of New Brunswick, Alberta, and Prince Edward Island." He doubts that even professed regionalist William Faulkner "would have approved the subsidizing of Alberta's best."

Talk about literary bigotry! Surely it's obvious that those regional guilds and publishers Metcalf finds so laughable are building the audience he claims doesn't exist. How many times do we have to go over this? In the world of hockey, Wayne Gretzky didn't just happen. First came Howie Morenz, Rocket Richard, Gordie Howe, Bobby Orr and countless others. And for every hockey star, thousands of kids played hockey at thousands of neighborhood rinks across the country. Gretzky exists because somebody erected and flooded those rinks—and the same is true of his audience. Nobody appreciates Gretzky better than an ex-hockey player, even one who never got out of the neighborhood rink.

Subsidized publishers, Metcalf argues, produce "a flood of books which would not be published in a normal literary environment." What, you may ask, is "a normal literary environment?" Why, that of Great Britain, of course—a country many centuries older than Canada, almost three times as populous, a fraction the size and far more homogeneous (even now). Just for starters. Look at Metcalf's authorities! Cecil Day-Lewis, Richard Hoggart, Kingsley Amis, Charlie Osbourne: scratch a Metcalf mentor and you'll find a worthy Brit of suitable psychological set, and never mind that he wouldn't know Oberon from Oolichan or NeWest Press. Subsidy, don't you know, is "destructive of the necessary relationship between writer and audience." Everybody has a place and had best be in it.

I could go on. But if Bharati Mukherjee is right, we Canadians have fostered Metcalf's elitist ranting by celebrating the mosaic rather than the melting pot. We're just going to have to live with it. Who knows? Maybe there's something healthy about having continually to confront such eloquent resentment.

***

Part Two

The Taking Of Wild Rose Country

I

First News Flash:
Opening Salvos

Remember Ontario in the 1960s? The emergence of Canadian nationalist publishers and the almost magical arrival of the Atwood generation of writers? Something similar happened in Wild Rose Country in the 1980s. Writers and publishers, backed by a new generation of readers, besieged a government preoccupied with oil and gas. Eventually, they stormed the barricades and seized the citadel of funding, and the ensuing explosion of literary activity transformed the cultural landscape. In this, Alberta was like other provinces in "outer" Canada—Saskatchewan, Nova Scotia, British Columbia—only more so.

Four studies have laid out the statistical evidence. In 1984, a national 448-page report called *Book Reading In Canada* revealed that if you scratch 100 Albertans you'll find 61 book readers—more than you'll turn up in any province except British Columbia (65). Two years later, a 235-page report called *Out Of The West* showed that 25 Alberta publishers had sold more than $15 million worth of books in the preceding year. In 1989, a 260-page report called *Word For Word* hailed a "second-generation literary flowering" in Wild Rose Country and listed 38 nationally recognized authors who are or have been based in Alberta. And in 1990, the first region-wide study of book publishing in western Canada, *Partners In Success*, discovered that Alberta's book publishing industry was poised to take over from British Columbia's as the largest in western Canada.

The province's literary community took the citadel in 1984, when under pressure the provincial government set up the Alberta Foundation for the Literary Arts (AFLA). It was a granting agency, a Canada Council of sorts, with an annual budget (in the end) of $1.325 million to spend on writers, publishers and libraries. AFLA's death in 1991 marked the end of an era. But the foundation, which transformed the province's literary community, would never have existed if well-known writers hadn't rallied the troops in 1980 and founded the Writers' Guild of Alberta (WGA). Ten years later, the guild boasted 800 members and an annual budget of $185,000.

Before the WGA there was only a provincial government department—Alberta Culture's film and literary arts branch, created in 1971 (also dismantled in 1991). John Patrick Gillese, who had been a freelance writer for 28 years, directed the branch through the 1970s. The first action Gillese took as a civil servant, he told me in 1981, was to set up the Search-For-A-New-Alberta-Novelist competition. Six or seven manuscripts, he expected—though he told Macmillan of Canada, which had agreed to publish the winning manuscript, that he anticipated 15 or 16. "You know how many we got? Ninety-eight!" He pounded his desk. "We got ninety-eight manuscripts!"

The original competition has gone through several incarnations and publishers. It has turned up some good novels. But its number-one success story remains Pauline Gedge's 1975 novel *Child Of The Morning*, which fetched $81,500 for U.S. paperback rights, more than $20,000 for British hardcover rights and $50,000 for the first four hours of TV rights—and launched an international career.

Encouraged by this, Gillese introduced more competitions—general-interest non-fiction, regional history, children's books. He began publishing, for developing writers, "and with special sympathy for the writer who has absolutely no one to help him," the bi-monthly *Alberta Authors' Bulletin* containing advice and market tips and upbeat, writer-success stories. He started running weekend workshops in places like Grande Prairie, Killam and Medicine Hat. And he initiated correspondence courses aimed at producing salable writing.

Trouble was, Gillese's emphasis on commercialism and competition infuriated writers interested in making literature—in producing books, not that would sell abroad, but that would reflect the community they came out of, and that would last. The best-known of Gillese's critics—they surfaced as such in the late 1970s—was novelist Rudy Wiebe, who had already published 13 books and won a governor-general's award for *The Temptations Of Big Bear*.

Wiebe was teaching in the English department at the University of Alberta and had the support of numerous writers and poets, most of whom were also teaching at universities. Among them were Stephen Scobie, Douglas Barbour, Ted Blodgett, Christopher Wiseman, Aritha van Herk and Myrna Kostash (the only non-academic). In 1978, at the University of Calgary, Wiebe publicly denounced the literary arts branch for its commercialism, its "safe" support of non-controversial writing and its "contest approach" to culture.

The battle between the literary arts branch and the university-based writers was escalating when, in 1979, Mary LeMessurier became minister of culture. It peaked early in 1980 after Gillese made some ill-considered remarks about poets and poetry that appeared in the *North American Review*, an Iowa-based writers' magazine. Ted Blodgett, chair of the University of Alberta's comparative literature department, and also an accomplished poet, denounced Gillese's statements in *The Edmonton Journal* as "disgusting, repugnant and contemptible." He demanded an apology. A flurry of letters to the editor followed. "Elitist!" "Philistine!"

Meanwhile, several writers—among them Wiebe and van Herk—had approached LeMessurier seeking changes in the policies of the literary arts branch. She responded by convening, in April of 1980, a one-day symposium of 35 writers and publishers. That symposium identified the problem and proposed a solution. Only two percent of Alberta's cultural development budget was going to the literary arts branch. Visual arts was getting seven percent and performing arts a whopping 24 percent. Everybody agreed. More money was the answer....

25. The WGA Is Born

They came to Calgary from Edmonton, Red Deer and Fort McMurray, from Lethbridge, Camrose and Water Valley. They came home to Alberta from Winnipeg and Vancouver. They came in blue jeans and sneakers, in cowboy boots and string ties, in slacks and skirts and fancy dresses. They came 160 strong, the writers of Alberta, and they came to do something that had never been done before.

They met in a stuffy classroom at the Southern Alberta Institute of Technology at noon on a Saturday in October of 1980. And when, after hours of emotional discussion and debate, they left that room for the last time, on Sunday shortly after 5 p.m., they had founded The Writers' Guild of Alberta.

No, the WGA is not the first writers' group to be formed in this province. But it is the first to be established without government funding. And it is the first to boast a broad-based membership that includes writers of national reputation—people like Robert Kroetsch, Myrna Kostash, Aritha van Herk and Rudy Wiebe.

Rudy Wiebe was elected president of the organization. "We want to develop a sense of community among writers, a sense of tribe," he said in an interview when it was all over. "We want to raise the profile of writers in this province, to make people aware of how important we are to what's happening here."

Wiebe said the turn-out of 160 writers, each of whom paid $10 to attend the meeting, "went far beyond our expectations." He noted that those present indicated a desire "to be strong and independent" by rejecting a proposed membership fee of $10, voting instead—overwhelmingly—to set the fee at $25.

"One of the main things we did was establish a grievance committee," Wiebe said. "If any writer has a problem, we're going to stand behind him." The WGA will also "exert pressure on government and private industries to encourage developing writers in this province."

Christopher Wiseman, Calgary-based poet and creative writing instructor, was elected WGA vice-president. He came away from the meeting "tired but exhilarated, and with a tremendous sense of possibilities."

Saturday was devoted to a general discussion of objectives, and Sunday to the formulation of the constitution, the election of the eight-member board of directors and the establishing of priorities and strategies.

Robert Kroetsch, who in 1969 won a governor-general's award for *The Studhorse Man*, opened the meeting with a characteristically spirited description of the benefits to be derived from a writers' organization.

He cited the example of the Writers' Union of Canada. The union, he said, has lobbied strongly for Public Lending Right, according to which writers will get paid for the use of their books in libraries (it later became a reality), and has improved the lot of writers as regards contracts and copyright. Kroetsch, who taught in 1979 at the University of Calgary, had come home from Winnipeg, where he was working at the University of Manitoba.

Representatives from the Writers' Federation of Nova Scotia and the Saskatchewan Writers' Guild—Greg Cook and Geoff Ursell, respectively—described how their organizations function and what they have achieved.

The most divisive issue discussed during the two-day meeting was that of eligibility for membership. On Saturday a straw vote showed that those in attendance were almost unanimously in favor of an "open membership" policy: Anybody who thinks he's a writer can join.

The debate resurfaced the following day as writers argued over the wording of the WGA's constitution. Edmonton poet Stephen Scobie argued forcefully for "the principle of having a criterion of some sort," backing a motion by fellow Edmontonian Barry Frizzell that demanded as a condition of membership the publication "of at least one item." Scobie had the support of novelist Aritha van Herk.

Poet Ted Blodgett pointed out that publication in itself means nothing. A woman in the crowd elaborated: What if someone publishes a recipe somewhere? Does that constitute an item? Rudy Wiebe stressed the administrative hassles that membership criteria would entail, and pointed out, in the face of skepticism from Scobie, that the Saskatchewan Writers' Guild has an open membership policy and is flourishing.

Advocates of open membership won the vote by a large margin, and the WGA's constitution says: "Membership in the guild shall be open to any writer resident or formerly resident in the province of Alberta." The $25 annual membership fee applies to everyone except full-time students and senior citizens, who may belong to the guild for $10 a year....

26. Shots Are Fired

By the spring of 1981, the Writers' Guild of Alberta was furiously active. Culture Minister Mary LeMessurier had sought a huge increase in the annual budget for the literary arts branch—from $148,000 to $404,000. She'd received $156,000. A slap in the face. Writers and publishers were outraged. The WGA held its second annual meeting. Margaret Atwood, incoming chair of the Writers' Union of Canada, visited Edmonton to rally the troops. "This province is loaded," she told writers. "You should have an arts program second to none. Instead you're getting the very, very short end of the stick."

EDMONTON—The Writers' Guild of Alberta sent a letter to Premier Peter Lougheed urging him to reconsider a recent budget allocation to the film and literary arts branch of Alberta Culture. The letter, approved by the 240-member guild at its semi-annual meeting, says funding for Alberta writers and publishers, frozen since 1975, is "totally inadequate."

Culture Minister Mary LeMessurier sought a budget of $404,000 for the literary arts branch, but cabinet approved only $156,000. In 1980, the figure was $148,000. WGA president Rudy Wiebe said LeMessurier "assured us there would be more funding available to writing and publishing—but firm assurances from the minister of culture seem to carry no weight."

Ted Blodgett, a guild executive member, said "the budget continues to foster the general Canadian view that the word 'Alberta' is synonymous with 'oil' and 'cattle.' Literature is the mirror of what a society thinks of itself. Literature projects an image of that society abroad. This is why Quebec, as well as Ontario, supports its writers and publishers. Literature is at once a cultural and a political product."

The WGA has a wide variety of projects in the development stages, and estimated operating costs for the year are $28,000, while projected income is $19,000. The Saskatchewan Writers' Guild, by comparison, has an annual budget of $125,000 to $160,000. Ven Begamudre, sent by that province's guild, said most of those funds come out of provincial coffers.

The WGA also hopes to set up a writers-in-residence program at the high-school level, and to back a series of mobile creative-writing workshops. Nicknamed the "Travelling Nude Project," after a story by Henry Kreisel, these workshops would happen in such small Alberta communities as Camrose, Edson, Fort McMurray and Grande Prairie (wherever the demand is greatest). Writers would run them one evening a week for 10 consecutive weeks.

These projects will generate funds, but others won't. For example, the 180 guild members who attended a meeting at the University of Alberta also voted to set up, in Edmonton, a combination business office, library and writers' centre staffed by one part-time person. "If we don't get extra funding for this," guild secretary Merna Summers said, "we'll be in desperate shape."

✳✳✳

II

The Alberta Volunteers

"We're not advocating breakup!" Don Braid declared. "We're strong federalists! We want to see the country saved. We want to see a new and united Canada. That's why we wrote the book!" Braid, political affairs columnist for the *Calgary Herald*, was talking about *Breakup: Why The West Feels Left Out Of Canada*, which he co-authored with fellow journalist Sydney Sharpe. "The time is ripe," he insisted late in 1990. "But if the rest of Canada, and particularly Ontario, doesn't listen this time, then the whole country could collapse."

This could happen, Sharpe said, not through political upheaval but by regions gradually drifting apart. "Here in the West fear of the U.S. is not as solid as in Ontario. We don't have the same loyalist traditions." Also, many Westerners have American-immigrant ancestors. *Breakup*, one of the most important non-fiction books of 1990, made a national statement from the West. That statement can be summarized in a single borrowed phrase: "The West wants in!"

The problem, of course, is that nobody willingly gives up capital-P Power. Certainly not Ontario politicians. The authors saw a glimmer of hope, however, in a stronger alliance between Quebec and the West. "If Quebec is out," Braid said, "or associated in some parallel system, there's no way Atlantic Canada or the West would stay in, not without some kind of regional equality in government—not with Ontario having half the population and 60 percent of the GNP. The moment Ontario realizes it's either going to lose this wonderful hinterland or give up political power, it might decide that it's better to give up some power."

Breakup devotes separate chapters to the West in relation to Quebec and Ontario. It argues that the National Energy Program not only damaged—and alienated, perhaps permanently—the oil industry, but that it led to the collapse of western Canadian financial institutions. The book points an accusing finger at eastern Canadian banks, arguing that they refused to finance the western Canadian oil industry in the 1950s and '60s—and by default forced American institutions to do it. As a result of that and the NEP, Braid said, "the oil industry is separatist. It wants to separate itself from the Canadian economic system."

Today people talk of various combinations of western provinces, and even of a new country, Cascadia, made up of British Columbia and Alberta and some northwestern American states. "But I don't think we should present these as active choices," Braid said. "We're at the mercy of forces we can't control. We should hook ourselves into Canada before it's too late."

But I'm not going to focus on non-fiction writers.

Here again, as in Part One, they deserve a book of their own. Even fiction writers I can't treat exhaustively. Merna Summers, Fred Stenson, Mary Riskin, Scot Morison, Judith Duncan, Dave Duncan, John Ballem, Reg Silvester, Candace Jane Dorsey—they all merit celebration here. And what of Monica Hughes, Martyn Godfrey, Marilyn Halvorson, Jan Truss, Myra Paperny, William Pasnak—that whole battalion of award-winning children's book writers? Apparently arbitrary exclusion! To Alberta poets, too, I'm compelled to give outrageously short shift. Consider Christopher Wiseman, an award-winning poet who for years has battled literary pretension in Alberta and elsewhere. "I want poetry to be so damned human it hurts," he told me in an interview. "I do not want obscurity. I want clarity, directness. I want poetry to be accessible."

The year was 1988. From a scattering of pages on his desk at the University of Calgary, Wiseman pulled a copy of a poem that pokes fun at postmodern poetry. He invited me to scan it, then elaborated: "Often, the more complex and difficult a poem, the less humanity there is in it. Any complexity should be in the feelings the poem generates. I want people to laugh and to cry, not to puzzle over the meaning of my poems."

Wiseman, who was born in England and educated at Cambridge University, has taught at the University of Calgary since 1969. When he arrived, the university offered no courses in creative writing and Wiseman started teaching poetry-writing as a continuing education course. In 1973, he taught it as a credit course for the first time. Four years later the English department expanded its creative writing offerings, adding fiction to the curriculum. And recently, Wiseman said, the university awarded its first master's degrees to students who wrote creative theses: "I feel we've come full circle."

When Wiseman looks around at literary Calgary these days, he finds it almost unrecognizable. The university, Mount Royal College, *Dandelion* magazine, the Calgary Creative Reading Series, the Writers' Guild of Alberta, the Alberta Foundation for the Literary Arts —so many different centres of activity: "I love the diversity of it," Wiseman said. "The energy is just fantastic."

But no, I'm not going to focus on poets....

27. W.O. Mitchell: His Own Best Character

In the spring of 1990, while congratulating W.O. Mitchell for having won a Writers' Guild award for According To Jake And The Kid, *Edmonton fiction writer Merna Summers spoke of the legacy that one generation of writers leaves for the next. "I didn't know you were allowed to put gophers in stories," she said, "until I discovered that Mitchell had done it." When the author himself stood up to speak, the audience of writers rose as one and applauded until there wasn't a dry eye in the place.*

Since he came home to Calgary in 1986, the grand old man of prairie fiction has been producing books at an astonishing rate: Ladybug, Ladybug *(1988),* According To Jake And The Kid *(1989),* Roses Are Difficult Here *(1990). "My agent in New York says it's my best book," he said of this last novel. "I think she's wrong—but it's up there with the best." Mitchell was whispering to save his voice for radio interviews. "How I Spent My Summer Holidays, The Vanishing Point, Who Has Seen The Wind," he croaked, citing the highlights of his own canon. "But it isn't bronze, silver and gold. Writing isn't an Olympic event."*

The 76-year-old author had recently been the subject of a massive tribute at Toronto's International Festival of Authors. He told me that, even with political heavyweights Joe Clark and Jim Coutts and publisher Douglas Gibson offering testimonials, his wife Merna had stolen the show.

He mentioned that in 1991 M&S will republish an edition of Who Has Seen The Wind *illustrated by William Kurelek. Mitchell, who these days does most of his writing in a small office at the University of Calgary, also said, "I've got two more novels in the oven." In 1986, he sat for a portrait....*

He's not a native son, exactly, having been born in Weyburn, Saskatchewan. But W.O. Mitchell, novelist, playwright and raconteur extraordinaire, has spent more time in Calgary and environs than anywhere else. Since 1979, he has been blackening pages in Ontario, where he is writer-in-residence at the University of Windsor. Recently, rumors surfaced suggesting that Mitchell, now in his 70s, might eventually retire to the East.

Utter nonsense, the author said in an interview. Mitchell not only spends part of each summer at a lakeside cottage which is a day's drive from Calgary, but he is often here in this city, at home in a comfortable old place facing onto a park in the southwest. And that's where I went one afternoon to discover what Mitchell was up to—and also to glimpse, if I could, the whole man behind the kaleidoscopic public image.

I'd interviewed Mitchell at home twice before, and described him in print as "scratchy-voiced, salty-tongued, dishevelled, a waver of arms, an unrepentant ranter—surely his own best character." Yet I'd never seen behind the persona, never discovered what links the author of that graceful classic *Who Has Seen The Wind* with the public performer who once got a blue-chip audience of 1,000 laughing uproariously at scatological passages which most of its members, individually, would have condemned as outrageous, vulgar, completely unacceptable.

In the mid-'70s, Mitchell was the subject of a film documentary called *Novelist In Hiding*. He dislikes that documentary, primarily because it implied that he was lazy—and in retrospect the work does seem obtuse. Yet its title is suggestive. During an interview, Mitchell is friendly and forthcoming—indeed, recklessly honest. But just try to pin him down. Politicians could learn from this man, who eludes probing questions with such style that he leaves an interviewer wondering how he did it, and wanting almost to see him do it again. Evanescence personified. Novelist in hiding.

"He is a serious novelist," publisher Douglas Gibson had told me. "But he is also W.O. Mitchell, character. And that character is not put on." Author Pierre Berton had elaborated. "There's only one Bill Mitchell," he'd declared, talking of how he and Mitchell became friends in the late 1940s. "But he was less of a character then than he is now. I think he's been building that character like he builds his fictional characters. And his persona has been sandpapered and honed and polished by his platform presence over the years. Back then, he was a little more rough hewn."

These were signposts—although I hadn't realized it when Mitchell's wife, Merna, ushered me into their home and hollered at her husband to come downstairs: the reporter had arrived. Two hours later, with Mitchell under a full head of steam and obviously prepared to ramble into the evening, Merna would surface with broad hints about Mitchell's getting back to work on his novel, until even the most reluctant of leave-takers would be forced to beat a retreat.

In between, Mitchell was Mitchell—discursive, rambling, impossible, his conversation sprinkled with unprintable expletives and lengthy asides aimed at benefiting the careers of those he loves. Mitchell also has arguments to make, scores to settle—but then, how could it be otherwise? The man has been a national figure for decades.

William Ormond Mitchell was born into a middle-class family on March 13, 1914. He spent what he calls his "litmus years" in Weyburn, Saskatchewan. "The whole context of the early years, the round billiard table of the Regina plains, the prairies, was very, very important to me, both as a person and an artist."

At age 12, Mitchell contracted tuberculosis of the wrist and his parents sent him to Florida to finish high school. The geographical effect was overwhelming: "If you have been used to just the rudiments of land and sky, just the horizon, and no trees unplanted by man, and then you go to the lush subtropics, as I did..." He shook his head.

In Florida, Mitchell developed an interest in acting: "I had the lead in the senior play, and was marked by a teacher, Emily Murray, for greater things. In later years, I did end up working with a little theatre in Seattle. And my first writing was for stage."

Meanwhile, each summer, Mitchell had been returning to Saskatchewan. "I worked at a great number of things, but the thing that saved us all in the West was harvest time. Then you'd go to work for a dollar a day, sleep in the hen house. And the result was, I knew a great many farm laborers."

In 1931, Mitchell enrolled at the University of Manitoba, intending to become a neuro-surgeon. But his wrist made this career a bad bet. He switched majors, won the university's gold medal in philosophy and promptly dropped out. He took a writing course at the University of Washington in Seattle, then hopped a freight to Montreal. From there he worked his way to Europe on a tramp steamer. In France, he worked as a high diver in a carnival show.

Back in Canada, Mitchell sold classified ads for the *Calgary Herald* and worked as a department store Santa Claus. In Edmonton, while selling *World Book Encyclopedia* door to door, Mitchell met his future wife, Merna Hirtle. She introduced him to "a professor Salter."

"I was never a student of his. But he talked me into going back to university and taking teacher training. He looked over my shoulder during the next two years or so. I worked on *Who Has Seen The Wind* (begun in 1937). It was growing. And then I married Merna, and I went to my first school in Castor, Alberta. And I worked on the book all that year. Then, the following year, I was principal at New Dayton, south of Lethbridge. I worked on it in my spare time. And then we moved to High River.

"By this time, besides working on *Who Has Seen The Wind*, I was doing short stories. And I had scored with *Liberty, New York* and *Maclean's*. I'd made, the last year, double from short stories what I'd made as principal of New Dayton High School. And we'd saved up 500 bucks, so we moved to High River and I totally committed myself to writing."

Years later, Mitchell's second son would tell his father a revealing anecdote about the period. "He'd come home after school, and around the corner from the kitchen was my office. And somebody would say, 'Who's in there with your old man?' And Huey was embarrassed because there was no one in there with his old man. It was me, reading aloud what I had done, to listen for sharps and flats. And to capture the voice. Because the sound of a unique voice is really what character is. But in a long-winded way, I'm getting to the fact that acting and writing are extremely, extremely close arts."

Mitchell completed *Who Has Seen The Wind* in 1946. Excerpts appeared that year in *Atlantic Monthly* and *Best American Short Stories*. The novel was published in 1947, and was a critical and commercial hit. "I knew then that I was going to go up on that trapeze again quickly, for a long haul, and that I would do both short stories and a novel."

Maclean's magazine, which in those days published a lot of fiction, invited Mitchell to Toronto to become fiction editor. He accepted, and while there became friends with Berton, then managing editor. "Mitchell didn't have much money," Berton said. "None of us did. He used to buy all his clothes from the Crippled Civilians or the Salvation Army. And they never quite matched. He'd buy a brown suit with the trousers coming from one suit and the jacket from another so they would be slightly off color. He was an eccentric."

Drawing on what he'd learned from his summer jobs on the prairies, Mitchell started writing short stories for *Maclean's* about two characters named Jake and the Kid. In 1949, to CBC-Radio, he sold the idea of a radio series based on those characters. Between 1950 and 1958, CBC broadcast more than 300 *Jake-And-The-Kid* episodes. Mitchell not only wrote the scripts, but at one point, at least, acted in them: "They couldn't find anybody else," Berton said, "and he played the part of a gopher or a prairie dog or something."

Berton calls *Jake And The Kid* one of Mitchell's great triumphs. "And who is to say that the radio series wasn't as important as any novel he might have written at the time? Certainly, it had 10 times or 100 times the audience, and made him a nationally known figure much more than *Who Has Seen The Wind* or any of the other novels he has written."

According to Mitchell, Berton was taking book, betting that this quintessential Westerner would remain in Toronto like everybody else. But Mitchell said that after two and a half years, "Merna came to me and said, 'Let's go back to the hills.' And I said, 'Let's stay another year and get some more fat on our bones.' And she said, 'Suit yourself, but I'm taking the little boys and moving back at Easter, and you can come when you like.' So we returned. We had our home in High River."

There is an apparent gap between *Who Has Seen The Wind* and Mitchell's next major novel, *The Vanishing Point*, published in 1973. That gap gave birth to the novelist-in-hiding thesis. But Mitchell was writing steadily—not only *Jake And the Kid*, but film documentaries, feature articles and plays. He published a second novel, *The Kite*; and yet another novel, *The Alien*, appeared serially in *Maclean's* and later evolved into *The Vanishing Point*. "I was still writing every day, every week, every month," Mitchell said. "But this was at a time when I had to do applied art, too. And, in fact, it wasn't a slow period. That's the way it goes. And it's only in the last 15 years that I have been able to address myself by choice to play-writing, to film and to the novel. I couldn't do it (financially) before."

But the documentary film-maker, Mitchell said, "had fallen in love with the idea that I had written a first novel and then was essentially a lazy guy and in hiding. It's B.S. I tried to tell him that at the time—that I had in the works a stage play, a film, and not one but two novels. But he loved his first thesis too much. It was a very fine film, incidentally. It really was—the fabric of it. But the thesis was really quite stupid."

According to Berton, "the problem everybody has when he produces a fine first novel is trying to top himself. And *Who Has Seen The Wind* is really the Great Canadian Novel. Certainly the Great Western Novel. And I don't think anybody has topped it, including the author."

Gibson put it this way: "Bill Mitchell has fought through the hardest thing that can ever happen to an author. The only thing that's worse than having a first book that's a bomb is having a first book that's a towering success." Every time Mitchell sat down to write another novel, he felt *Who Has Seen The Wind* hanging over his shoulder. This remained true until 1981, Gibson said, when Mitchell published *How I Spent My Summer Holidays*. The novel, Gibson declared on the dust jacket, "is to *Who Has Seen The Wind* as *Huckleberry Finn* is to *Tom Sawyer*."

Many critics, including Jamie Portman of Southam News, share this view. "There is a dark side to *Huckleberry Finn*, which is why it's never been as popular a novel as *Tom Sawyer*," Portman said. "Yet it is the novel which ultimately has achieved the highest critical reputation in the years since it was written."

After *Summer Holidays* came *Since Daisy Creek* (1984), which received mixed reviews. And now Mitchell is at work on still another novel, as yet untitled, which Gibson privately calls the "Great Mark Twain Novel" and hopes to publish next fall. (It became *Ladybug, Ladybug*.)

Meanwhile, there have been plays— the best known among them being *The Kite*, *Back To Beulah* and *The Black Bonspiel Of Wullie MacCrimmon*. "W.O. as playwright is just a damn nuisance," said Gibson, his tongue firmly in cheek. "Because if he's writing plays, he's not writing novels for me to publish." Gibson admitted that Mitchell's plays are enormously successful: "Across the country, if you put on a W.O. Mitchell play, you get full houses. That's the entertainer giving people what makes them feel good—and also making them think."

Portman regards Mitchell as an accomplished playwright who honed his craft doing *Jake And The Kid*. "And this carries through to the best of his stage works. *Back To Beulah*, certainly, and the stage adaptation of *The Kite*, which I think is probably superior to the novel of the same name."

"When writing a play," Mitchell said, "you're only half finished when you leave the typewriter. And then it's bounced against a director, and then there's the read-through with the kids. And you can stand apart from it better than you can from a novel. By the time you get to the dress rehearsal or the opening, you can sit in the audience and say, 'Hey, that guy's not a bad playwright.' You're that far removed from it. So it's less painful, it's collaborative. And the trick with play-writing is to hold back, and leave room for a fine director and fine actors to make their contributions."

Portman drew attention to Mitchell as teacher, to the fact that, until 1985, he was head of the writing program at the Banff Centre. "I think there are a lot of people across the country who have benefited from their experience with him."

Alistair Macleod, a short-story writer who taught with Mitchell at the University of Windsor, describes the novelist as an inspirational teacher.

"Sometimes you get writers who are very good themselves but they are very selfish with their time or they're not interested in encouraging other, younger writers. And he's a very, very exceptional individual in that way."

What of Mitchell as performer? Has the energy he has expended as an entertainer cost him as an artist? "I don't think so," Macleod said. "Because what you do is you write first, and the writing is a very quiet and a very private act. Then when you go on stage to give a performance, as he calls it, you move from being a private person to a public person. And I think the writing is done in a very private, perhaps anguished way. And then when he gives the performance, he becomes almost someone else. So I don't think there's a contradiction at all."

Portman calls Mitchell "a natural performer," and Macleod agrees: "He's very gifted in that way. He can change and modulate his voice and do certain physical gestures and become part of a piece that he is reading in a manner that a lot of other writers are unable to accomplish." Said Berton, "The thing is, he's very, very good at it. It may be that this is what he should be doing anyway, not writing any more novels. Who's to say? He has been preserved now on film and in television, and I think the time will come when people look back and say, 'My God, we produced a public performer named Bill Mitchell.'"

"Many novelists do not ever develop or practice the acting art," Mitchell said. "But it's interesting how many novelists have been good performers, too. I'm thinking of Charles Dickens. I'm thinking of Mark Twain...."

Later, as he sifted through his notes, the forgotten reporter found himself thinking, in that context, of Mitchell himself. "Extremely, extremely close," the author had said of acting and writing. Maybe that was it, the unity in the diversity, the face behind the many masks: Mitchell as actor—a born empathizer with the gift of the gab. The novels, the plays, the teaching, the public performances, the impossible, larger-than-life persona—yes, the actor lurked behind them all.

If that seemed a modest insight, it was the only one the reporter had to offer. And he sat down to write.

28. Rudy Wiebe: Where Is That Voice Coming From?

In 1990, Rudy Wiebe's Playing Dead *was a co-winner—with* This Was Our Valley *by Shirlee Smith Matheson—of Alberta Culture's award for best non-fiction book of the year. For Wiebe, it was another in a long list of honors that includes a governor-general's award for his 1973 novel* The Temptations Of Big Bear *and the Lorne Pierce Medal from the Royal Society of Canada.*

Also in 1990, Wiebe retired from teaching after 24 years at the University of Alberta. Early in 1991, he visited south India to participate in a seminar at what he described as a very active Canadian Studies Association. These days he is working on several projects, including a novel about the North.

Novelist doing groundwork

Rudy Wiebe is singing the North. The author says he feels about the Arctic the way he felt in 1967 about the West, when he returned to Alberta after teaching for four years in the United States.

"It's the same kind of kick," he said in an interview. "Back then I discovered Big Bear. It seems to be my destiny, or my sentence, to be ticked off by historical things and try to make a modern story out of them."

Wiebe was in Calgary to promote *Playing Dead: A Contemplation Concerning The Arctic.* It's a book of essays about the North which incorporates everything from Inuit myth to reflections on the so-called Mad Trapper to personal experience.

Written originally as a series of special lectures, the essays will appeal not only to those interested in the North but to anyone intrigued by signs flashing, "Novelist doing groundwork."

Wiebe, born near Fairholme, Saskatchewan, in 1935, has always been more "North" than most Canadians. In 1969, he said, "I published an essay in which I said (to Canadians), 'We've got to start looking North.'"

The second of his eight novels, *First And Vital Candle*, includes a long sequence focusing on a Hudson's Bay Company trader in the Arctic. And in 1980, Wiebe published *The Mad Trapper*, a novel about "Albert Johnson" and the most famous of northern mysteries.

In *Playing Dead* he returns to Johnson. "First, there is the mystery of the man and the extraordinary lengths to which he went to hide his identity," Wiebe said. "But for me, Johnson's the classic example of White Man thinking he can hide in the North. You can't hide in the North! It's endless, two-dimensional open space! Johnson made the typical white man's mistake—thinking you can live alone and be left alone in the North."

Wiebe drew attention to one of the Inuit myths he includes in *Playing Dead*. It describes how a male hunter creates a snowshoe frame but requires a woman/mate to web it for him. "That's it right there," he said. "In the North you can't survive alone."

In *Playing Dead*, so-titled after another key myth, Wiebe is contemptuous of British "exploration" of the North. It was a by-product of the search for the Northwest Passage. "They didn't want anything to be there," he said, and then quoted one of his book's memorable lines: "I desire true North, not passage to anywhere."

Wiebe paraphrased his major theme, suggesting that Canadians have never quite escaped the British attitude. "We keep wishing the North was something other than it is," he said. "We do not have an imaginative vision of what the North is about. We've got to recognize that we really are a nordic country, to stop pretending that winter isn't a normal season—to accept our nordicity."

In *Playing Dead*, Wiebe turns this statement into a wonderful jeremiad, inveighing against Canadians who "go whoring after the mocking palm trees and beaches of the Caribbean and Florida and Hawaii...." That passage alone is worth the price of admission.

In the final sentences of *Playing Dead*, Wiebe suggests what his next project will be: "To walk into the true north of my own head between the stones and the ocean. If I do, I will get a new song. If I do, I will sing it for you."

The Mad Trapper

Alberta's Rudy Wiebe, considered by at least one literary critic to be among Canada's six most significant contemporary novelists, was born in 1935 in a one-room log cabin in northern Saskatchewan.

His Mennonite parents had emigrated from Russia in 1930. In 1947, the family moved to Coaldale, Alberta, where Wiebe attended a Mennonite high school and became seriously interested in writing.

The Mennonite experience informs certain of Wiebe's novels—*Peace Shall Destroy Many, First And Vital Candle, The Blue Mountains Of China*. Others, including his two most successful, go further afield.

The Temptations Of Big Bear explores a crucial period in the history of the Canadian prairies (1876-88) from the perspective of the Plains Indians. *The Scorched-Wood People*, published in 1977, treats roughly the same time (1869-1885) and place from the Métis point of view.

The sheer size of these two books, their Tolstoyan breadth and ambition, is impressive, almost overwhelming. Too, as John Moss, the critic mentioned above, notes in his critical anthology *Here And Now*, "We experience the worlds he populates with an uncanny sense of immediacy."

The Mad Trapper, Wiebe's 13th book, doesn't have the epic dimension of *Big Bear* or *The Scorched-Wood People*. The author concentrates here, not on the sweep of history, but on the ramifications of a single event.

The book's immediacy, however, the feeling it imparts that *you* the reader are *there*, is stunning. *The Mad Trapper* is destined to become a classic of the North.

The story, based on events that actually happened during the winter of 1931-32, is a Canadian legend familiar to many, at least in its outlines. It takes place in the Northwest Territories, north of the Arctic Circle, in the land of four-hour days, 24 nights and temperatures of 50 below zero.

A stranger known as Albert Johnson, recently arrived in the North by raft with thousands of dollars in his pocket, builds himself a snug one-room cabin 80 miles from the nearest settlement.

When he deliberately springs another man's animal trap and hangs it defiantly from a tree, two Mounties pay him a call, seeking an explanation.

Johnson shoots one of them, wounding him seriously. Then he escapes into the howling wilderness and becomes the object of the largest manhunt in RCMP history.

For 50 days, alone on foot, Johnson defies capture, traversing hundreds of miles of frozen tundra in numbing cold, and becoming the first man to cross the Richardson Mountains in winter.

Much of the novel focuses on Johnson's pursuers—on Spike Millen, a humane and likable Mountie who becomes obsessed with capturing the Mad Trapper, as Johnson comes to be called; and, later, on Wop May, a First World War flying ace who joins the manhunt, the first involving an airplane, in the hope of securing a place in history.

And this is where controversy arises. In reality, Johnson killed one Mountie before he himself was shot to death. In Wiebe's book, Johnson kills two Mounties before he dies. But in the movie *Death Hunt*, filmed near Banff, Johnson kills no Mounties at all—and he escapes.

Wiebe has criticized the movie as a "horrible rip-off" of Canadian history. It's difficult to see how this criticism can be justified, however. If Wiebe can add one dead Mountie to The Truth, why can't somebody else subtract one?

Other problem areas exist—the choice of 56-year-old Lee Marvin, for example, to play Millen, who was 32. But the fine line between the legitimate use of poetic licence and the felt need to remain true to at least the spirit of historical fact is not going to be definitively drawn here.

Anyway, Wiebe's frustration probably stems from the simple fact that a *Mad Trapper* movie has been made at all. Why? Because his own book is so visual—and this is the key to its immediacy—that it could be turned into a film almost scene for scene.

In fact, three years ago Wiebe finished a *Trapper* screenplay for a $5-million movie starring Oliver Reed and Len Cariou. The project died for lack of funds. Who wouldn't be angry?

In the past, criticism of Wiebe's work has usually included a suggestion that his prose is Germanic, turgid, heavy. But consider this passage from *The Mad Trapper*: "By six o'clock the four pursuers were awake; they had eaten and broken camp in the darkness by eight and when the long blue shadow that precedes the glimmer of dawn broke high on the cliffs above them they had broken up the third fight between their dogs and were at the brush heap on the frozen creek where they had turned back the evening before.... It was forty-nine below zero, but for once not the slightest wind; not a grain of snow moving. The track had been wiped away during the night."

Could that be made clearer? No, and neither could it be made more evocative of the North. And there lies the novel's great achievement. At the end of the book, the Mad Trapper remains an enigma. But to our knowledge of the North, Wiebe has added a dimension.

War In The West

"Canadians will spend eight hours watching *The Blue And The Grey*," Rudy Wiebe said, "and they come away knowing all about the American Civil War. But the same people know virtually nothing about the small but vicious war that helped create their own country."

Wiebe was talking about the Northwest Rebellion of 1885. "It was the last stand of the native hunter against the immigrant agriculturist," he said over lunch. It was also the war that led to the hanging of Louis Riel.

The Rebellion is the subject of Wiebe's 22nd book, which he co-authored with historian Bob Beal: *War In The West: Voices Of The 1885 Rebellion.*

A couple of years ago, as the 100th anniversary of the war approached, Wiebe decided "something had to be done about it." He fixed on the idea of putting together "a book of pictures and stories about ordinary people, not big shots."

He wanted to work with an historian, someone comfortable with hard facts. Enter Beal, who had just finished researching the Rebellion for another book: *Prairie Fire.*

Beal teaches history at the University of Alberta, where Wiebe teaches English and creative writing. The two pooled their resources. Both had turned up original documents focusing on the Rebellion: newspaper accounts, tapes of interviews, journals.

They decided to structure the book chronologically, to let participants tell the story in their own words. These accounts had to be chosen from a plethora of material, and then edited. Wiebe focused primarily on that. Beal concentrated more on the photos and illustrations.

For most of a year, they met three or four times a week. Gradually, the book took shape.

If the landscape here is familiar, at least to those interested in the story of the West, seldom has a writer evoked it so vividly.

The most dramatic event of the Rebellion, the Frog Lake Massacre of nine unarmed people, is told from several points of view, and becomes more real than in any other version I've read.

Then there's the eye-witness account that Wiebe unearthed of the Battle of Batoche. A Métis survivor, known only as Mrs. William J. Delorme, left a two-page deposition with her children in which she described running to the river carrying one young child in a washtub.

So many bullets were hitting the water, she said, that it looked like it was raining. "You don't get an image like that," Wiebe noted, "except from someone who was really there."

29. W.P. Kinsella: Shaking The Dust Off His Feet

*The expected confrontation didn't happen. Fiction writers Rudy Wiebe and W.P. (Bill) Kinsella had been trading insults and angry words through newspaper articles for months. Wiebe had charged that Kinsella's depiction of native peoples was racist. He had urged residents of the real-life Hobbema Indian reserve to take legal action to stop Kinsella from using the name of the community in his fiction. Also to seek a part of his royalties in damages. Kinsella replied from White Rock, British Columbia, that Wiebe was "a petty little academic drone" driven either by jealousy of his material success (*Shoeless Joe *had become the hit movie* Field Of Dreams) *or anger at his pro-free-trade politics.*

But come the spring of 1990, when both Wiebe and Kinsella were in Calgary for the annual general meeting of the Writers' Guild of Alberta, the two writers never appeared in the same room at the same time. Wiebe gave a Friday night address in which he rehearsed the WGA's 10-year history of accomplishment. At a Saturday afternoon luncheon, Kinsella read from a just-completed novel called Box Socials, *the first volume in a semi-autobiographical trilogy about a boy growing up in rural Alberta. Neither said a public word about the other.*

A couple of months before, after laying out the issue as clearly as I could, I'd summed up my own feelings about it: anti-censorship, pro-responsibility. I also suggested that Kinsella had been used as a whipping boy: "Through five books of 'Indian stories' Kinsella was hailed almost everywhere, including on Indian reserves from coast to coast. Then, for a sixth book of the same, he gets thrashed? Okay, times have changed. But the message has been delivered. Let's give the fiction writer—as opposed to the public talker—a chance to respond."

In 1990, Kinsella the non-fiction writer did the text for an artbook celebrating the work of a native artist: Two Spirits Soar: The Art Of Allen Sapp/The Inspiration Of Allan Gonar. *Richard Wagamese, an Ojibway journalist, reviewed the book for the* Calgary Herald. *He wrote that in his fiction Kinsella had perpetuated stereotypes: "This time, however, he displays a sensitivity for and an appreciation of the spiritual nature of the paintings of Allen Sapp."*

Seven years before, when he moved out of Calgary, Kinsella shook the dust off his feet. He'd been teaching English at the university and wasn't sorry to put that behind him. Since 1983, he has lived in White Rock, British Columbia. In summer, he and his wife, journalist Ann Knight, often drive around the United States visiting major league baseball parks. "I work best on the road," Kinsella told me once. "I set a quota for myself, two pages a day, six days a week. When you have to check out of a motel by 11:30, it provides a lot of inspiration."

In Calgary we knew him when...

The door to W.P. Kinsella's office at the University of Calgary is a clutter of cartoons, many of which poke gentle fun at academia. I'm standing there reading them, chuckling, when the man himself, bearded and side-burned, turns a corner and scuffs down the hall toward me in old brown corduroys, a flannel cowboy shirt and sneakers that have seen better days. Kinsella is not your typical English-department type.

Books line the walls of his office all right, but dozens of them are copies of his own four collections of short stories, including the latest work, *Born Indian*. And others clearly have nothing to do with Shakespeare or Chaucer—*The Encyclopedia Of Baseball*?

Baseball, you see, is the subject of Kinsella's first novel, *Shoeless Joe*, which grew out of the title story of his third collection, *Shoeless Joe Jackson Comes To Iowa*. After narrowly missing the $50,000 Seal Books Award, not given in 1981, the novel won its author a $10,000 Houghton-Mifflin fellowship, and will be brought out by that Boston-based publisher, the author says, "in the spring of '82 to coincide with the opening of baseball season."

Kinsella says the magic-realist Shoeless Joe Jackson story is the first section of the novel. An Iowa farmer builds a baseball field on his acreage and his idol, the long-dead left fielder of the title, rewards him with a visit. In the second section of the novel, called "They Tore Down the Polo Grounds in 1964," the farmer-narrator goes to New Hampshire and kidnaps J.D. Salinger. And that's just the beginning.

If all of this makes Kinsella sound like the most exciting writer in Alberta, that's because I think he is. Born in Edmonton in 1935, he grew up on a farm in the bush near Lake Isle, 95 kilometres west of the Alberta capital, and didn't go to school until he was 10. In 1954, he graduated from Edmonton's Eastbrook High, then did "all sorts of vile things." He sold real estate and life insurance and advertising for the yellow pages, managed a retail credit agency, drove a taxi and, after moving in 1967 to Victoria, bought and ran a pizzeria.

Kinsella had been writing all along, but it wasn't until 1975, after he'd picked up a degree in creative writing from the University of Victoria, that he started selling his stories regularly. He'd found a narrative voice—that of Silas Ermineskin, a teenager who lived on the Indian reservation at Hobbema, halfway between Edmonton and Red Deer.

Kinsella says he's never been to Hobbema. He sets his Indian stories there for convenience, and learned what he knows about Indians from sitting in hotel bars and driving a cab.

He published the first of the Hobbema books, *Dance Me Outside*, in 1977, while he was earning a graduate degree at the University of Iowa. Four years later, it had sold 10,000 copies, the best-selling book Oberon has ever published. Kinsella published *Scars*, the second Hobbema book, in 1978, when he started teaching at the University of Calgary. Silas Ermineskin, a cross between Holden Caulfield and Huckleberry Finn, narrates the stories in both collections.

Shoeless Joe Jackson Comes To Iowa (1980) contains stories written over several years, and features a wide range of subjects and points of view. But with *Born Indian* we're back on the reservation again, with Silas and his friends Sadie One-wound, Frank Fencepost, Louis Coyote, Connie Bigcharles and Mad Etta.

It's more of the same, but it's wonderful—tragic and touching and funny all at once. An Indian child is taken away by social workers and dies of Sudden Infant Death Syndrome. A man badly crippled after getting involved with somebody else's woman talks Silas into helping him commit suicide, but decides in the end to go on living. The gang from Hobbema visits Silas's sister Illianna in Calgary, and in her absence turns her house into a stable.

It's not content that makes these stories exceptional, but language. Silas has a unique voice and a gift for the arresting simile: "My mouth is dry as a brown paper bag from talking so much"; "her eyes be dark and blank like mud puddles."

Kinsella says, and I agree, that *Born Indian* is the best of his Hobbema books. It contains no weak stories. Its language, while still authentic, is more refined than hitherto, less choppy. And the book is the funniest yet, with humor lacing even the starkest stories.

Born Indian, Kinsella says, may be the last of the Hobbema books. He wants to tell other, more "audacious" tales. "I'm going to write about Flannery O'Connor some day," he says. "I don't know how soon."

Shoeless Joe goes over the fence

First there was W.O. Mitchell. Then came Rudy Wiebe and Robert Kroetsch. Now we get W.P. Kinsella, who teaches creative writing at the University of Calgary. His first novel, *Shoeless Joe*, won its author a $10,000 Houghton-Mifflin fellowship, the first ever awarded to a non-American. And the book reads as if that's just the beginning. It's a wonderful work, hilarious, human, wildly original, about baseball and magic and crossing the line between fantasy and reality—about, Kinsella suggested the other day, "the power of love."

The novel *Shoeless Joe* grew out of the title story of the last collection but one. Narrator Ray Kinsella, an Iowa insurance agent turned farmer, hears a disembodied voice telling him to build a baseball field on his land, that if he does so his idol, the long-dead left-fielder Shoeless Joe Jackson, will pay him a visit. And so it comes to pass.

That's where the short story ended. In the novel, The Voice speaks again, sending Ray Kinsella—are you ready for this?—to kidnap the reclusive writer J.D. Salinger and take him to a baseball game. This fictional Salinger, who's incredibly well-drawn, gets caught up in the narrator's mad quest. He travels north with Kinsella in search of the truth about Moonlight Graham, who in 1905 played a single inning of baseball in the major leagues. And so it goes, with all the logic of a dream.

"To translate this situation to reality," Ray Kinsella notes at one point, "would be like trying to stuff a cloud in a suitcase." Quite so. But that brings us to the author's language, to his gift, as I've called it elsewhere, for the arresting simile: "Eddie Scissons slid into my dreams as gently as if he were stealing second base in slow motion." Or again, when Ray Kinsella meets Salinger, he blurts out what he wants, knowing as he does that he sounds wrong, all wrong, completely wrong: "I feel like a rookie runner caught off first base by a wily pitcher, hung up in that vast area between first and second...."

Yes, the language is stunning—but language alone does not account for this novel's greatness. Here, too, we have a wacky, wonderfully inventive story-line. We have Ray Kinsella himself, a beautiful dreamer if ever there was one, admittedly "a little eccentric where baseball is concerned." He's a man who wonders "if there are soft-spoken voices who deliver assignments to all of us at various times, and if my problem is one of hearing too acutely."

Or suddenly we're in the middle of a brilliant set piece, a scene at once funny and moving, as when the Oldest Living Chicago Cub declaims a fundamentalist sermon praising the name of baseball: "Have you the word of baseball living inside you? Has the word of baseball become part of you? Do you live it, play it, digest it, forever? Let an old man tell you to make the word of baseball your life. Walk into the world and speak of baseball. Let the word flow through you like water, so that it may quicken the thirst of your fellow man."

Finally, though, it's Kinsella's vision that sets this work apart—his vision, if you will, of the power of love to work magic, to change the world. "I wish I had your passion for baseball," Salinger tells Ray Kinsella at one point. "However misdirected it may be, it is still a passion. If I had my life to live over again, I'd take more chances. I'd want more passion in my life. Less fear and more passion, more risk. Even if you fail, you've still taken a risk."

Amen, W.P., Amen.

I telephoned Kinsella after I read *Shoeless Joe*. He told me Houghton-Mifflin, on the advice of its sales people, had printed 25,000 copies of the book—twice the usual run. That he'd finished another collection of Indian stories, tentatively entitled *The Moccasin Telegraph*. And that he'd just returned, uncompleted, an application for tenure at the University of Calgary.

Ah, well. There's no denying what Kinsella has said, to anyone who'll listen, more than once—that he deserves to live in a warmer climate. At least he'll be with us until June, 1983.

***

III

Second News Flash:
The Good Guys Advance

Scratch 100 Albertans and you'll find 61 book readers. That's more than you'll turn up in any province except British Columbia, where you'll come upon 65. In Ontario, you'll discover 59 and in Quebec 54. These and thousands of other obscure facts turned up in *Book Reading In Canada*, a 448-page study of the Canadian book trade that appeared in 1984. The report, written by publisher James Lorimer, was based on a survey of 17,600 adult Canadians carried out by Statistics Canada. Most national surveys, to put this one in perspective, involve 2,000 people.

Book Reading In Canada generated a couple of wire-service stories. But they were written in Toronto and that made a difference. I noted, for example, that if you lumped Alberta together with Manitoba and Saskatchewan and sampled 100 "prairie dwellers," you'd find only 56 people who had read a book in any given six-week period. If that were the only fact reported, a reader might take away the impression that Ontarians are bigger on books than Albertans—and that would be wrong.

Other Alberta angles hadn't received any attention at all. Surely, it was worth reporting that, contrary to popular opinion, Calgary had a greater number of educated book readers than Edmonton. Ignoring education levels, Edmonton had a slight edge—248,000 book readers to Calgary's 233,000. But when you considered readers who had completed some high school, Calgary was on top by a wide margin—226,000 to 131,000. And Calgary had the edge, as well, in readers with some university education—66,000 to 63,000.

That report crossed my desk in April, 1984.

In May, as a result of the siege begun in the early '80s, Alberta Culture Minister Mary LeMessurier announced the creation of a literary arts foundation to aid the province's publishers, libraries and writers. In June, the Alberta Foundation for the Literary Arts (AFLA) became a reality under the *Cultural Development Act,* which received royal assent in the legislative assembly just before summer recess. The act empowered Le-Messurier to appoint a 7- to 10-member board of executives and spend $800,000 annually through the foundation over the next five years.

Money for the foundation—whose annual budget had grown by 1991 to $1.35 million—came out of provincial lottery profits. The department of culture received 32.5 percent of all such monies, and AFLA got 12 percent of that. Some people questioned the morality of this arrangement: lottery funds? But most reacted like Christopher Wiseman, then president of the 425-member Writers' Guild of Alberta. "We're really excited about this!" he declared. "We're just overjoyed! It's a tremendous boost for Alberta writers and readers."

Early in 1985, a take-charge guy was appointed to secure the citadel. Ex-publisher and author George Melnyk became executive director of AFLA on April 1, having been chosen from about 60 people who applied for the job. Born in 1946, Melnyk had founded Edmonton's NeWest Press in 1975, and had served variously as editor, publisher and president. He'd edited *Of The Spirit: The Writings Of Douglas Cardinal* (1977) and written *Radical Regionalism,* a collection of essays on the West (1981). He'd just finished writing *The Search For Community,* an exploration of the international co-operative movement. By mid-1985, Melnyk had moved to Calgary, set up an AFLA office and was handling grant applications.

30. Out Of The West

SPRUCE GROVE, Alberta—Alberta publishers sold more than $15 million worth of books in 1985, according to a report on the province's publishing industry. Twenty-five publishers did $7.75 million worth of business in 1984 and more than doubled that figure the following year, says *Out Of The West,* an exhaustive, 235-page report released in April, 1986.

James J. Douglas, the Vancouver publisher who wrote the report, said the jump was due partly to sales of Hurtig Publishers' *Canadian Encyclopedia*, but that another publisher also did $3 or $4 million worth of business.

The $4,000 report was sponsored by Alberta Culture, the Alberta Publishers' Association and the Writers' Guild of Alberta. Much of the funding came from the Alberta Foundation for the Literary Arts.

Douglas, interviewed at the annual meeting of the Writers' Guild of Alberta, expressed astonishment at the number of publishers, their combined sales volume and the variety of books they publish.

The co-owner of Douglas & McIntyre said he expected to find 10 or 12 publishers in Alberta. He thought Hurtig Publishers would be the only significant operation, as it was a decade ago. But he found three publishers whose annual revenues exceeded $1 million.

In his report, subtitled *The Business Of Publishing And Writing In Alberta*, Douglas deliberately omits names. But the two largest publishers after Hurtig are based in Calgary: Best of Bridge, which specializes in cookbooks, and ACTA Press, which publishes engineering books for American and European markets.

In *Out Of The West*, which uses final figures from 1984, Douglas makes 26 recommendations on publishing and eight on writing. These include developing provincial grants programs to complement federal ones, setting up a guaranteed loan program and publishing an annual list of Alberta books recommended by librarians and teachers.

But he said the real value of the report is that it offers a statistical, in-depth profile of the industry. Jack Lewis, president of the Alberta Publishers' Association, echoed this sentiment: "It enables us to show others that we have a vital, thriving and important industry here. We're very well diversified. It's just that we're at an earlier stage of development than some other areas."

Out Of The West shows the Alberta publishing industry is doing as well financially as the industry nationally. And in some cases it's doing better. But it's still a young industry and does require some nurturing. Twelve

Alberta firms publish trade books (for sale in bookstores). Four produce educational books for schools, four are literary houses and one focuses on children's books.

In 1984, six Alberta publishing companies earned from $50,000 to $250,000, three from $250,000 to $500,000, two from $500,000 to $1 million and three more than $1 million. The province's publishers had 618 titles in print and brought out 89 new books each year. Of the titles in print, 57 percent were in paperback only, 26 percent in hardcover and 17 percent in both.

Alberta publishers had 85 full-time and 31 part-time employees. They paid a total of $1,840,000 in salaries, including those to owners, managers and part-time staff. They received more than 700 manuscripts a year, 80 percent of them from Alberta writers. And they commissioned, on average, about 50 percent of their titles, editing 90 percent of them in-house.

Monty Reid, president of the Writers' Guild of Alberta, praised the report. But he noted that it dealt exclusively with business values: "I wouldn't want to see decisions made on the basis of this report alone." To make *Out Of The West* as comprehensive as possible, the Writers' Guild of Alberta sent questionnaires to its 475 members, as well as to 30 writers who are not members. It received 210 completed questionnaires.

Alberta publishers scored well among writers for consultation on such matters as design, prices and print runs, and for such courtesies as returning original manuscripts and paying interest on late royalty payments. But writers criticized marketing, promotion and distribution efforts.

31. AFLA Makes A Difference

Hard times returned to Alberta in 1987 as a result of falling oil prices, but the province was enjoying a renaissance in writing and publishing. Alberta publishers generated annual sales worth $15 million in 1985 (the latest figures available), and the Writers' Guild of Alberta had more than 500 dues-paying members.

Much of the book-related activity could be traced to the Alberta Foundation for the Literary Arts (AFLA)—the province's answer to the

Canada Council's writing and publications section. Since giving out its first grants in June 1985, the foundation had awarded almost $2 million to writers, publishers and libraries.

"In a province of two and a half million people, $1 million a year is a significant amount of money," said George Melnyk, the foundation's executive director. "I really believe we have made a significant difference in the literary arts."

Melnyk said "the creation of the foundation is the most positive thing that's happened in the past 10 years. It signalled a new era."

Rudy Wiebe, chair of the Writers' Union of Canada, shared this view. A decade ago, he said, the provincial government was spending much of its cultural budget on the Calgary Stampede and on Edmonton's Klondike Days. Wiebe, whose intensive lobbying led to the creation of AFLA in late 1984, said writers all over Canada "very much envy" the foundation.

Foundation chair Ted Hart said "we're really beginning to see results." Writers were buying time to work, and publishers were bringing out books they would not otherwise have produced. (NeWest Press, for example, received $25,000 to publish an anthology of short stories called *Alberta Bound*, which appeared as a mass-market paperback at $4.95.)

During the last half of 1986, AFLA awarded 50 grants ranging in value from a few hundred to tens of thousands of dollars. The high end included $60,000 to the Alberta Library Trustees' Association, $42,400 to the Alberta Publishers' Association and $35,000 to the Writers' Guild of Alberta.

Among the other grants were $6,600 to the Calgary Public Library to fund a writer-in-residency for Fred Stenson; $21,078 to popular historian James Gray to research and write a biography of R.B. Bennett; and $13,300 to Hurtig Publishers to fund a feasibility study for a Canadian encyclopedia for young people.

Out-of-province organizations and individuals were also eligible for funding, Melnyk said, "as long as there's an Alberta connection." For example, $6,475 went to the Association of Canadian Publishers to fund an annual general meeting in Alberta and $4,430 to the Writers' Union of Canada to fund travel costs for the chair and a national council meeting in Edmonton.

Grant recipients had to submit a report within six months of completing their projects, explaining how they spent the money and how the project turned out. They also had to agree to have their financial records audited if necessary and to return any unspent funds. Melnyk said grant recipients were scrupulous. Ninety-nine percent of them have completed the reports, and a couple even returned money.

AFLA, one of several provincial arts foundations, was receiving $1 million a year from Alberta lottery profits in 1987. The operating budget took 10 to 15 percent of that, and included the salaries of two full-time staff members (an executive director and an assistant), plus office rental in Calgary and honorariums and travel expenses for board members.

The board comprised 9 to 15 voting members appointed by the minister of culture—mostly publishers, writers and librarians—and one non-voting government representative. They served for a two- or three-year term, and met four times a year to assess grant applications (someone from out-of-province usually lent a hand).

During the first few "grant runs," the bulk of the money went to writers. But AFLA had a mandate to fund writers, publishers and librarians equally, and (using the $1 million figure) earmarked $250,000 for each of its constituencies, with $150,000 slated for joint projects.

***

IV

More Alberta Volunteers

32. Katherine Govier: Maverick In Exile

Katherine Govier is the Mavis Gallant of Alberta. Born and raised in Wild Rose Country, she's the writer who left and succeeded and never returned—except for visits and in her fiction. During the 1960s, when Govier was coming of age in Calgary, she felt Real Life was happening elsewhere. The images shown on TV and in magazines—"patent leather pumps you couldn't even buy here"—reflected the realities of other places. "The imagery around me was not projected anywhere," Govier told me in 1989. "I got so hungry to see my reality, my life made real. I felt I had to go somewhere to be reckoned with."

Since 1971, Govier has been based in Toronto, though she has also lived in London, England and Washington, D.C. She published her first novel, Random Descent, *in 1979. Since then she has published two more novels—*Going Through The Motions *(1982) and* Between Men *(1987)— and two collection of stories:* Fables Of Brunswick Avenue *(1985) and* Before And After *(1989).*

Early in 1991, Govier was completing her sixth book, a novel called Hearts Of Flame. *She said the title comes from the name of a fictional Alberta folk-rock group, now disbanded, one of whose ex-members has disappeared. Has she been murdered? Abducted? The novel is not a mystery, Govier said, but explores the nature of community.*

Fables Of Brunswick Avenue

Nobody would guess that this attractive, soft-spoken woman wearing white slacks, a white blouse and a red Mickey Mouse wrist watch is a maverick Albertan making a name for herself as a Canadian writer. Not that Katherine Govier, who was born in Edmonton and attended high school in Calgary, is a newcomer to the literary scene. After all, she published a first novel in 1979 (*Random Descent*) and a second (*Going Through The Motions*) in 1982.

Still, her 1985 book, a superb collection of stories called *Fables Of Brunswick Avenue*, is somehow deeper, wiser, closer to the bone than her novels. It's attracting an unusual amount of favorable attention across the country, and is quietly turning its author into a Writer To Watch.

Maverick Albertan? "I was born here, and my father was born here, and yet I felt there was no place for me here," Govier said over lunch, explaining why she moved to Toronto in 1971. "Maybe it's different now, but then, people who wanted to do what I wanted to do had to leave." Leaving Alberta was, nevertheless, "a first betrayal. It's only a series of betrayals after that—a refusal to fall into line, to do what was expected of one."

Govier, born in 1948, said her family (including two sisters) still lives in Calgary, and "I feel like an impostor anywhere else." Yet, after spending more than a decade in Toronto—except for one year in England and two in Washington—"I've made my place there."

Yes, it's all quite complicated. In Calgary, Govier attended William Aberhart Senior High School for three years. She had moved to Calgary from Edmonton with her family after her father, a chemical engineer, became head of Alberta's Oil and Gas Conservation Board.

Govier's mother, Doris, is one of Calgary's best-known teachers of Canadian literature. "She taught me to love books," Govier said, "though I used to think Canadian literature was extremely boring."

After graduating from high school in 1966, Govier wanted to attend Carleton University in Ottawa and become a journalist. To her parents, Ottawa sounded like the far side of the world—"and we compromised on the University of Alberta." There Govier took a degree in honors English. She worked a year for the university's alumni publications, then moved to Toronto to take a master's degree in English at York University.

Much of what happened during the next few years can be discerned in her latest book, which Govier stoutly denies is autobiographical. There was a first marriage, and along with it a bohemian period spent living on

Brunswick Avenue in downtown Toronto (ah, youth!). Later, there was a second marriage—to a journalist (hence the two years in Washington). And most recently, there were two children, born 18 months apart in 1982 and '83.

Not long ago, Govier spent several months adapting her novel *Going Through The Motions* for the stage. Toronto's Factory Theatre Lab gave it a showcase production. Govier found writing for the theatre difficult, however, because "so many people are telling you what to do." Compared with writing fiction, it's "like working on Mean Street. People are really out to get each other."

Now Govier is working on a third novel, a contemporary comedy of manners set in Calgary. It also draws on history, focusing on the story of Calgary's second murder—that of a young Indian woman in 1889. "She's emblematic of something to me."

Maybe the choice of subject has something to do with what Govier calls Alberta's "outsider or outlaw mentality: not in the sense of anything illegal—a handshake is a handshake and a deal is a deal, God knows—but in that feeling of not having access to power. People in central Canada don't know what that's like, that double colonization."

Govier finds Calgary "less pretentious than establishment Toronto. Here, you're only as good as what you do." Besides, the drive from Calgary to Banff "is one of my favorite things in the whole world."

As for the red Mickey Mouse wrist watch, "it cost only $14.95 and keeps perfect time. Look, you push this button and it pops open. It's digital, really up-to-date. And the kids love it. They keep asking me, 'Mommy, let me push the button.'"

Putting Calgary on the map

Several fine writers have set novels in and around Calgary, among them W.O. Mitchell, L.R. (Bunny) Wright and Aritha van Herk. But Katherine Govier is the first novelist to place Calgary at the heart of a full-length fiction, to make it the focus of attention in a work designed to put the city on Canada's literary map.

Govier, an expatriate Albertan based in Toronto, establishes her controlling metaphor early in *Between Men*. "This matter of getting on the map," one of her narrators writes: "first it was the railway that was going to do it, then the boom, then the fire of 1886. And still it hadn't happened. There was a sense of something owing." Later, he notes: "Calgary will be the first Western town to have streetlights. The power project will put us on the map."

Between Men is a complex, well-crafted novel with two intertwined story-lines. The first of these, the framing tale, is a contemporary love story which focuses on Suzanne Vail, a 35-ish history professor recently returned to Calgary after an absence of 10 years. She is torn between two men. One is her businessman husband, Ace, whom she is divorcing. The other is a jaded, 53-year-old politician named Simon, with whom she has an intense affair.

This contemporary story is rich and detailed. It includes vignettes from Suzanne's past (most of them involving Ace) and an ongoing skirmish in the present, with Suzanne battling an attempt by her departmental chairman to cut the most significant course she teaches (Reinventing The West). This tale features memorable minor characters, notably Suzanne's oil-man father-in-law, Block, and her friend Gemma, a shameless gold-digger who founds a group called SWARM (Single Women After Rich Men), incidentally providing light relief.

Suzanne is researching an historical paper about the brutal and mysterious murder of an Indian women named Rosalie New Grass. She is obsessed with this real-life event, which happened in 1889 at a down-and-dirty Calgary bar called the Turf Club. Her search for facts becomes a quest for truth, and her imaginings make up the story within the story, and eventually reveal the death to have been "something that happened between men."

Govier links Suzanne's quest with her larger purpose: "This murdered Indian woman, that dark club and the men who frequented it, the town's panic: it was one of those occasions where the layers of custom broke open, and one could see straight to the core of the place. But to see that core, Suzanne would need a way in."

To this end, Suzanne creates a newspaperman/narrator named Murphy, who is present at key historical scenes and comes vividly to life. Murphy's dark, brooding chapters are among the novel's chief attractions and demonstrate the power of Govier's imagination.

Dipping her brush now in the dark colors of the past, now in the bright ones of the present, the author creates a multi-hued portrait of the city in which she became a woman. Riding in hot air balloons, canoeing in Bowness Park, camping in the nearby Kananaskis mountains—all of the distinctive local tones are here. "Stampede was not just another rodeo," Govier writes. "It was 10 days of scheduled mayhem to which the city was tradition bound."

When Suzanne pushes her bicycle up 11A Street toward Riley Park, those who know Calgary will exclaim: "Yes! I see it! I see it happening!" But the author doesn't forget those unfamiliar with the city, for she immediately rounds out the image: "She intended to go to sit by the playground and watch the mothers and children...."

Govier combines an insider's intimate knowledge of Calgary with an outsider's cool detachment. Her depiction of the city is profound.

> Calgary was a club. Membership meant holding dear a few tenets: the mountains were beautiful, and business was good.... Further tenets were a handshake meant a deal, and art without a horse in it was pretentious....
>
> Anyone could do business in Calgary. But although making money was Calgary's credo, and a continuous influx of fortune-seeking strangers necessary to its functioning, the seekers after gold were disdained.... Club members were more than willing to do business with you but until you'd lived through a bust and lost your money and started again, you wouldn't belong...
>
> This exclusivity was, like all exclusions, a defence. It was the Calgarians' answer to the national assumption that they were lesser because although they had made it big they had only done it in this out-of-the-way place. Nevertheless it was there.

If Govier is hard on her old home town, she is even more coolly scathing in treating conventional Eastern Canadian attitudes about the

West. When Simon learns that Suzanne has spent the past 10 years down East, he relaxes: "There were common assumptions then, she wasn't an untutored Westerner after all but someone who had been in the centre, who had learned the proper order of things."

Between Men isn't an allegory. It's far too subtle. Yet, Simon is quintessentially an ugly Easterner—older, experienced, smugly superior, he has come to teach the local yokels a thing or two: "The West will never get power. Power doesn't travel from east to west. Only the sun and eager young men do that."

Ace, on the other hand, is 35 but looks 20. He's a maker of mistakes—but also vital and alive. And he's identified with Calgary and the West. "Ace looked ahead. Both he and the city were tuned, engineered, bright with progress. He belonged to the good times, and hadn't been hit by the bad."

Govier's novel is notable, finally, for its insight into male-female relations. One example: "Fidelity was an invention of men to ensure an otherwise unprovable paternity, embraced by women because they needed a man's protection. Until (Suzanne) had agreed to that fidelity... she had had the power. But now she had given up her power. Without Ace, she could not make Simon jealous. Instead she made him fearful."

No ambitious novel is without flaws. In this one, Ace's possessiveness is hard to believe, given his years-long separation from Suzanne. There's also a curious, whimsical scene between Ace and his mother which Govier might have omitted. Some will object to certain supernatural effects, others to the author's habit of occasionally using commas to separate complete clauses.

But these are quibbles. *Between Men* is a powerful, multi-faceted assertion of identity by a gifted fiction writer. When all of the clever but placeless novels churned out this decade have been forgotten, *Between Men* will still be showing up on Canadian literature courses. It puts Calgary on the map.

33. Aritha van Herk: The Prodigal Returns

Alberta's prodigal daughter eventually came home. Aritha van Herk, who left Alberta in 1980 vowing never to return, moved to Calgary three and a half years later and, with her geologist husband, promptly bought a house. Van Herk, who in 1978 won the $50,000 Seal First Novel Award for Judith, *began teaching at the University of Calgary in 1983 and has been there since.*

In 1980, when van Herk left Alberta, she had lots to say about "the oppressive and dangerous political atmosphere" of her native province. She was especially critical of the film and literary arts branch of Alberta Culture. Times have changed, she said soon after returning. The formation of the Writers' Guild of Alberta, for example, "pressured Alberta Culture into being much more responsive" to writers' needs.

And Calgary? "Who would have thought a bust could do so much to improve the character of a city?" she asked rhetorically over lunch. "The best things have stayed, the worst have gone away. Calgary has undergone a maturing process. It's quite, quite different. The people are friendly again. They've stopped talking about nothing but money, about how many properties they've flipped in the past month. And the cultural life! The city's so alive!"

In 1990, van Herk published "a geografictione" called Places Far From Ellesmere. *A departure from the mainstream novels (*Judith, The Tent Peg, No Fixed Address) *that have earned her an international audience, the book explores the shaping influence of geography on The Writer. Much of the work consists of a feminist re-reading of Leo Tolstoy, The Writer, and his creation,* Anna Karenina. *Literary and cerebral, if not downright academic,* Ellesmere *will take its place in van Herk's opus as a stimulating digression.*

No Fixed Address

Aritha van Herk was tired of reading about nice, middle-class women. She was fed up with heroines who sit waiting at home while their husbands run through jobs, adventures and mistresses. She wanted to write about "a really bad girl."

In her third novel, *No Fixed Address: An Amorous Journey*, she gives us Arachne Manteia, who sells panties but resolutely refuses to wear any. "I am not Arachne," van Herk stated flatly. "But I do like her passionate approach to life. She doesn't sit at home waiting for life to come to her. She goes out and gets it."

Arachne roars around the Canadian West in a classic Mercedes Benz, flogging undies for Ladies' Comfort Limited and screwing whenever, wherever and whomever she pleases—and damn the would-be husband waiting at home. "Why can't a woman behave as badly as a man and get away with it?" van Herk said over lunch. "Arachne is amoral, but so what? She's an earthy, sensual, exciting woman. If she were a man, we'd be saying, 'Oh, God, isn't he virile and interesting!'

"With most novels about women, you know right away that the heroine will leave her husband and go find herself, or else have a baby. But you can never predict what Arachne's going to do. She refuses to behave according to the usual narrative, contextual, or formal rules."

This last is also true of the author herself. Van Herk was the youngest author (32) selected for the 45 Below promotion in 1986, when judges came up with a list of the 10 best Canadian fiction writers under the age of 45. But she is best-known as the author of *Judith*, which in 1978 won the first Seal Books $50,000 First Novel Award.

Judith has been published in nine countries and seven languages; van Herk's second novel, *The Tent Peg*, in six countries and four languages. With their total sales approaching 200,000 copies, the novels have earned van Herk an international reputation.

Born in Wetaskiwin, Alberta, van Herk was the first Canadian-born child of Dutch immigrants who arrived speaking only a smattering of

English. She grew up on a farm in Edberg, about 140 kilometres southeast of Edmonton (and a mere 24 kilometres from Heisler, boyhood home of novelist Robert Kroetsch).

After graduating from high school in 1971, van Herk spent a year working as her father's "hired man"—out of necessity, not because she relished farm work. Then she attended the University of Alberta in Edmonton. There she studied with Rudy Wiebe, became friends with Marian Engel, who was writer-in-residence, and earned a B.A. and an M.A. in English. Van Herk has always been a voracious reader, she said, and always obsessed with wanting to write. She published a poem when she was 12.

In 1977, van Herk won the *Miss Chatelaine* short-fiction contest with a nuts-to-marriage-and-motherhood story called "The Road Out." The following year she took the Seal First Novel Award. "It was a mixed blessing," van Herk said. It launched her career in spectacular fashion—and enabled her to buy a Porsche—but it also took a heavy physical and mental toll. To promote *Judith*, she made three cross-Canada tours and one European tour. When it was all over, she remembered, "I went to bed for three months."

Since then, in addition to *The Tent Peg*, van Herk has published many essays and a dozen short stories. Two of these, "Never Sisters" and "Waiting For The Rodeo," have been anthologized repeatedly. Van Herk has also co-edited two collections of short stories: *More Stories From Western Canada* (with Rudy Wiebe) and *West Of Fiction* (with Wiebe and Leah Slater).

Meanwhile, van Herk has embarked on a second career—as an academic. For two years, beginning in 1980, she was a sessional lecturer in the English department at the University of British Columbia. Then she accepted a full-time post at the University of Calgary—replacing W.P. Kinsella. She teaches three courses (freshman English, Canadian literature and creative writing), and in 1985 she won the superior teacher award for the faculty of humanities, an honor bestowed by student vote.

Van Herk has also found time to do an astonishing amount of travelling. Since 1978, she has given over 100 public readings and lectures in North America and Europe. In 1983, she occupied the guest chair in Canadian studies at the University of Kiel in Germany. In 1986, she visited Singapore for the Triennial Conference of the World Association of Commonwealth Literature. And so it goes.

Van Herk and her husband (they married in 1974), exploration geologist Robert Sharpe, recently bought a house in Calgary. There, when she isn't on the road, van Herk reads a book a day—"but that includes manuscripts," since she's on the editorial board of NeWest Press, Alberta's largest literary publisher. She's also on the editorial board of *NeWest Review*, a monthly journal of culture and current events in the West, and co-editor, with Kroetsch and poet Monty Reid, of *The Dinosaur Review*, a literary magazine based in Drumheller. And, of course, she writes, rising daily at six a.m. and working all morning (she teaches in the afternoon).

That's how van Herk wrote much of *No Fixed Address*. In this novel, she eschews images of castration (those in *Judith* left male reviewers wincing) and all talk of tent pegs being driven through men's skulls. Instead, she gives us a heroine as sexually casual, as vengeful and ruthless, as any Jerzy Kosinski hero—a funhouse-mirror image of a macho man. The difference is, Arachne is very human, and thus almost redeems herself.

Is van Herk mellowing? "As a feminist, I'm getting tougher," she said. "My anger was more evident three or four years ago, but I'm much more formidable now. I know better how to channel and direct it."

Van Herk began writing *No Fixed Address* in 1981. "They say second novels are hard," she said. "Let me tell you, third novels are hell. They're awful. I never want to write another third novel. I've rewritten this book more times than the other two put together."

When van Herk started to work on the novel, she had in mind only Arachne, "a funny little street rat" who grows up longing for normalcy and has almost as many lives as a cat. She hit upon the name Arachne, derived from Arachnida, the class of insects that includes spiders, because she had discovered during some research that spiders are traditionally linked with rogues. She knew that this born-feminist rogue, an all-in-one answer to Tom Jones and Don Quixote, would figure in a picaresque novel, travelling around Alberta and British Columbia. But doing what?

At Vancouver's Centennial Museum, van Herk stumbled upon a show called "Underwear Through The Ages": "Imagine a museum putting on a show called that!" Now, with an idea of how her heroine would occupy herself, she made a few phone calls. A rural B.C. shopkeeper solved her problem when she confided that the WonderBra man called on her twice a year.

Arachne begins her adult life as a Vancouver bus driver (this emerges in an extended flashback) and eventually ends up on the back roads of Alberta selling underwear. "The litany of the places she visits is the poetry of my novel," van Herk said. "Rumsey, Ryley, Heisler, Edberg—poetry is the epitome of the prairie town."

Arachne is a strong, well-defined character—impulsive and unpredictable, but consistently so, and very real. But here the novel runs into difficulty. Having taken pains to make Arachne real, the author deliberately calls her reality into question.

We're ready to believe she would have a torrid affair with a coppersmith old enough to be her grandfather; this fits with the parody of macho. As the novel unfolds, however, Arachne's adventures become increasingly fantastic. In one sequence she's handed a cheque for $25,000—and is later able to cash it. In another, she shares a motel room in Kamloops with a hitch-hiking woman and her pet bear.

It's as if van Herk started to write a picaresque novel that would stand the traditional male rogue on his head. Then, growing bored with that idea, she got swept up in the rhetoric of postmodernism. So she dragged in an unnamed female narrator obsessed with underwear—a narrator who is piecing together Arachne's story from various interviews and research, and creating her in the process.

This is all very interesting, but it's a different novel—one concerned not with mirror images of macho but with reality and narrative. This second, superimposed novel is at odds with the first. The aroused reader, led to expect some resolution, however fantastic, of key relationships, emerges baffled and unsatisfied.

Arachne shows charity in befriending Josef, the old coppersmith. But he proves to be merely a catalyst for fantastic adventures. Worse,

Arachne's relationship with Thomas, a cartographer who plays Penelope to her Odysseus, is left unresolved. Arachne's quest for normalcy, which Thomas represents, is abandoned—and with it goes all coherent meaning.

Arachne loses reader sympathy toward the end of the novel, when she behaves ferociously. But by then, we're not sure what is real and what is not, so it hardly matters. Arachne is no longer a reverse role model, but has become merely words on a page.

On the positive side, van Herk's sense of the West is palpable. Her language is muscular—always the single word where a lesser writer would use two or three. And she also turns up a welter of funny set-pieces, as when Arachne tries to buy her first brassiere and ends up stealing it, or when she takes a poor, babbling poet to bed and has her way with him.

This time out, van Herk was waylaid by her own ambition. But make no mistake. *No Fixed Address* gives evidence of a tremendous talent slouching—no, driving a Porsche hell-bent—toward maturity.

34. Samuel Selvon: The Janitor Is World Famous

A native of Trinidad, Samuel Selvon was well-established as an author long before he settled in Calgary in the late 1970s. Many of his novels, published in Great Britain in the '50s and '60s, have been unavailable in Canada and the United States. In 1990, two were reprinted for the North American market: The Housing Lark *and* Those Who Eat The Cascadura. *In 1989, Selvon published* Foreday Morning: Selected Prose 1946-1986, *which included both fiction and non-fiction. Early in 1991 Selvon was at work on a novel—working title:* A High of Zero—*set in Calgary and Trinidad.*

In 1982, Samuel Selvon found himself running short of cash. He scanned the want ads, saw that the University of Calgary was looking for a janitor and applied for the job. He got it, and for the next four months, he worked from 11 p.m. to 7 a.m. cleaning blackboards, washing floors and doing the things that janitors do.

Nothing odd in this except that Selvon is an internationally known author. Originally from Trinidad, he lived in England for 28 years before moving to Calgary in 1978. He has published countless short stories, articles and plays for radio, stage and screen, as well as three non-fiction books and 10 novels. Selvon has won many awards, including two Guggenheim Fellowships.

The year after he moved here with his family, Selvon taught creative writing as a visiting professor at the University of Victoria. When that appointment ended and the bills kept coming in, he took the janitorial job at the University of Calgary.

"It didn't bother me to work as a janitor for a few months," Selvon said over lunch. "In fact, I rather enjoyed it. A job like that, you don't really have to think. And if I needed money tomorrow, I'd do the same thing. Or I'd go and dig ditches, and I'd do it without any qualms. That's part of who I am. I wouldn't go to the unemployment office and say, 'I want a job as a writer.' I'd take anything I could get."

Selvon, a tall, slim, unassuming man who laughs easily, delivers all this in the lilting cadences of the West Indies. He quit cleaning classrooms, he said, only after a senior arts grant came through from the Canada Council. In 1985-86, he went back to work at the University of Calgary—not as a janitor, but as writer-in-residence. There he could be found in a book-lined office in the English department, reading manuscripts and dispensing advice to aspiring writers.

It was the first time the university had a writer-in-residence since 1978-79, when Rudy Wiebe held the post. Aritha van Herk said Selvon was more than welcome: he was necessary. "I had room for 19 students in my senior writing class," she said "and I received 90 applications."

Selvon is an old hand at playing outrider to a university English department. In 1976-78, he served as writer-in-residence at the University of Dundee in Scotland. He was at the University of Alberta in 1983-84, and the University of Winnipeg in 1984-85. Both jobs meant lots of commuting, and he was happy to walk to work from his home in suburban Charleswood, where he lives with his wife and three offspring.

Selvon has been writing for over 40 years. He began selling short stories to the British Broadcasting Corporation while still in Trinidad working as a copy editor on a newspaper. "I felt I was too young to fall into a contented way of life—parties and drinking rum and going to the beach on Sundays." And so, he became part of "an influx of writers from the Caribbean" who went to England in the 1950s. Among his contemporaries were George Lamming, Andrew Salkey and V.S. Naipaul. "I didn't go as a writer," he said, "though I was partly trained as a journalist. I went prepared to do any job. And I did a lot of things—cleaning and working in factories."

Meanwhile, he was getting up at 4 a.m. to write. (When working on a project he still rises at that hour.) Gradually, book by book, Selvon developed a reputation. "I got splendid reviews," he said. "All my first printings sold out. But only 5,000 or so copies. I'm not saying they were bestsellers. It's only recently, through reprints and cheap editions, that I've started to earn royalties."

Selvon's novels are acclaimed for their humor and vernacular rhythms. "Some critics call them 'dialect novels,'" the author said, though he clearly doesn't like the term. He published his first novel, *A Brighter Sun*, in 1952. The book has gone through five printings and is still available in the United States. Three other novels remain in print there, and can be ordered through bookstores: *Turn Again Tiger* (first published in 1958), *Moses Ascending* (1975) and *Moses Migrating* (1983), named best novel of the year by the Writers' Guild of Alberta.

It wasn't until the mid-'70s that Selvon began thinking about leaving Great Britain. In 1976, he went to Scotland for a two-year stint as writer-in-residence at the University of Dundee. On returning to London, he found that most of his West Indian contemporaries had left the city, many to university appointments in the United States. "I'd spent 28 years inculcating the English tradition and European ways. There was a lot I still hadn't experienced in the western way of life. I wanted to get back to this side of the world—but not to Trinidad or the Caribbean. Too small."

Selvon's Anglo-Indian wife had relatives in Calgary—her mother, a brother and a sister. "She'd visit them, and then she'd come back and say, 'They're doing fine and we're struggling here. Let's go to Canada.' So finally I said, 'OK, Canada seems as good a place as any. Let's go.'"

Selvon was sporting a small Canadian flag in his lapel and said "we're rooted" in Calgary. In 1981, he said, "the day I became eligible, I took out Canadian citizenship. Not just me, all of us. That tells you my feelings about the place. In 28 years, I never wanted to take out British citizenship."

Selvon said he has "much more freedom here" to write. "It's much more difficult to earn a living in England. They don't have very many resident-writer appointments, for one thing. And the whole cultural upheaval in Canada. I feel part of it. You don't get that sort of thing in England. I find it so exciting, the feeling about writing that exists here."

Selvon doesn't miss England. "Canadians are much easier (than the English) to get along with," he said. "I find Canadians warm, tolerant and friendly. They're more relaxed and open-minded. We've all found this. Certainly there's prejudice and it needs watching. But compared with England, it's like nothing."

✳✳✳

V

Third News Flash:
Victory Is Ours!

35. Volunteers Launch New Assault

The Writers' Guild of Alberta shifted into high gear in 1988 in its drive to increase the political clout of writers in Wild Rose Country. Roughly 150 of the WGA's 650 members attended the organization's eighth annual general meeting, the most intense and emotional since the early 1980s.

Members voted to push for improved representation on the board of the Alberta Foundation for the Literary Arts; elected a highly politicized executive; and approved funding for a detailed study of the economics of writing in Alberta for use in negotiations with government.

The two-day meeting took place in Red Deer, a small city halfway between Edmonton and Calgary. Emotions boiled over during business-meeting discussions about the Alberta Foundation for the Literary Arts, which since 1985 had been channelling roughly $1 million a year in lottery funds to writers, publishers and libraries.

WGA members empowered their executive to lobby Alberta Culture Minister Greg Stevens for better representation on the foundation's board. Writers felt they were being short-changed as the 11-member board included—by their count—only one writer, Rudy Wiebe. As the largest, most active writers' organization in Alberta, the WGA wanted to be able to select two board members.

Wiebe argued forcefully that the new appointments should be "writers who are politically aware," not stooges chosen to placate MLAs. He noted that the foundation was slated to receive a budget increase, with an additional $140,000 earmarked for publishers and $85,000 for writers. The additional writers' funds were to be spent on novices, Wiebe said: "Our responsibilities are increasing while the pot isn't getting that much greater."

What angered Wiebe and others is the idea that the provincial government should dictate how grant money is to be spent. Guild members wanted to see the foundation operating at arms-length from the government, much like the Canada Council, and voted unanimously to reaffirm the "arms-length principal."

The issue had moved off the back-burner when foundation chair Howard Platt, a medical doctor with a history of involvement in the arts, accepted a job as a senior civil servant. Platt argued that the government had the right to oversee the overall allocation of lottery funds, while admitting that specific grants were "entirely the responsibility of the foundation."

Platt spoke, some thought courageously, at the guild's Saturday night banquet, where he urged writers to pursue their ends through negotiation rather than confrontation. Glenn Buick, assistant deputy minister of culture, also spoke at the banquet. Afterwards, privately, he insisted that Alberta's foundations were not created as "arms-length" organizations like the Canada Council, and denied that writers were being treated differently from other constituents.

Against this background, WGA members chose two of the most politically active writers in Alberta to lead the guild through the next year. Calgary fiction writer Aritha van Herk was acclaimed president and Edmonton non-fiction writer Myrna Kostash was elected vice-president. Kostash, chosen in absentia while researching and lecturing in eastern Europe, also won the WGA award for non-fiction with her book *No Kidding: Inside The World Of Teenage Girls*. (Out-of-province writers picked the $500 winner.)

Van Herk, whose three novels have won several awards, pledged to enhance the profile of Alberta writers and to show just how much they contribute to the cultural life of Alberta. In a fiery speech at the awards banquet, she climbed onto the head table to show off her snake-skin running shoes. "I put these on special," she said, "to show how hard and how fast I intend to run on behalf of the writers of Alberta."

Guild members also approved the hiring of B.C. writer Andreas Schroeder to do a study of writers and writing in Alberta. Schroeder, author of nine books and outgoing chair of the national Public Lending Right Commission, told the meeting he would gather "solid, hard data" on the local literary scene, including how much money authors received and how much they put back into the economy.

36. Over The Top

During the past 15 or so years, Alberta has experienced a "second-generation" literary flowering so rapid and extensive that even the province's writers and publishers don't appreciate its magnitude. Word For Word, *a wide-ranging 260-page report published in 1988, said that if such a phenomenon had occurred in central Canada, it would have been "determined, announced, itemized, tracked, analyzed and thoroughly celebrated" years ago.*

The $15,000 report, prepared by Vancouver author Andreas Schroeder, said Alberta continues to be derided as "an intellectual swampland" when in fact the province is a national leader in cultural use, purchase, production, spending and attendance. The report, subtitled The Business Of Writing In Alberta, *was a companion volume to a 1986 study of Alberta's publishing industry called* Out Of The West. *Sponsored by the Writers' Guild of Alberta and Alberta Culture and Multiculturalism, it was funded by the Alberta Foundation for the Literary Arts.*

"People just don't know about the burgeoning of Alberta," Schroeder told me. "The province is one of Canada's best-kept cultural secrets." In Word For Word *he declared: "Clearly, it's time the rest of Canada stopped thinking of Alberta as an intellectual swampland. If that assessment was ever true, it's now many decades out of date." He blamed Albertans for not celebrating their own successes, but also blasted the "national media" for propagating stereotypes.*

Schroeder was putting it strongly. But the visceral skepticism of the eastern media as regards the West was duly illustrated in a report that appeared in Canada's national newspaper. The writer, H.J. (Jack) Kerchhoff, was an old friend of mine from a shared stretch at The Montreal Star. *I decided to write him an open letter.*

Dear Jack:

The headline on your story in the *Globe And Mail* hit me like a bucket of cold water in the face: "Report on writers holds few surprises." My shock increased when I discovered that the head accurately reflected the contents of your article on *Word For Word*.

Few surprises? The 260-page report describes Alberta as "one of Canada's best-kept cultural secrets," and argues that this province has been wrongly derided for too long as "an intellectual swampland."

Andreas Schroeder, the Vancouver-based author of the work, said his findings blew him away. In a telephone interview, he told me he was "amazed" and "absolutely staggered" by the numbers. The literary wunderkind who masterminded Public Lending Right, Schroeder described Alberta as "a wheat field shooting up green like never before."

Of the three prairie provinces, the usual control group, Alberta had the most writers, the most publishers, the most bookstores. During the previous 25 years, 500 writers had produced the most titles: 1,600.

Between 1971 and 1988, Alberta writers won no fewer than 86 national and international awards. The report listed 38 "well-known and nationally recognized authors" who were or had been based in Alberta.

Schroeder estimated that 65 writers made a full-time living in Wild Rose Country. This was astounding, he wrote, "and would have been unheard of a mere decade ago." Including part-timers, the province had about 625 published or produced freelance writers working in all genres. And when one included writers who held other jobs, that number quadrupled to 2,885. Five short decades ago, there were 169 writers in the province, and even in 1971, only 1,000.

Few surprises? *Word For Word* showed that Alberta leads the country in virtually every category of per-capita cultural use, purchase and attendance.

In 1986, Albertans spent more on books and magazines than any other Canadians—an average of $222 per family compared with a national average of $205. They also spent most on home entertainment ($450 compared with a national average of $388) and cultural events. Per-capita spending on live theatre here was second only to that in Ontario, and on visiting museums second only to that in British Columbia. In 1985-86, Albertans went to movies more often than any other Canadians: four times per person, clicking the turnstiles 9,556,800 times.

In 1983-84, Alberta government spending on culture was the highest in the country: $51 per person, the same as Quebec and well ahead of the next nearest competitor (Manitoba) at $39. In 1985-86, Alberta again shared first place, this time with P.E.I. at $65. Include municipal funding and Alberta was clearly ahead at $72 per person.

Between 1971 and 1981, the cultural labor force in Alberta increased by 124 percent (more than doubled) while nationally the average increase was 39 percent. *Word For Word* was wrong when it said the Edmonton Public Library had the highest rate of circulation in English Canada. In 1988, that honor went to the Calgary Public Library for the second straight year: 8.5 million borrowings compared with Edmonton's 7.8 million. Yet the result remains the same. When it comes to library use, Alberta is Number One.

Much of the above came from unpublished figures compiled by StatsCan. Published but unpublicized figures reveal another surprise: that most of these trends were well-established by 1982. Albertans spent $611 million on culture that year, or $263 per person. The closest competitor was British Columbia at $247 per person.

Also in 1982, Albertan families spent the most on reading materials ($169 to Ontario's $157), on admission to cultural events ($102 to Ontario's $97) and on home entertainment, equipment and services ($318 to $265 for both Ontario and Saskatchewan).

Jack, you're not surprised? Let's get together and hoist a few next time you're in town.

Sincerely, your old pal, etc....

***

VI

Those Volunteers Just Keep Coming

37. Joan Clark: Swimming Toward The Light

A Nova Scotia native who lived in and around Calgary for over 20 years, Joan Clark published her first book in 1969 and never looked back. Today, she has nine books behind her—three for adults, six for children. Her 1988 novel, The Victory Of Geraldine Gull, *won the Canadian Authors' Association award for fiction and was short-listed for both a governor-general's award and the Books In Canada first-novel award. Her 1990 book,* Swimming Toward The Light, *drew raves across the country— though reviewers weren't sure whether to call it a story-collection or a novel. "I see it as a collection of stories," Clark told me, "because that's the way I wrote it. It's a novelistic collection of stories."*

Since 1985, Clark has been based in St. John's, Newfoundland. Now past-president of the Writers' Alliance of Newfoundland and Labrador, Clark has drastically reduced her non-writing commitments—"it's not so much the time as the imagination they take hold of"—and rented an office away from her home to write an historical novel about the Norse who settled in Greenland 1,000 years ago. Tentatively entitled Freydis, *it focuses on the half-sister of Leif Eiriksson, the daughter of Eirik the Red.*

"It took seven years and six complete drafts," Joan Clark said in 1988, "but finally it's finished. And boy, am I glad!" Clark was brimming with enthusiasm—and rightly so—for her eighth book, *The Victory Of Geraldine Gull.*

It's set in a tiny settlement in northern Ontario populated by about 100 Swampy Cree Indians and two whites—a priggish Catholic priest and a gruff Hudson's Bay trader. Into this fictional village, called Niska, comes Willa Coyle, a young woman who has been invited to teach summer art classes to the local children.

Willa looms large in the novel, emerging as the eyes and ears of "liberal" Canada: educated, well-meaning and white. But Willa doesn't dominate the book, for Clark set out to write what she described as "a group novel." We get to know Father Aulneau, who has spent years pining for rice pudding made properly; Patrick Eagle, a college graduate who has returned home "from outside" to better the lot of his people; and, of course, Geraldine Gull, a maverick Ojibway woman, big and brawny, fond of flouting the law.

All of these people, Clark said, have a basis in reality —although really they're fictional, because she has transformed them for the novel. The seed of the work was sown in 1958, Clark said, when as a 23-year-old bride she spent three months with her new husband—then a junior officer in the air force—in the northern Ontario village of Peewanik.

This was a particularly intense period of her life. Clark vividly remembers sitting at home one night while outside a local wild-woman raged, hammering on the door to get in; and also a priest who warned her sternly not to wear shorts because she was setting a bad example for local teenagers. Both incidents figure in *Geraldine Gull*.

But Clark didn't plan it that way. She put her northern interlude behind her and began raising a family. In 1965, newly settled in Calgary, she found herself writing a story about a young girl: "I was as surprised as anyone." She filled three scribblers, then typed her opus and sent it off to two publishers, seeking a reaction. To her amazement, one of them published it—under a title, unfortunately, that makes her blush to this day: *Girl Of The Rockies.*

"When I reached Page 26," Clark said of the first time she read the published book, "I burst into tears. It was awful. I was horrified. That's when I knew I was serious."

During the next two decades, while raising her three youngsters in Calgary and nearby Bragg Creek, Clark established herself as a writer of children's novels, winning acclaim for such works as *The Hand Of Robin Squires*, *Wild Man Of The Woods* and *The Moons Of Madeline*.

She also co-founded Calgary's *Dandelion* magazine, which today is the foremost literary magazine in Alberta, and published a book of stories for adults called *From A High Thin Wire*. This largely autobiographical work showed real promise. With *The Victory Of Geraldine Gull*, her first novel for adults, Clark delivered. Five of the drafts she wrote while living in Calgary, and from the first she had almost all of the material.

The challenge, she said, was "to achieve the necessary distance," and so find a way to evoke "the texture of the whole village." Clark turns this trick by standing well back from her material, zooming in and out as suits her purpose.

Here she is at a distance: "Looking out the plane window at the roadless map unrolling below, you see shadows of cloud moving across the river, spreading over the muskeg, staining it grey. The shadows look like the ghosts of giant animals drifting above the sand. You see lakes that look as if they have been made by the paws of a giant Wapusk as he roams the land in search of food. You see the cold blueness of Hudson Bay, the horizon blocked with rotting pack ice."

Here she is up close: "Geraldine comes out of the brushes, scoots down the side of the church and tries the front door. Sucker. He left it unlocked for evening mass. She finds the catechism books stacked neatly on a table inside the door. She looks around for something to carry the books in, but there's nothing."

The Victory Of Geraldine Gull is ambitious, complex, notable for the scope of its vision, the multiplicity of its voices. It's the work of a mature novelist with a vision all her own.

Clark, who was born and raised in Nova Scotia, lives now in St. John's, Newfoundland, where her husband teaches and does research at Memorial University. She misses Calgary, she said, although she sees it now as "awfully American." In Newfoundland, she finds herself becoming more political, "more engaged," and enjoys the people for their "great sense of hilarity."

Still, she expects eventually to return to the West. She has one son in Calgary, another in Vancouver, and her university-student daughter is bent on returning. Then there's the family cottage on Lake Lillian, six kilometres north of Invermere, British Columbia: "I have a feeling we may end up there."

38. Darlene Barry Quaife: Celebrating Similarities

With her first novel, Bone Bird, *Alberta author Darlene Barry Quaife won the Commonwealth Writers Prize for best first work of fiction in the Canada-Caribbean region in 1989. The award was worth about $1,050 in cash—and also a free trip to Australia. "When I heard that," Quaife said, "that's when I really got excited." Quaife has been teaching writing at Mount Royal College for 12 years. In 1991, aided by a Canada-Council grant, she will devote herself to writing almost full-time, teaching only a single writing course at the University of Calgary. Quaife hopes to complete a picaresque novel,* Roadsigns, *and to make progress on a collection of short stories called* Dancing Trap: An Erotic Journey.

Most readers of *Bone Bird* will assume that the book's author is a native of Vancouver Island. That's where this wonderfully evocative first novel takes place. But don't be deceived. The author of this impressive debut is a third-generation Calgarian whose grandfather served with the Northwest Mounted Police during the Riel Rebellion.

Born in 1948, Quaife grew up mostly in suburban Killarney. She attended Viscount Bennett High School and later the University of Calgary, and these days she lives with her husband (an environmental scientist) and two sled dogs on an acreage in Priddis, just south of the city.

"I find that if I write about places I don't know intimately, it allows my imagination to work. I know this place (Calgary) intimately, and I didn't want to be a recorder. I wanted to be an inventor."

Besides, Quaife used to visit the West Coast as a child and has always had strong feelings about it: "I see that place as one of the characters in my novel."

Thematically, Quaife wanted to explore native spirituality, and also to show that people of widely different backgrounds and cultures—Yaqui Indian, Chinese, East European—can unite as a community when given half a chance: "I wanted to say, 'Look, our differences are not important. Our similarities are important.'"

Bone Bird takes place in Tanis Bay, a dying logging town. The book focuses on Aislinn Cleary, a young woman who keeps a general store, cares for her dying mother, identifies with and learns from her Indian grandmother, and both hungers and fears to join the larger world beyond the island.

In more ways than one, *Bone Bird* is a coming-of-age novel. First, Aislinn herself grows up. But, in a way not at all heavy-handed, she also represents western civilization. The message is that it's time for our society as a whole to grow up, and to begin doing so by adopting certain native Indian attitudes—those toward the environment, for example.

Bone Bird, which served Quaife as a creative thesis for her master of arts degree at the University of Alberta, is also notable for its language: tight, vivid, imagistic and rhythmical. "My first love was poetry," said Quaife, who didn't write her first short stories until 1980, when she took a creative writing course from W.P. Kinsella at the University of Calgary.

Quaife has also written plays, radio scripts and scores of non-fiction articles, and for the past 12 years has taught in the English department at Mount Royal College (literature, creative writing and composition).

These days, when she's not teaching, Quaife is toiling in three genres. She's writing poems (one of them will be performed in Edmonton as part of a National Book Festival program); short stories ("I'm exploring the erotic from a female point of view"); and, yes, another novel, "a picaresque" entitled *Roadsigns*. Her heroine starts in northern Alberta and ends up in Brazil—but, no, she doesn't sell lingerie.

This project sounds especially exciting because *Bone Bird*'s strengths are atmosphere, language and theme, not narrative drive. Indeed, a rather slight story line carries a lot of historical freight.

By definition, though, a picaresque novel is relentlessly eventful. And given her other powers, Quaife just won't be able to miss.

39. Pauline Gedge: Returning To Ancient Egypt

If Alberta novelist Pauline Gedge has been cast as Cinderella in more than a few newspaper articles, it's because that's the most inspiring way to tell her story. Picture a single mother on welfare, struggling to support two young children, who wins a first-novel competition and is magically transformed into a best-selling novelist.

"It's an old story," Gedge said late in 1990, hinting politely that she's tired of telling it. But the New-Zealand-born author, who was in Calgary to promote *Scroll Of Saqqara*, her third novel set in ancient Egypt, graciously filled in the blanks one more time.

Born in 1945, Gedge moved with her family to Canada in 1959, settling in Edmonton seven years later. In 1972, recently divorced, Gedge found herself in the tiny Alberta town of Edgerton, three hours east of Edmonton.

That year, she submitted a contemporary novel to the first Alberta Search-For-A-Novelist competition and placed fourth in a field of 98. "I'd been writing poetry for 20 years," she said, "but that was my first attempt at fiction."

The following year, Gedge submitted a second contemporary novel, a work she now dismisses as flawed and arrogant. In 1974, she began writing a third contemporary novel, but didn't like the way it was developing. "I'd been interested in ancient Egypt since I was 11," Gedge said. She turned to that old obsession and in six weeks, while living on welfare, pounded out *Child Of The Morning*.

That novel, which focused on the only woman ever to be pharaoh, not only won the Alberta contest but was translated into seven languages and went on to sell over a million copies around the world.

Gedge published two more moderately successful novels—*The Eagle And The Raven* and *Stargate*—before producing *The Twelfth Transforming*, which was again set in ancient Egypt and again topped the million mark in sales.

Now, six years later, comes a third Egyptian novel: *Scroll Of Saqqara*. Why so long between books? Gedge, looking far more relaxed and comfortable than during previous interviews, explained that in 1984, for the sake of her teenage sons, she moved to Edmonton: "As soon as I got to the city, I dried up. I just couldn't write."

Gedge, who works at night, said, "Maybe it wouldn't have been so bad if I'd got a place downtown, where day and night merge. But I was in the suburbs, where everyone was on the same schedule—get up at seven, leave for work at 7:45, at 8:15 the kids go off to school—and I felt so eccentric, so strange. I guess I felt threatened."

She worked for a year as writer-in-residence at the St. Albert Public Library—but still couldn't write. Then, in 1987, she moved back to Edgerton, into a house on the outskirts of town, "and the ideas just came pouring out of me." Her two sons, now young adults, remain in Edmonton, and last June, having entered into a relationship "that was a beautiful surprise," Gedge remarried: "I'm the happiest person in the world."

Gedge's first two Egyptian novels took place in the 18th Dynasty: "That's my favorite period." This time out the author intended initially to write about Ramses II, who was part of the 19th Dynasty and lived about 1200 B.C. Gedge did her research and was about to start writing when, first, she learned that Norman Mailer was about to publish *Ancient Evenings*, which also centred on Ramses: "Who wants to compete with Mailer?" Second, "the book I planned would have been derogatory to Ramses, because I have no admiration for the man."

Finally, Gedge had discovered "this wonderful legend about Ramses's favorite son, Prince Khwaemwaset." The legend, which describes how the prince stole a magical scroll and paid a terrible price, gives shape to Gedge's latest novel—though the author has massaged the ending, she said, "to make it more satisfying, more credible to a modern audience."

This latest Egyptian novel, Gedge said, is more domestic than the other two, and far more intimate. Where both *Child Of The Morning* and *Twelfth Transforming* covered many years and dealt with political traumas and dynastic upheavals, *Scroll Of Saqarra* focuses on relationships within a single family.

The novel also has an occult strain, which Gedge identified as arising naturally out of ancient Egyptian views of the world. "One of the reasons I'm successful as an historical novelist," she said, "is that I can enter other worlds without bringing along modern philosophies, preconceived notions and judgments."

Not long ago Gedge began writing a contemporary horror novel. "I wanted a rest from research," she said, "and from the responsibility of getting the facts straight." Will she again return to ancient Egypt? "Oh, yes! Because I like money!" Gedge laughed. "Egypt always means big sales for me, especially in Europe."

Something about her facial expression, her eyes, suggested that this was only part of the reason. But the rest she left unsaid.

40. Elona Malterre: The Best Sex Scenes?

Early in 1991 Calgary author Elona Malterre completed Twisted Paradise, *a contemporary novel mentioned below, and began working on a sequel to* The Celts *called* Mask Of Fire. *Her children's book,* The Last Wolf Of Ireland, *won an American Library Association Choice Award as one of the best books of 1989.* Mistress Of The Eagles, *described below, is now being translated into German, Swedish and Norwegian.*

In the spring of 1989, Elona Malterre was still rising daily at 4 a.m. She'd don a tattered orange dressing gown, fill a beer stein with coffee and sit down at her computer to write for three hours. Then she'd head out to teach writing at Mount Royal College.

These days Malterre doesn't get out of bed until 6:30 a.m. She dons the same dressing gown and drinks just as much coffee—but she remains at her tube until 4 p.m.

The Calgary author owes this improved schedule to *Mistress Of The Eagles*, her second novel. It's an historical romance for which she received an advance of "nearly $50,000"—money that enabled her to quit her full-time teaching job.

Malterre, who has published "literary" stories and won poetry prizes, now devotes herself exclusively to commercial or popular fiction and refuses to apologize for it. "For me writing is a business," she said at her home in suburban Montgomery Heights. "I work seven days a week."

Malterre was born in France but raised north of Calgary in Simon's Valley, near Balzac. After graduating from high school, she worked at "six jobs in five years"—was a cost control clerk, a receptionist, a production typist. "Also I sold Leggs panty-hose all over southern Alberta. I was 22 or 23, drove a van. Wore mini-skirts up to here and high-heeled red shoes. The men loved it."

In the mid-'70s, Malterre quit work to study English at the University of Calgary. While earning first a bachelor's and then a master's degree, she fell in love with Irish literature—with the work of William Butler Yeats and James Joyce, but most of all with Celtic mythology: "All those stories I'd never even heard. I was swept away."

She had also taken a creative writing course from W.P. Kinsella and started to write. In 1987, while completing her master's thesis on the late Canadian poet Alden Nowlan, Malterre wrote an historical novel which she called *The Stones Of Erin*. It was snapped up by Dell in the United States, retitled *The Celts* and published as a mass-market paperback—the kind sold mostly in supermarkets and drugstores.

For *The Celts*, Malterre received a $25,000 advance. By now she was well aware that a first "literary" novel, with its far smaller potential market, would at best command maybe one-tenth of that sum—and so decided to stick to "popular" fiction.

What distinguishes commercial from literary fiction? Malterre said that in popular works the hero or heroine overcomes all obstacles ("they're never overwhelmed by circumstance"). The heroes and villains are clearly identifiable as such ("there are fewer grey areas"). And the plots are faster moving, more action-oriented.

A real-life Irish pirate queen named Grannia O'Malley who lived in the 1500s inspired *Mistress Of The Eagles*, Malterre said. "She was the germ. My original title was *The Pirate Queen*."

Malterre's first draft of 800 pages was rejected. "I was just devastated," the author said. But she pulled herself together and spent a year revising the work.

Set in 15th-century Ireland, *Mistress Of The Eagles* focuses mostly on the beautiful and spirited Arrah O'Donnell. She flees an arranged marriage, as the dust jacket tells us, "to seek her fortune on the high seas."

Arrah finds plenty of adventure and passionate sex, and Malterre has both a penchant and a gift for describing sexual encounters at length and using detail that may shock fans of conventional historical romance. "I want to be known," Malterre said, "for writing the best sex scenes in Canadian fiction."

For the rest, Malterre recently completed her first children's novel, *The Last Wolf Of Ireland*. And she was hard at work on a contemporary novel. Commercial? "Of course! I'm not writing anything else!"

41. Sarah Murphy: Tomorrow's Fiction Today

In 1992, Sarah Murphy will publish a novel tentatively entitled Lilac Summer: A Tale Of Forsythia, Bedbugs, Faded Cotton And Time. *It's about a New York performance artist who cracks up, and her relationship with the female narrator, who lives in Alberta. Alternatively, it's about a friendship among three women, or about sexuality and power. "Boxes within boxes," was the way Murphy put it. "Boxes within boxes within boxes."*

Sarah Murphy isn't just another breath of mountain-fresh air. She's the future of fiction in Canada arrived early—and right here in Calgary.

But don't take my word for it. Check out Murphy's second book, *Comic Book Heroine* (NeWest Press). It's a collection of short stories that combines technical sophistication and political awareness, stream-of-consciousness pyrotechnics and the toughest of tough subjects.

That's what I mean about the future of fiction. Here and now, even serious fiction writers can ignore such problems as alcoholism and sexual abuse and the long-term effects of torture. But tomorrow? Murphy makes language dance while staring down the day-after. Influenced by the great South Americans? By Marquez, Cortazar, Asturias? Only profoundly.

What's more, the book's publication by Alberta's top literary press signals vigorously that publishing in this province has shucked off its early parochialism to welcome the world: Murphy's making it here, not elsewhere.

Before meeting the author, ponder a single quotation from "Figures in a Central American Lottery," one of the best stories in the collection. Our female narrator is deep in discussion with a Mexican woman friend—a university lecturer who's about to become a guerrilla. She worries about revealing herself to be "just another North American reductionist," like students who for years urged her friend's "circuitous exuberance to come to the point, asking what was the point, are you making a point, over and over. With the straight and narrow always the shortest distance between whatever points there were to be made, while she tried to distill experience, pointless perhaps, or at least not very sharply defined, out of chaos."

Yes, Murphy admitted over coffee, yes, this could be construed as a credo. But now, of course, we want just the facts.

Murphy, whose first book was a novel called *The Measure Of Miranda*, has almost completed a second novel. It takes place in Calgary and New York, focuses on a performance artist who has cracked up and explores the nexus between the emotional, the ethical and the political.

From the top? Born and raised in New York City, Murphy was 14 when in 1960 she joined the left-wing Students for a Democratic Society (SDS), and 17 when she became an executive member of the SDS board. She attended the University of Chicago (general studies) and then a prestigious art school (Parson School of Design) in New York. In 1965, as an SDS organizer, she became part of the anti-Vietnam-war movement. In 1967, exhausted, burned out, she moved to Mexico City, "fell in love with the sense of color and design"—and remained for six years.

Murphy married a Canadian and, in 1973, pregnant with her first child, moved with him to Toronto. There she remained, mothering (in 1975 she had her second child) and teaching (Spanish and English at Berlitz) and mounting the occasional one-woman show, "mostly collage and construction."

In 1979, her husband landed a job in Calgary and, the following year, after holding a one-woman show at the Muttart Gallery, Murphy decided— she laughs now—"to take a three-month vacation and write a novel."

The projected book focused on the Mexican student movement, and by the time it went off the tracks, "at about the 800-page mark," Murphy was hooked on writing.

Not yet coherent? It helps to know that both Murphy's parents were journalists. They met and married while working for *Time-Life*. Her father became a staff writer for *The New Yorker*, but in 1952, on his 40th birthday, while on assignment in South Africa, he died of hepatitis.

Murphy's mother went into a slide, but eventually she married again— a self-educated Choctaw seaman who taught Murphy the history of native Americans.

Murphy grew up spending half her time with the intellectual elite of New York, the other half with "the dislocated poor" in down-and-dirty Brooklyn bars. She got a scholarship to a progressive uptown prep school (Dalton), and there the contradictions intensified.

Her stepfather had told her the saga of the Trail of Tears, and how in the 1800s the American government uprooted thousands of native Americans from the east coast and compelled to move to Oklahoma. On the trail, Murphy said, "between two-thirds and seven-eighths of them died."

Her progressive prep school taught the history of both labor and of slavery, she said, but not a word about native Americans. And when with her classmates she attended a production of the musical *Oklahoma!*, Murphy sat remembering her stepfather's stories of the Trail of Tears—and so of course she joined the SDS.

Flash forward 30 years and here's Murphy praising ... Calgary? "I'm not into Toronto-bashing," she said, "but of all the places I've lived..." She wrinkled her nose and shook her head. What about the Big Apple? "People say, ah, New York! But all I ever wanted to do was get out of that city. To be poor and in New York—it's the most inescapable place imaginable!"

But still, Calgary? "There's a wonderful openness here," Murphy said. "Also, I feel very much part of the communities I work with on immigration issues and women's issues. And the physical! The other day, out driving in the mountains, I found myself telling my daughter, 'Do you have any idea what I would have given at your age just to be in a place like this?' I don't think anything in the world could get me to move back to the States."

***

VII

Final News Flash: New Horizons

When George Melnyk finishes a job he doesn't hang around. So it was with Edmonton's NeWest Press, which he set up on a shoestring in 1975 and left, seven years later, when it was flourishing as Alberta's top literary publisher. So it was with the Confederation of Alberta Faculty Associations, where Melnyk served as first executive director (1982-84). And so it was with the Alberta Foundation for the Literary Arts, where after three years as executive director, Melnyk resigned early in 1988 to devote more time to writing and editing.

The foundation board accepted Melnyk's resignation with regret and hired him to work for three months as a consultant on revamping the grants program. Melnyk said he was leaving the organization on four pillars. It was in excellent financial shape; it had an experienced, well-informed board; it had a new grants program in the works, which he described as "the culmination of the whole start-up period"; and it had on staff author Shirlee Smith Matheson, who provided experience and continuity. Melnyk noted that the organization had the smallest staff—two—of any cultural foundation in the province, and said he was proud of not having turned it into a large bureaucracy: "I've always run it as a small business."

In April of 1988, in a move that implied an expanded mandate for the foundation, the provincial government appointed a new executive director—a man with more than 20 years experience in television. Ron Robertson had spent the past 11 years as a senior manager with the publicly owned ACCESS Network. He was also chairman of the Canadian Literature Consortium for the Council of Ministers of Education of Canada, which two years before had produced a superb series of videotapes on Canadian writers together with a large-format textbook called *Canadian Literature: A Guide*.

In announcing the appointment of Robertson, board chairman Howard Platt noted that "we are entering a period of major growth and increased responsibility," and indicated that Robertson's "background and experience will be most valuable." People speculated that AFLA might become responsible for the Banff Television Festival or a new film and video arts fund, but eventually both were added to the film and literary arts branch of Alberta Culture, while AFLA continued to fund script-writing.

42. The Army Grows

In the late 1980s, the Federation of B.C. Writers grew explosively and became the largest regional writers' organization in Canada. In 1990, with more than 800 members, the Writers' Guild of Alberta regained that distinction. Today, the WGA has an annual budget of $185,000, with $65,000 coming from AFLA, $15,000 from Alberta Culture, $10,000 from corporations and $4,000 from the City of Edmonton. It raises $25,000 through memberships, and most of the rest through conference registrations, workshops and retreats. The WGA holds an annual meeting and publishes a 16-to-20 page newsletter six times a year. In Edmonton, executive director Lyle Weis heads a three-person office, and the WGA has smaller operations in Calgary and Red Deer. Weis said the provincial government was looking for ways to cut costs, and the WGA was watching closely.

More than 200 writers turned up in Calgary in the spring of 1989 for the largest-ever annual general meeting of the Writers' Guild of Alberta. "We are no longer the WGA we were when we began," outgoing president Aritha van Herk told an enthusiastic audience. "We now have more than 700 members from all over the province and we are growing all the time." Van Herk noted that the WGA now has an annual budget of over $170,000. The weekend meeting, which ran from May 5 to 7, featured the usual workshops, panel discussions, literary readings and business meeting, as well as a splashy Saturday night awards banquet.

A total of 59 books by Alberta writers were entered for the 1988 awards, with each winner receiving a $500 cheque and a leather-bound copy of his or her winning book.

At the Saturday night banquet, van Herk passed her presidency—and a chain of office consisting of four well-worn running shoes—to Edmonton writer Myrna Kostash, author of *All Of Baba's Children*, *Long Way From Home* and *No Kidding: Inside The World Of Teenage Girls*. Kostash, who has sojourned extensively in eastern Europe, said she hoped the WGA, now well-established as a professional organization, would begin to address broader concerns. "We have the eyes and ears of the corporate and political world," she said. "Now we can look forward to developing our relationship with public issues."

In her report to the membership, van Herk hailed the *Word For Word* report on the business of writing in Alberta as the WGA's major accomplishment of 1988. She described this exhaustively detailed work as "the most valuable tool we have," a sentiment that surfaced repeatedly throughout the weekend and was shared, notably, by Ruth Bertelson Fraser, director of the film and literary arts branch of Alberta Culture and Multiculturalism.

Guild members, among them fiction and non-fiction writers, poets, playwrights, script-writers and children's book authors, conducted most of their business during a grueling five-hour session Saturday afternoon. Among other things, they resolved:

— to prepare a detailed plan for a province-wide readings program.

— to set up WriteBank, a computerized clearing house of information on the business of writing.

— to investigate setting up a joint awards program with publishers, librarians and booksellers.

— to cancel YouthInk, a literary magazine for young writers, which has been projected for the past three years (at a cost of $5,000) but has not got off the ground.

— to increase basic membership fees from $35 to $45, thereby raising over $30,000 for projects (seniors and students pay lower fees).

One of the highlights of the weekend was a Friday night reading featuring Kristjana Gunnars, a Regina-based poet, translator and fiction writer; L.R. (Bunny) Wright, an ex-*Herald* staffer and Edgar-award winning novelist who recently completed her seventh book, *States Of Exile*; and Edna Alford, 1988 winner of the Marian Engel Award.

Alford and Wright participated, along with Edmonton novelist Rudy Wiebe, in a lively seminar exploring the social role of the writer. Other workshops focused on non-fiction and poetry, new writers, screenplays and scripts, markets and trends, grantsmanship and cross-over writing. Toronto literary agent Bella Pomer gave a workshop on contracts that was a model of concision.

43. First We Took Alberta...

A decade of astonishing growth left the Alberta book publishing industry poised in 1991 to become the largest in western Canada. That was the biggest surprise in the first region-wide study ever done of the book and periodical publishing industry.

Calgary publishing consultant George Melnyk did the study in the spring of 1990 for Western Economic Diversification Canada (WD), a federal government department. In 1984, Melnyk wrote, Alberta's book industry boasted 85 full-time employees and gross revenues of almost $8 million. By 1987-88, the province's publishers had over 100 full-time employees, and in 1990 they projected gross revenues of $15 million.

In 1987-88, by comparison, the B.C. book publishing industry had 144 full-time employees. Between 1982 and 1987, it had grown quickly, increasing sales from $6.9 to $15.8 million. Then, because it was receiving the lowest level of provincial government support in western Canada, the B.C. industry levelled off.

If these trends continue, Melnyk wrote in May, the Alberta industry will surpass that of British Columbia: "Alberta is quickly closing the gap."

That gap closed more quickly even than Melnyk anticipated. Nik Burton, executive director of the 29-member Book Publishers' Association of Alberta, said in December of 1990 that a recent survey showed total sales for 1989 were between $22 and $25 million. And those figures did not include *The Junior Encyclopedia Of Canada*, which Hurtig Publishers of Edmonton brought out in 1990.

Margaret Reynolds, executive director of the Association of Book Publishers of British Columbia, said that for 1988-89, B.C. book publishers had net sales of roughly $16 million. That suggests gross sales of between $24 and $27 million.

Melnyk's study, called *Partners In Success: A Directions And Opportunities Study Of The Book And Periodical Industry In Western Canada*, was released as a consultant's report, not as government policy. Its views, WD's Joyce Bateman Hancock noted, "are not necessarily endorsed by the department of Western Economic Diversification."

Burton expressed disappointment at this, but Melnyk said in an interview: "The ball is in the publishers' court. It's up to them to take the information in the report and use it to lobby WD to implement my recommendations." In a sense, WD has gone beyond what it originally promised, Melnyk said, by releasing the entire report, including some implied criticism of WD.

"Western Canadian publishers need a new support program for the '90s," Melnyk said. "That program should be tied to interest-free loans. Grant programs should remain, but the industry has grown so fast that it has outstripped them. It's unrealistic to expect grant programs to triple and quadruple in size."

In his report, Melnyk wrote: "The major entrepreneurial problem facing western Canadian publishers is not oversubsidization but undercapitalization, a problem that WD is able to address." WD could disburse between $2 and $5 million to western publishers during the next two years, he said.

Hancock said WD commissioned *Partners In Success* to determine whether western Canadian publishers could make better use of the department, which in 1987 was given $1.2 billion to diversify the economy of western Canada. By late 1990, WD had distributed about $700 million, mostly in repayable contributions, for diverse projects that met five complex guidelines.

Publishers most likely to take advantage of WD funding are in Alberta, Melnyk said. Burton confirmed that "some publishers are working with WD right now on various projects"—focusing mostly on marketing, distribution, import replacement and technological advancement. "There's lots of possibilities. But we have to stay within the five guidelines."

B.C. publishers, Reynolds said, "have talked about a variety of things we'd like to do, but most of our members are not big enough to take advantage of the program." One British Columbia publisher used WD funding for an industry-wide feasibility study of expanding the market in the Pacific Rim, she said, "but most find the red tape prohibitive."

Melnyk noted that the two western-most provinces have different windows of opportunity. The provincial government in British Columbia is taking steps to rectify past neglect, while publishers in Alberta are "pushing at the edges of everything."

The book publishing industries in Manitoba and Saskatchewan, both with fewer than 25 full-time employees in 1987-88, and gross revenues of just over $1 million and $2-$3 million respectively, are the least likely to avail themselves of WD funds, mainly because they are so small.

Melynk wrote that the rapid expansion of the Alberta industry in the late '80s owed much to "the phenomenal growth of educational publishing." Burton elaborated, noting that a decade ago, Alberta had only one publisher producing books for use in schools. The recent survey showed nine Alberta publishers reporting educational sales. "We're looking at total estimated sales of $5 million."

Burton said this growth can be traced to the "spectacularly supportive policies of the province's department of education." Those policies—like buying Alberta-produced books for native studies programs—have been instrumental in getting several educational publishers off the ground, Burton said. "That's been the big boost."

Both Burton and Melnyk also underlined the importance of the Alberta Foundation for the Literary Arts (AFLA). Created in 1984, AFLA spent roughly $350,000 of its annual budget on book publishers and another $34,000 on periodical publishers.

But Melnyk warned that this growth will level off unless governments launch new initiatives—like that of WD. "The industry isn't strong enough, even at its present size, to be self-supporting."

Melnyk said western Canada's publishing industry should aim to draw even with the Canadian-owned segment of the Ontario industry during the next decade. "That's the goal. It will never surpass the Ontario industry as a whole, because you always have that foreign element. But if you take out the Canadian component, it's not improbable that the whole region could match it—though it would have to double or triple in size."

44. Tomorrow, A New Advance

Journalists are paid to be suspicious. But in March of 1991, when Alberta Culture Minister Doug Main announced the birth of the Alberta Foundation for the Arts, professional journalists weren't the only people who heard alarm bells. Because, while proclaiming the birth of AFA, Main reported (incidentally) the deaths of three foundations, one of them the Alberta Foundation for the Literary Arts (AFLA).

The rhetoric spoke of a "one-window approach," of bringing arts funding under a single roof, mixed metaphors notwithstanding. But what was the real agenda? One clear signal was that, though existing programs would initially remain in place, Main projected annual savings of $400,000. Which would be channelled, he said, straight back into the arts.

I wasn't alarmed by the loss of two jobs locally, or even by the closing of AFLA's Calgary office, the only visible bit of literary infrastructure in southern Alberta. No. The death of AFLA came on the heels of a radical restructuring of arts support through the department of Alberta Culture and Multiculturalism. That restructuring wiped out the department's film and literary arts branch.

Put it all together and you've got the end of one era, the beginning of another. Not necessarily a bad thing. But AFLA, a product of fierce grass-roots lobbying, has been wildly successful. Now it has been swallowed by AFA, a Tory government initiative that came as a complete surprise to the people it's supposed to serve.

AFLA, with its annual budget of just over $1 million, had disappeared into the giant maw of AFA, whose $16 million budget will go mostly to visual and performing arts institutions (there lie the other dead foundations). Can this be good for the literary community? How can a mammoth, other-focused foundation remain sensitive to the needs of writers, publishers and librarians?

Jon Whyte, president of the Writers' Guild of Alberta, said he was optimistic. He hoped the new organization would be "as efficient, effective and friendly" as AFLA was. And he applauded the introduction of a jury-system for the awarding of grants. Still, Whyte noted that the province's literary advisory committee died a couple of years back, and said he'd like to see the return of a ministerial forum for community input.

But let's return to the disappearance of Alberta Culture's film and literary arts branch. The government has abandoned its 20-year-old system of organizing support by arts-discipline in favor of a functional approach. No more literary, visual arts or performing arts branches, but rather a single arts branch with five "program groups." These are artist development and organizational support, cultural literacy and education, marketing and audience development, cultural industries development and support, and communication and government services. Got that? Know where to find what you're looking for?

In literary Alberta, it's common knowledge that the branch and some elements of the community have occasionally been at odds. These turf disputes will become a thing of the past. But so will a great deal of discipline-specific expertise. And user-friendliness.

One of the dangers here is that Alberta's literary community—writers, publishers, booksellers, librarians—will lose their hard-won sense of, "Hey! We're all in this together!" That the grass-roots whole will be fragmented, the body politic divided and conquered.

No, I don't think that's the hidden agenda here. But if the literary community doesn't act to ensure its survival—and its continued flourishing—it could well be the end result.

Fortifications today. Tomorrow, a new advance.

***

Part Three

The International Front

Sprinkle angel dust on the controlling metaphor of this book and presto! the English language becomes an ocean. Writers sail over it in sailboats and sloops, in slippers and schooners and galleons, bringing news of faraway places. The news they bring is always of war—of war against tyranny and racism, war against censorship and intolerance and repression. Everywhere and always it's the same war. Writers bring news of the war against various shades of darkness.

Over the Sea of English in the not-so-long-ago came Jerzy Kosinski, abandoned as a child in war-torn Poland, author of *Steps* and *The Painted Bird* and *Passion Play*, holed up for years in a New York City apartment, battling for his life against trumped-up charges of plagiarism. Over the Sea of English came the Afrikaner Andre Brink, who went to Paris an almost-dilettante and returned home a Sartrean existentialist, committed to reversing apartheid. Over the Sea came Salman Rushdie, arguably the greatest writer of a generation, now banished to an unholy solitude—and here words fail me.

But even war has its magic moments. I think of visiting Niagara Falls in the company of Nobel-Prize-winner William Golding, how he clapped his hands like a small boy at the sight of them. I think of playing De Alfonce Tennis with the man who invented the game, The Ginger Man, J.P. Donleavy. I think of rambling the streets of Old Quebec City with the ghost of Jack Kerouac during a four-day celebration that some called a sacramental experience, others an old-style happening, and still others a rip-roaring wake....

✳ ✳ ✳

I

A Rip-Roaring Wake
In Vieux Quebec

45. Jack Kerouac: Still On The Road

QUEBEC CITY—Jack Kerouac, the controversial American novelist who died in 1969, turned up here in October, 1987. He sprang vividly to life in the minds and hearts of roughly 200 people—among them, poets, novelists and scholars of international reputation—who gathered in the author's ancestral homeland to celebrate his work.

Participants came from the United States: from California, Ohio, Wisconsin, Massachusetts and New York. They came from Ontario and New Brunswick and Alberta. But the majority came from Quebec, where French-Canadians recently awakened in numbers to shout: "Ciboire! Kerouac's one of us!"

This was no academic conference, with professors delivering esoteric papers and scoring debating points. Nor was it a literary festival, with big-name authors reading from their works on a dais, socializing among themselves and granting the occasional interview.

Brilliantly conceived and orchestrated by the *Secretariat permanent des peuples francophones*, the *rencontre*, or gathering, was a way for French-speaking Quebecers to affirm themselves as North Americans, a way to open a dialogue with the world.

The *rencontre* took place in the back rooms and bars, the streets and small hotels of Vieux Quebec. It featured lectures and panel discussions at the international youth hostel, lunch-time debates at a downtown pub and late-night shows at an aptly named bar, Le Grand Derangement. There was a five-man Kerouac-reading by the Toledo Poets Centre; an evening of

Kerouac and jazz with San Francisco bop artist Mark Murphy; and a night-long poetry extravaganza broadcast live on radio in both French and English.

Videos, film premieres, book launchings, slide shows, book-and-photo exhibits, posters, cassette tapes, T-shirts—for four days Jack Kerouac took over Quebec City. Nobody who attended the celebration left untouched. Poet Allen Ginsberg declared: "I haven't seen anything like this since the 1960s." Kerouac biographer Ann Charters, a renowned authority on the Beat Generation, said the gathering represented "a true rebirth, a renaissance."

The occasion had as many meanings as participants, all of them underscored by its historical significance: the confluence of two great rivers of thought—one essentially American, the other French-Canadian—each roiling with tensions and contradictions, all of which were contained in the author himself and many of which were personified here.

The man who inspired this extravaganza was born Jean-Louis Lebris de Kerouac in 1922 in Lowell, Massachusetts, a mill town on the Merrimack River. His parents were French-Canadian, born in Quebec and raised in New Hampshire. Kerouac didn't speak English until he was six, and into his teens he spoke the language with a French accent.

Kerouac published his first novel (*The Town And The City*) at 28 and went on to conduct audacious experiments in his adopted tongue, most notably in *Visions Of Cody* and *Old Angel Midnight*. Best-known for *On The Road* and *The Dharma Bums*, Kerouac wrote more than 20 books, most of which are autobiographical novels belonging to his *Legend Of Duluoz*. He lived both hard and religiously, and eventually drank himself to death at age 47—but only after he'd been lionized as leader of the Beat Generation: King of the Beats.

Most serious discussion of Kerouac has treated him in this American context—as a Beat Generation writer who rebelled against the consumerism and conformity of the United States in the 1950s. The sub-themes here have been well-articulated—spontaneous prose, Zen Buddhism, autobiographical fiction, colloquial language, identification with the underdog—and most perspectives were represented in Quebec City.

Charters, the only serious biographer of Kerouac who ever met the man, was the most popular of the American intellectuals. She marvelled at "the emphasis on culture," and said the intensity of the debate underlined Kerouac's importance. She drew attention to Kerouac's life-long love of French literature, and at one point even suggested that perhaps the author's mother should never have left Quebec.

Other American intellectuals also made a strong impression. Midwesterner Gerald Nicosia, author of the biographical tour-de-force *Memory Babe*, painted a moving portrait of Kerouac's last years, describing the torturous demise of a holy wanderer. And New Yorker Regina Weinreich, who recently published a brilliant textual study called *The Spontaneous Poetics Of Jack Kerouac*, reminded listeners of the importance of Kerouac's writing, and that his prose merits attention.

A California contingent included the poet, publisher and bookseller Lawrence Ferlinghetti, once a friend of Kerouac's, who delivered an emotional Canticle To Kerouac. Ferlinghetti wondered if the gathering "might be exaggerating Jack's Quebecois-ness too much," and noted that one of the great problems for all immigrant Americans is "the fantastic speed with which they lose their roots."

Among the other Californians were Kerouac's friends Jack Micheline, a white-haired street-poet who proudly declared: "I'm coming out of Jack's closet!"; and the bookish and famously distracted John Montgomery, who figures in *The Dharma Bums*.

Carolyn Cassady came from England, where she lives to indulge her love of theatre, and offered what for many was the most moving testimonial of the gathering. An elegant, well-spoken woman, Cassady is the ex-wife of Neal Cassady, real-life model for Kerouac's most famous hero, Dean Moriarty. In describing her long, complex love affair with Kerouac, Cassady evoked an indisputable truth: Kerouac was a great spirit, a great heart.

Several scholars came from France, where Kerouac went in 1965 in search of his roots. Yves Le Pellec, author of a book on the Beat Generation, emerged as a particularly sensitive interpreter of Kerouac, noting, for example, the incredible expressiveness of the author's face as preserved on videotape. Le Pellec reviewed criticisms he'd heard of Kerouac—sentimentality, naivete, mysticism, lack of understanding of women—but insisted on the greatness of much of his work, citing particularly the virtuoso description of "Joan Rawshanks" in *Visions Of Cody*.

Outstanding collectors of Kerouac's works were represented by Joy Walsh of New York and Dave Moore of England, both of whom edit magazines exploring the author's life and work, and by Rod Anstee of Ottawa, whose first editions formed the basis for a museum exhibition.

The second great river of Kerouac interpretation flows directly out of the decades-old Quebec-independence debate and focuses on the author's French-Canadian heritage. Franco-Americans from Lowell have insisted for years that the Beat-American interpretation of Kerouac is inadequate. But no heavyweight intellectual has arisen among them to state the case convincingly or to explore its implications.

All that changed in Quebec City as French-Canadian poets, novelists and scholars exploded into the debate, challenging Kerouac buffs from around the world to explore questions about "Le Grand Jack" that, as Ferlinghetti observed, "nobody in America has ever asked." Does Kerouac symbolize what happens to French-speaking Quebecers who leave their province? Was he unable to return to Quebec because the province wasn't mature enough to welcome him?

The crucial document in this awakening was a videotape of an interview that Kerouac conducted in 1967 in Montreal for the French television program "Le Sel de la Semaine." The truth was there, in gesture and expression, and despite a unique accent, for all to see: Kerouac was a French-Canadian—*un de nous autres*.

And so the debate was joined.

Novelist Victor Levy-Beaulieu reiterated the intransigent Quebec-nationalist position he developed 15 years ago in his book *Jack Kerouac: essai-poulet*. He insisted that Kerouac should be read not because he has anything to do with Quebec but simply because he is a great artist. Award-winning poet Lucien Francoeur depicted Kerouac as a minor writer experimenting in a major language, and stated flatly that Quebec has no place for him as a Beat writer. And Denis Vanier, a Montreal pop poet who hides a fine mind behind tattoos, a red-scarf and a black-leather jacket, described Kerouac as a literary Elvis, and seemed bent on celebrating the author's self-destructive streak.

Others countered these dark visions. Geographer Jean-Maurice Morriset drew parallels between Kerouac and Louis Riel, regarded by most French-Canadians as a martyr. Morriset argued that Kerouac could not return to Quebec during his lifetime because the province wasn't mature enough to accept him. Conference organizer Eric Waddell elaborated, claiming that until now French-speaking Quebecers have not been secure enough to perceive themselves as Franco-Americans, and thus to accept Kerouac. He described Kerouac as a universal genius who wrote a unique blend of literature and lived truth: "vecriture."

Franco-Ontarian Fernan Carriere viewed the whole exercise as the first sign of a new openness of spirit in Quebec; and Graham Cournoyer, a Montreal composer who was one of Kerouac's best friends in New York City in the '50s, told moving anecdotes about the author. Acadian film-maker Hermenegilde Chiasson unveiled his new film *Le Grand Jack*, a clever melange of drama and documentary footage from "Le Sel de la Semaine" that concentrates on Kerouac's French-Canadian heritage. And there were two separate slide shows from Lowell, Massachusetts, where Kerouac grew up and Franco-Americans are building a park (now completed) in the author's honor.

Three people who had hoped to attend the gathering were absent for health reasons: Father Armand "Spike" Morissette, who counselled Kerouac as a boy; John Clellon Holmes, one of Kerouac's best writer friends; and Pierre Vallieres, author of *White Niggers Of America*, a Kerouac buff whose quest has taken him from politics to Buddhism. A fourth would-be participant, Pradip Choudhuri of India, was refused a visa by Canadian authorities.

Taken as a whole, the *rencontre* recalled an experiment once conducted by Quebec playwright Michel Tremblay. Tremblay took actors who had appeared in two radically different, autobiographical plays he'd written, put them on stage and told them to interact, remaining in character. The experiment ended in disaster as one set of actors drove the other from the stage.

Part way through the *rencontre*, as tempers flared (see below), some observers couldn't help wondering whether a similar debacle was about to unfold. That it didn't was a tribute to the spirit of the author himself. Jack Kerouac is still On The Road.

46. Allen Ginsberg Pays Homage

Many of those who regard Jack Kerouac as a wacky saint of sorts see American poet Allen Ginsberg as his prophet. Others perceive the author of *Howl* as Kerouac's dark angel and accuse him of having helped destroy the Franco-American writer.

Ginsberg, born in 1926, stressed at the *rencontre* that Kerouac was not only his friend but his teacher, and that he was there to pay homage. The celebrated poet, who has been a favorite target of anti-homosexual and anti-Jewish sentiment, was present throughout the gathering, and for some he embodied that largeness of heart and spirit which in the end made the occasion what it was.

Ginsberg delivered a spontaneous, hour-long, Zen-Buddhist interpretation of Kerouac that focused on the author's spiritual greatness. For those who hadn't heard him on the subject, his talk was a revelation. The poet also addressed the recurring questions: "What happened to Kerouac? Why did he drink himself to death?"

Quebecois author Victor Levy-Beaulieu had suggested it was because Kerouac was Quebecois, *un de nous autres*, and that he suffered because the English-speaking world has never understood or accepted French-Canadians.

Ginsberg responded with parables. He offered the Buddhist view that Kerouac despaired because all life is suffering, and he never found a teacher to resolve certain contradictions.

He anticipated poet Lucien Francoeur, who argued forcibly that Kerouac is a minor, experimental writer. Ginsberg asserted that the Beat King was a great writer who was misunderstood, undervalued and ridiculed, and insisted that even today he is not properly appreciated.

The turning point in the conference came after a brilliant but resolutely nationalist discourse by Beaulieu reiterated the interpretation he offered in 1972 in *Jack Kerouac: essai poulet*, raising the temperature in the crowded hall by about 30 degrees.

He ruffled the feathers of Quebecois who consider his nationalist politics outdated; of French-Canadians who live outside Quebec and intend to survive as themselves; of Anglo-Montrealers who don't believe every trace of their existence should be obliterated; and of Americans who object to being stereotyped.

While lauding Kerouac as a great artist, Beaulieu dismissed Ginsberg's work with a supercilious shrug and a wave of his hand. Others leapt to the microphone and his defence, but Ginsberg remained in his seat, leaning on his cane. Questioned immediately afterwards, tension still in the air, Ginsberg spoke of Beaulieu's sensitivity, beautiful language and great talent and said he was "like Jack."

Then he hurried off to find Beaulieu in the throng, to congratulate him and, it turned out, invite him to dinner. Beaulieu went—but for most observers the symbolic, incidental lesson was still unclear.

Next day, without seeming to do so, Ginsberg elaborated. He described how, when attacked, Kerouac never fought back. He talked of the author's "panoramic awareness," of his incredible empathy, and finally of his ability to hold contradictory ideas in his mind.

"Yes, Kerouac is yours," Ginsberg was saying to Beaulieu and his followers. "But he is not yours alone. Le Grand Jack belongs to the world."

❋ ❋ ❋

II

Fabulous Festivals In
A World-Class City

On the northernmost shores of the Sea of English is located the world-class city of Toronto. The Harbor Master there is one Greg Gatenby—famously an impossible man who does undoable things. Impossible? Outer-Canadians, at least, are apt to smile tightly when told from a public stage that, for 10 days each year, Toronto is "the literary capital of the world." Or that during the International Festival of Authors, writers read from their works before "the most sophisticated and erudite audience in the world."

Trouble is, this un-Canadian chest-thumping has some excuse. The festival, held at Harbourfront and the Harbour Castle Hilton Hotel, is the biggest and most respected annual gathering of authors in the world. It has been happening since 1980, when 18 writers turned up from around the globe. That number has been steadily growing, and in 1990 more than 80 writers participated.

In addition, a series of weekly readings brings to the world-class city another 170 writers annually. Harbor Master Gatenby, who doubles as the maestro behind all this magic, says that for Torontonians, the festival "is not an isolated event, but a crowning adjunct to the regular series." And he knows from private discussions that many regular attendees—audiences average 300 per night—read the works of the visiting authors. Which lends plausibility, I suppose, to his "sophistication" claim.

In 1990, the 10-day festival drew over 12,000 paid admissions, and every year sees another box-office record. Always there are more authors than ever before, more public interviews, more readings, more events. In 1989, Gatenby added a wildly popular Lives-and-Times series featuring biographers talking about their subjects. In 1990, he introduced an annual

Winter's Tales Program for English-language fiction writers in the first week of February, and in 1991, he conjured the fourth annual World Poetry Festival, with over 25 poets attending.

The International Festival of Authors, held in October, features the awarding of three major literary prizes: the Marian Engel Award ($10,000), the Festival Prize (roughly $22,500) and the Lionel Gelber Prize (at $50,000, the largest in Canada). Winners of the Booker, the Pulitzer and the National Book awards—more than 50 of them over the years—grab most of the remaining headlines, unless a Nobel laureate turns up (Saul Bellow, Wole Soyinka, Joseph Brodsky, Czeslaw Milosz and William Golding have done so). Yet one of the strengths of the festival is its avant-garde eclecticism, and participants have included writers as different as Kathy Acker, George Lamming, Chinua Achebe, Alison Lurie and Jerzy Kosinski.

47. William Golding Visits Niagara Falls

William Golding is author most recently of An Egyptian Journal *(1985) and two novels:* Close Quarters *(1987) and* Fire Down Below *(1989). The Nobel Prize-winner granted only one interview when he visited Toronto, a round-table circus in the hotel cafeteria. Half a dozen journalists turned up but only two of us asked questions—myself and the late Ken Adachi of* The Toronto Star.

I'd stumbled across and investigated allegations of plagiarism, but when I pushed it to a third question Golding narrowed his eyes. Adachi asked me about it later and I was relieved that I could fill him in on something, anything. I was relieved to express my thanks that way because Adachi knew Golding's work far better than I did, and if he hadn't been present the interview would have devolved into a major embarrassment.

NIAGARA FALLS—William Golding, winner of the 1983 Nobel Prize for literature, was sitting in the back of a van with his wife and half a dozen other writers when he got his first glimpse of Niagara Falls.

"Jolly good show!" he exclaimed and spontaneously led his fellow travellers in applauding the two Canadians in the van, as if they had helped to create the thundering natural wonder visible through the windshield.

"I hadn't realized it went round like that, like a horseshoe," Golding said a few minutes later, out of the van and leaning over a stone railing. "Magnificent! Wonderful!" Excitedly, Golding called for a reporter to take his photo with his wife, Ann—first with his back to the falls, then facing them, pointing joyfully at nothing at all for the sake of the pose.

For Golding, the 1985 headliner at Toronto's International Festival of Authors, this display of excitement was uncharacteristic, yet somehow not surprising. Present throughout the nine-day festival, the phlegmatic British author most often projected the image of a grand old man of letters: a serious sort, best-known as author of *Lord Of The Flies*, who well deserved the world's largest ($240,000) and most prestigious literary award.

But it was Golding's ability to respond to experience with child-like wonder and enthusiasm that made him a creative writer in the first place, as is apparent in such novels as *Pincher Martin, The Inheritors, Freefall* and *Rites Of Passage*. Hence, no surprise.

Two nights after visiting Niagara Falls, as he ended the festival with an authoritative reading that drew a standing ovation, Golding again revealed his paradoxical nature. He opened his reading with a hilarious description of his early school days, in which he figured as a strangely sensitive bully, and closed with an intensely intellectual essay on creativity which he described in a round-table interview as "a sort of manifesto."

Golding, born in 1911, has been the focus of two controversies since he received the Nobel Prize. The first involved the award itself. The committee cited Golding's several novels, "which with the perspicuity of realistic narrative art and diversity and universality of myth, illuminate the human condition in the world today."

But one committee member, Artur Lundkvist, made an unprecedented break with protocol to protest the award, calling Golding "a little English phenomenon of no special interest." Lundkvist was backing an experimental French novelist named Claude Simon, who won the Nobel Prize in 1985.

"I don't know Simon's work," Golding said, "but I understand he's highly thought of in some French circles, not in others. When you win the Nobel, the first thing you find out is who your enemies are. I imagine Claude Simon is finding out just that."

The second controversy erupted early in 1984, when English critic Auberon Waugh raised the question of unconscious plagiarism. Waugh noted that *Lord Of The Flies* bears an uncanny resemblance to a forgotten English novel called *Children Of The Morning* by W.L. George, published in 1926.

Golding said he'd "never even heard of" that work and that the similarities must be coincidental. "There are lots of books about boys on islands." This is the answer he has been giving to this question all along. He said he hasn't read *Lord Of The Flies* "for a generation: I can re-read my essays, but not my novels."

Indeed, Golding doesn't read much contemporary writing of any kind. "I read ancient Greek, mostly," he said—and he wasn't kidding.

These days he and his wife, married for 46 years, live in "an 1828 Regency house" in Cornwall. Together, they have raised a son and a daughter, but Golding said he doesn't count that among his major achievements: "That was dead easy."

48. Jerzy Kosinski Fights Plagiarism Charge

TORONTO—Jerzy Kosinski writes his own books. The controversial American novelist, who came under attack as a plagiarist in 1982, devoted the next six years to showing how he does it.

If his demonstration—a 527-page "autofiction" called *The Hermit Of 69th Street*—is difficult and defiantly unconventional, Kosinski is happy to explain.

The book is "about the making of a work of art," he told about 400 people at the International Festival of Authors. "It's about the spiritual halo, the intellectual topography which precedes arriving at the plot, at the knowledge that you have a story to tell."

Earlier, in an interview, Kosinski described *Hermit* as "a new literary instrument—one that allows the reader to participate, not in the mysteriously finished work, but in the climate that leads up to it."

With notable exceptions, book reviewers remain unimpressed. They describe *Hermit*, which is larded with footnotes and quotations from other authors, as unreadable and self-indulgent.

Kosinski, who has written eight previous novels, including *The Painted Bird* (1965) and *Steps,* which won the 1966 National Book Award, shrugs and notes that *Hermit* is outselling all his other books. During its first two months in print, *Hermit* sold 37,000 copies.

Kosinski, who taught at Yale for seven years and was president of International PEN for two, has always regarded himself—and been regarded by the literary establishment—as an outsider, a maverick, an experimental writer with a large cult following.

Born in 1933 in Poland, Kosinski survived the Holocaust with harrowing difficulty, a Jewish child travelling alone, constantly in danger of discovery. (He fictionalized this experience in *The Painted Bird*.)

In 1957, Kosinski defected to the United States under circumstances he declines to clarify—maybe by creating fictional referees, maybe by winning a photography contest and doctoring the amount of money involved to justify going abroad to accept the prize.

The author has always regarded plot "as a naive device" and most of his novels—among them *Being There*, which became a popular movie starring Peter Sellers—celebrate accident rather than meaningful continuity. "If there is an order in nature," Kosinski said, "God is the only author who could authorize it."

Chance and accident have shaped Kosinski's own life. While reading at Harbourfront, the author revealed that all his relatives except his parents were among 80,000 Polish Jews who were almost, but not quite, saved by advancing Russian troops toward the end of the Second World War.

Again, for three years, as a traumatized youth, Kosinski was mute. A serious ski accident restored his voice. Then, in 1969, because his luggage went astray, Kosinski missed being at the home of friend Roman Polanski the night the Manson gang murdered Polanski's wife Sharon Tate and several friends.

Kosinski said plagiarism charges planted by the Polish press have swirled around him since he defected. But in 1982, the food critic at New York's *Village Voice* built a story on them.

Two of the three people quoted denounced the article as sheer fabrication. But by then, *The New York Times* had picked it up and Kosinski was embroiled in a newspaper war—another accident.

Most Kosinski heroes are amoral sexual predators—ingenious, manipulative, ruthless and sometimes vengeful. But *Hermit* is Kosinski's most personal work, and here we find Norbert Kosky, a hero much tamer than usual, a Kosinski without the "sin."

Kosky is a 55-year-old Holocaust survivor holed up in New York and wrestling not only with charges of plagiarism but with the narrative tradition. Kosky comments endlessly on his own work-in-progress about Jay Kay, and "J.K." comments in turn on Kosky's remarks. The heavily footnoted result repeatedly flings the reader out of the text to other sources.

If *Hermit* is the author's least vivid, least accessible work, Kosinski regards it as the pinnacle of his achievement, and as a work that "closed the cycle" begun with *The Painted Bird*. (In May of 1991, Jerzy Kosinski killed himself. He had been suffering from a debilitating heart condition.)

49. D.M. Thomas Denies Arrogance

In 1990, British author D.M. Thomas published Lying Together, *the final installment of his "Russian Nights" quintet, which includes* Ararat, Swallow, Sphinx *and* Summit. *None of these novels elicited the raves inspired by* The White Hotel, *published in 1981.*

TORONTO—World-famous author D.M. Thomas publicly denied here that he is "arrogant, shifty and dislikable." Thomas, whose 1981 novel *The White Hotel* has sold 1.25 million copies around the world, said he was "surprised and bewildered" by this allegation, which appeared in a recent review of his book *Memories And Hallucinations: A Memoir*.

"Other reviewers have picked up on a more sympathetic character," Thomas said at the International Festival of Authors. "Certainly, my cats like me."

Maybe it was all just an act, but the British author, who by 1988 had published seven novels, five volumes of poetry and two book-length translations, emerged as diffident, sensitive and sincere during an hour-long public interview at Harbourfront attended by 300 people.

Thomas said that serious fiction "is not just chit-chat." It elicits strong emotions because the writer "goes quite deeply into his experience and feelings, and readers bring their own obsessions to the resulting work."

Controversy has dogged Thomas ever since he vaulted to international prominence—his work has appeared in 14 languages—with *The White Hotel*. Detractors have attacked him as a pornographer and a plagiarist.

An avowed Freudian, Thomas said that sexuality links "the highest and the lowest in man." It's primitive and uncontrollable, which is why people "like to tame it, to turn it into recreation or an expression in a marital relationship."

He said the sex in his novels is not mechanically detailed, but is there because sexuality "reveals people in ways that aren't available through social intercourse."

The plagiarism charges arose over the Babi Yar section of *The White Hotel*, in which Thomas drew on an eye-witness account of the slaughter of Jews by Nazi troops in 1941.

"Plagiarism is an unacknowledged borrowing of someone else's work," Thomas said. But in *White Hotel*, he clearly stated that he was using an historical document.

"Therefore, it's not plagiarism. The only controversy is over the validity of my approach. I would have felt immoral inventing Holocaust scenes at that point in the novel."

Thomas, born in 1935, didn't begin writing fiction until he was 40. Initially, the idea terrified him: "I feared writing prose for 15 or 20 years."

Finally, he was driven to it by boredom. "All my poetry is in one voice. The novel opened up possibilities."

Thomas's novels feature a multiplicity of voices and points of view. Asked if this implied a potentially dangerous loss of control, Thomas said: "Four years ago, I would have said no." But then he had "a breakdown, a big depression, a writer's block."

Thomas underwent Freudian analysis: "I don't see it as therapy, but as exploring the depths of the soul. You can't cure, but you may heal or make whole."

Thomas's new book, *Memories And Hallucinations*, grew out of that analysis. Framed by the experience of analysis, it paints a complex self-portrait using memories, dreams, reflections and poems.

"It's a watershed," Thomas said. "I'm moving towards a fresh beginning, exploring ideas without feeling confident yet."

50. Salman Rushdie Finds Himself Banned

The whole world knows about the holy war of Salman Rushdie. In February, 1989, Ayatollah Khomeini called on Muslims around the world to assassinate the author for blaspheming Islam in his novel The Satanic Verses. *This outrage and its consequences have made headlines around the globe. The bodyguards and the secrecy, the violent demonstrations, the break-down of Rushdie's marriage to Marianne Wiggins, his attempts to secure a truce (though not at any price)—they've all been documented, analyzed, explained.*

Through it all, and regardless of his changing attitude toward Islam, Rushdie has persevered as a working writer, as a warrior. In 1990, he published the short books In Good Faith *and* Is Nothing Sacred?, *respectively a defence of free speech and a meditation on the act of writing. And also* Haroun And The Sea Of Stories, *a bright, lively and magical children's book that appeals across generations and cultures in ways reminiscent of* The Hobbit.

Dozens of writers have painted verbal portraits of Rushdie and more will do so. Still, I treasure my single blurry snapshot of the author, which I took at the International Festival of Authors. I'd contacted Rushdie—we were both staying in Toronto at the Harbour Castle Westin Hotel—imme-

diately after arriving to request an interview. And discovered that, given his desperately busy schedule and several other interviews I'd arranged in advance, our schedules clashed. The only possible time was now, during the next hour, and Rushdie had already told me that he was resting between appointments.

On one end of the telephone line, then, we had Salman Rushdie—international star, winner of the Booker Prize, toast of the literary jet-set. On the other, we had a newspaper reporter from some obscure city in western Canada. Rushdie didn't need me. But when the scheduling problem—and, I suppose, my own anxiousness to meet him—became clear, Rushdie said: "Give me 15 minutes. I'll meet you in the lounge."

TORONTO—Award-winning novelist Salman Rushdie is at war with the government of his native India. Rushdie, who won the prestigious Booker Prize in 1981 for *Midnight's Children*, is fighting the banning in that country of his new novel *The Satanic Verses*.

"The one thing that unites those who support the ban is their refusal to read the book," Rushdie said at the International Festival of Authors. "They admit they haven't read it," Rushdie said during a panel discussion, "yet they feel able to say that it's not a work of art, that it's 'abusive filth,' that it's the product of a diseased mind—mine."

The Satanic Verses, a stylistic tour de force that mixes myth and reality in ways reminiscent of James Joyce, had been short-listed for the 1988 Booker Prize (it didn't win). And recently banned by Indian prime minister Rajiv Gandhi after complaints by a handful of Muslim politicians, who claimed visionary sequences depicting a fictional prophet maligned Mohammed, founder of Islam.

Rushdie, himself of Muslim heritage, wrote a 1,000-word open letter to Gandhi denouncing the ban as a flagrant attempt to buy the votes of India's 100 million Muslims. It appeared in newspapers throughout India.

That letter, Rushdie said in an interview, was being reprinted in *The New York Times*. What concerned the author most was that the controversy would create the impression that *Satanic Verses* is "abstruse, very heavy."

The novel is "at least partly comic," Rushdie noted. "It's a book about migration, metamorphosis, London, Bombay, coming to terms with death, learning how to love—all sorts of things politicians are not interested in." And only 70 of its 547 pages relate to Islam.

Rushdie, whose faded blue jeans and relaxed demeanor gave him the appearance of a counter-culture American, speaks English with a British accent. Even in the company of celebrated authors, he stands out as formidably erudite, remarkably eloquent.

Born in Bombay in 1947, Rushdie went to school in England. He graduated from Cambridge University in 1968, and since then has lived mostly in London. Until 1981, when the success of his second novel, *Midnight's Children*, enabled him to write full time, Rushdie worked as an advertising copywriter and an actor.

The Satanic Verses, which quietly displays extensive knowledge of the literatures of both East and West, is most influenced by the work of James Joyce, notably *Ulysses* and *Finnegans Wake*. "I think Joyce is the greatest English-language writer of the century," Rushdie said. "He was always The Master for me."

The Satanic Verses started, Rushdie said, with "an image I had of two men falling out of an exploded airplane and surviving. That wasn't just a Finnegan-like fall, but the most dramatic act of emigration I could think of."

The two men, Indian movie star Gibreel Farishta and Saladin Chamcha, Anglophile supreme, are magically transformed. While remaining themselves, they also become the archangel Gabriel and Satan himself, locked in an everlasting struggle that cuts from England to India and back again.

"The question is," Rushdie said, "which (of them) is good and which is evil? The tiniest shifts cause a reversal in the moral judgments one makes."

In *The Satanic Verses*, Rushdie paints a devastating portrait of Margaret Thatcher's England. "The deterioration has been spiritual rather than material," he said. "The anger and stress are much closer to the surface. The place feels like an explosion waiting to happen."

Rushdie, who in 1987 married American novelist Marianne Wiggins, said he is "toying with the idea of crossing the Atlantic" to live. North America offers "a culture of migrants," he said. "Here there are lots of people like me. Everybody is three or four things at once."

✱✱✱

III

International PEN
In Central Canada

In 1989, Salman Rushdie asked that he *not* be the main focus of attention at the 54th International PEN World Congress, which drew more than 600 writers to Toronto and Montreal. Yet Rushdie's name arose in two forums as the public business of the writers' congress got underway. Indian novelist Anita Desai, whose country was one of the first to ban *The Satanic Verses*, said at a panel discussion that she had spent the past six months agonizing over the role of the writer as a result of the Iranian death threat against Rushdie. At a panel on "The Writer: Freedom and Power," Desai said that Rushdie had in effect been banned from society because he did what a writer was supposed to do. "What is a writer's responsibility?" Desai asked. "To seek the truth. To go on questioning."

Later, at a press conference attended by about half of the 200 journalists in Toronto from around the world, PEN's international secretary Alexandre Blokh said the Rushdie case "is an offence to all men of conscience—though we must be very careful not to turn our reaction into an anti-Muslim campaign." Blokh spoke of Rushdie after deploring the slaughter of innocents that had occurred not long before (June 4, 1989) in China's Tiananmen Square, a bloody repression he described as having set back the clock by decades.

The variety of international concerns was evident throughout the conference. At the press conference a British journalist asked angrily why PEN—the acronym stands for Poets, Playwrights, Essayists, Editors and Novelists—was conducting its business behind closed doors. Graeme Gibson, president of Canada's English-speaking centre, explained that much of that business is delicate because it concerns writers in prison. Gibson also said that a protest by half a dozen non-white Canadians (Vision

21) at an opening night benefit was organized before the participants had a chance "to see fully what is going on here." And Blokh of France noted "the very great number of participants from developing countries."

At the panel on "Freedom and Power," American playwright Arthur Miller declared that conflict is the essence of writing. "The mission of literature is to maintain the playing field, to keep the arena open so the crushing of the opponent doesn't take place." He summed up his message in two words: "Beware orthodoxy." And Claribel Alegria of El Salvador gave a passionate description of the horrors facing writers in her country, where, she said, 23 journalists had been killed in the past 10 years, and others had disappeared.

Tadeusz Konwicki of Poland, who spoke through an interpreter, said that in Soviet bloc countries, "a certain kind of totalitarianism is crumbling." Polish writers feel that they are joining the world, he said, but feel threatened by the infantilization of art as exemplified in the movies of Stephen Spielberg (*Jaws, Close Encounters Of The Third Kind, Back To The Future*). The film-maker started by making interesting psychological pictures, Konwicki said, but turned to creating "cinematic fairy tales." These "may be very pleasant and entertaining to the world which is not suffering hunger," he said. "But there are places where they meet with impatience."

51. Women Writers Unite

TORONTO—Women writers stole the show at the 54th World Congress of International PEN. Led by American Betty Friedan, Quebec's Nicole Brossard and Ontario's Margaret Atwood, about 20 of them gathered to announce the formation of an International Network of Women Writers.

Atwood, who spoke last, after about 10 others from as far away as China, Senegal and El Salvador, said the network was a direct result of "the Norman-Mailer circus in New York" in 1986. At that Congress, Atwood ended up speaking on behalf of "foreign women writers" because so few had been invited—less than 10 percent of the guests.

Atwood said Mailer argued that more weren't invited because they simply didn't exist. She and Brossard—"my Francophone sister"—promised themselves that this year, at least half of the guests of honor would be women. "Women are now a majority at this Congress," Atwood said. "It can be done, Virginia. And I hope that it will be done again."

The new network will contact women writers around the world who are both inside and outside PEN to investigate the status of women's literature. It will also participate in international conferences of women writers.

Brossard, Quebec's foremost feminist writer, hailed the formation of the network as "a historic event." Speaking in French, she said that the participation of women can make a difference to the direction of any debate.

Friedan, a leading American feminist, lambasted "the symbolic annihilation of women" at the Mailer-led Congress and said the women's movement is in peril throughout the world. "Women are threatened in so many places," Friedan said, "that it's very important to have a network to say, 'We will get you a hearing somewhere in the world. We will keep the flame alive.'"

She said that in the United States women's rights "are in great danger." The threat to freedom of choice in abortion implies a threat to other rights, like that of birth control and research on birth control.

American Meredith Tax said the network is not "a split from PEN." Rather, it will work to strengthen that world-wide organization, whose primary purpose is to defend freedom of speech.

At a later press conference, PEN officials announced 16 resolutions that had arisen out of a closed meeting of delegates. Among them were motions calling on China to cease persecuting writers and others, and on Turkey to stop its brutal treatment of Turkish and Kurdish prisoners.

Graeme Gibson, president of the English-speaking PEN centre, drew special attention to a motion protesting and deploring an obscure rule of Canadian law that allows anybody to prohibit publication of an unpublished manuscript. Gibson also read a full-page statement in which he deplored news reports focusing on a small group of protesters (Vision 21) and asserting PEN Canada is richly representative of all Canadians.

52. The Good, The Bad, The Ugly

MONTREAL—More than 100 women writers from around the world spoke at the first meeting of the International Network of Women Writers. Organizers conducted a round-the-room survey at which writers—among them a handful of men—welcomed the creation of the network that will focus attention on women writers.

The network was hailed as the crowning achievement of the 54th World Congress of International PEN by authors from Cuba, Finland, El Salvador, Ghana, Mexico, Thailand, Australia, England, Nepal, Mexico and South Africa, as well as Canada and the United States.

Margaret Atwood, who vowed in New York in 1986 that this Congress would have more than 50 percent women participants, drew applause when she said: "I made the promise, but most of the people who carried it out were men. I hope the aim of this network will be inclusion rather than separatism."

Maureen McTeer, who is not a PEN member but is the wife of External Affairs Minister Joe Clark, sparked a debate when she suggested that the network be run by a board based in Canada instead of New York. But John Ralston Saul, vice-president of English-speaking Canadian PEN, said the executive had not considered taking on this job. And Atwood carried the day with a proposal that the well-organized American feminists run the network for one year and then let some other country do the job.

Among those who spoke at the meeting were Betty Friedan, Adrienne Clarkson, P.K. Page, Myrna Kostash (in fluent French), Ama Ata Aidoo, Maxine Hong Kingston and Alison Lurie.

The nine-day PEN Congress, which began in Toronto and then moved to Montreal, was the first ever held in two cities. Because it attracted more than 600 participants from more than 60 PEN centres, many of whom have never visited North America, it has had the effect of putting Canada on the literary world map.

Besides the nuts-and-bolts business of the organization, whose principal aim is to defend freedom of expression, the Congress featured a whirl of readings and panel discussions, book launchings and informal debates.

While many of Canada's best-known English-speaking writers participated in the Congress, either as guests or delegates or both, their Francophone counterparts from Quebec stayed away in droves. Roger Lemelin, creator of the Plouffe family, was on hand, as were two leading women writers, the expatriate Anne Hebert, a Margaret-Laurence figure in Quebec literature, and Nicole Brossard, a leading feminist. But those absent included most of the leading writers of the Atwood/Brossard generation, among them Michel Tremblay, Yves Beauchemin, Roch Carrier, Victor Levy-Beaulieu, Jacques Godbout and Marie-Claire Blais.

The Congress passed two resolutions focusing on Canada. The most significant was one calling on the Canadian government to jettison an obscure law that allows any person who gets an injunction to prevent the publication of a manuscript. The resolution derives from the $102 million libel suit brought by Toronto's Reichmann family against *Toronto Life* magazine. Writer Elaine Dewar turned the article into a book-length manuscript which was then seized.

The biggest red herring of the Congress was the charge of racism levelled at Toronto PEN by a tiny group, Vision 21. Canadian writers of Mennonite, Ukrainian, Dutch, Chinese and other backgrounds found themselves lumped together under the rubric White Anglo-Saxon Protestant. Visiting foreigners hailed the Canadian centre for the astonishingly high number of delegates from developing countries.

The highlight of the Congress for a dozen visitors was a trip to the Arctic sponsored by Petro Canada. Emily Nasrallah of Lebanon, for example, couldn't stop talking about the three days she spent with the Inuit.

Alberta writers at the Congress included Rudy Wiebe, Aritha van Herk, Sharon Pollock, Robert Kroetsch (now in Winnipeg) and Kostash (temporarily in Regina). Several of them read publicly in Toronto, although always as part of an all-Canadian line-up. One observer noted that every Canadian writer who read with high-profile foreign authors was based in Toronto, though non-Ontarian writers like Wiebe, Kroetsch and van Herk were frequently better-known internationally.

53. Just Paint A Placard

Back in Calgary from the 54th World Congress of International PEN, a nine-day literary extravaganza held in Toronto and Montreal, I find I'm still reeling. Talk about non-stop activity. Meetings and panel discussions started early each day and ran late, and then came readings and receptions.

The Congress meant different things to different people, but it's a safe bet that few foreigners went away without an altered sense of Canada. By playing the role of host for the first time, this country made its presence felt in an international forum.

One thing disturbed me: the attention paid to June Callwood's admittedly intemperate response—she said the F-word—to a handful of hecklers (from Vision 21) charging the English-speaking Canadian PEN Centre with racism.

No matter that they had their facts all wrong and that so-called "ethnic" Canadians had been invited to join the PEN executive, that organizers had found ways to pick up the tabs for delegates from a dozen developing countries, that this was the most pluralistic PEN Congress ever held.

No matter that, for the first time, women writers represented more than 50 percent of participants and began to change the face of PEN, or that a whole mini-conference celebrated young writers. No matter that more than 360 writers are in jail around the world, and that PEN spent countless hours trying to do something about it.

No matter. All non-participants wanted to hear about was this minuscule, wrong-headed protest, whose leaders had managed to provoke a high-profile writer to anger and so to bask in unwarranted publicity.

What a lesson in the power of the media—and, worse, in how easily the media can be manipulated.

The trouble, I think, is endemic to incident-oriented journalism. Nothing makes a better 10-second television clip or an easier 12-inch story than a confrontation.

Want to get your name in the newspapers or your mug on the TV news? Nothing to it. Just paint a placard, pick a public event and proclaim a protest.

On the other hand, freedom of expression—which most journalists consider a sacred right—means that minority voices, especially in opposition, must be heard. And the last thing a good journalist wants to see is more quotes from officially approved sources.

No easy answers here, folks. You figure it out.

***

IV

Winter Olympics In
Wild Rose Country

54. The Writers' Festival

When Trevor Carolan, co-ordinator of the Olympic Writers' Festival, told a closing night audience of 450 people "something very special has happened here," he was speaking for virtually everyone who'd participated in the five-day celebration. The $300,000 festival and book fair, part of a larger, month-long arts festival mounted with the 1988 Olympic Winter Games, was easily the most spectacular literary extravaganza ever held in western Canada.

More than 60 writers took part, over 20 of them from outside Canada: J.P. Donleavy, Lawrence Ferlinghetti, Jan Morris, Jaan Kaplinski, Jay McInerney, Emily Nasrallah, Rodney Hall, Ryszard Kapuscinski, Sven Delblanc, Kazuko Shiraishi, Blanche d'Alpuget—the list goes on. Canadians included W.O. Mitchell, Pierre Berton, Marie-Claire Blais, June Callwood, Rudy Wiebe, Alberto Manguel, Robert Kroetsch, Spider Robinson, Gaston Miron, Sid Marty, Aritha van Herk, Guy Gavriel Kay, Robert Bringhurst—and on and on.

More than 1,700 tickets were sold for the five gala readings by well-known writers (four per night). Another 2,516 went for the 21 seminars and panel discussions held (in both official languages) during the day. Some 2,440 students visited the book fair on formal school visits—1,680 elementary, 760 high school. Opening day celebrations, when volunteers were counting because of fire regulations, drew over 4,400 people to Calgary's downtown convention centre for a family day. Organizers estimated that another 1,200 visited during the next three days, with 1,800 clicking through the turnstiles on closing day.

Observers familiar with Toronto's International Festival of Authors were struck, not so much by the calibre of participants and level of discussion, which were comparable, but by the variety of formats and sheer numbers of people who attended. Alberto Manguel, for example, the Toronto-based editor, anthologist and author, said that in some ways he liked this festival better than the one held annually at Harbourfront. Manguel noted that, with secondary readings happening all day long at the book fair on two separate stages, a book-lover could drop in, catch a single reading and then head for home. "And I'm amazed at the turnout," he said, glancing around the 250-seat Glenbow Theatre, which at mid-morning was almost full. "This is a working day. It's astounding."

David Carter, co-ordinator of the Book Fair, could hardly contain his jubilation: "We brought in 14,000 (Canadian) books and sold 30 percent of them. We would have been delighted with even 20 percent." Carter said that after returns to publishers, the book fair—which occupied 22,000 square feet—would earn $12,000. It would have made even more, he said, if it hadn't closed nightly at 7:30.

Calgary's Sandpiper Books, which set up a booth and sold works by the 60 authors participating in the festival, also reported spectacular results. Co-owner Kerry Longpre said the store brought in 3,000 books and sold almost 2,000 of them. "We did about $1,500 a day for five days." Longpre said these sales "far outstripped" those at Harbourfront. "We were absolutely boggled by the whole thing—not just the commercial success, but by meeting the writers, all these people who came from outside the country."

The Canadian Children's Book Centre did a booming non-profit business. Debbie Rogosin said the centre received over 1,600 entries in its jelly-bean counting contest. Hundreds of children visited the large booth in groups, and the centre gave away 1,000 copies each of several posters and magazines. Book-fair readings for both children and adults—mostly by Alberta authors—attracted audiences which ranged from two dozen to 150 or more throughout the day. Edmonton writer Merna Summers said one such reading—by American poet and translator Sam Hamill—was the highlight of the week. Meanwhile, across the hall and upstairs at the festival, seminars and panel discussions ran simultaneously—often with two choices available in English, one in French. These attracted crowds of up to 300.

For most people, of course, the evening readings were the main attraction. Three of five nights were sold out, despite the addition of extra chairs. On opening night, W.O. Mitchell, the grand old man of prairie fiction, kicked off the festival with a reading that drew on the accessible, humorous side of his work. Quebec's Marie-Claire Blais, the prodigiously talented author of 30 novels, followed with an intense, difficult reading from *Deaf To The City*, demanding more of her audience than was wise. Robert Kroetsch got the evening back on track with energetic good humor (and impressive self-discipline), and Irish novelist J.P. Donleavy capped the program with a reading that ranged from the scatological (excerpts from *The Unexpurgated Code*) to the elegiac (the ending of *The Ginger Man*), and left scores of people howling for an encore.

Two nights later, the highlights of the program were readings in the Beat tradition. Accompanied by a local jazz trio, Kazuko Shiraishi read in her native Japanese in a be-bop style. Her "beatific" content, communicated by a translator, included everything from sexual imagery to mentions of Gary Snyder and Henry Miller. San Francisco's Lawrence Ferlinghetti, one of the original Beats, closed the evening with a powerful—and popular—reading of poems on a Dionysian theme. Ferlinghetti, who has a master's degree from Columbia University and a doctorate from the Sorbonne, decried the value of self-discipline in numerous asides: "What we need is hunger and passion."

Of the seminars and panel discussions, the best organized was undoubtedly "Publishing in the Eighties," put together by Linda Cameron of the University of Calgary Press. Four panel members from the Association of Canadian Publishers addressed publishing issues in detail. Rob Sanders of Vancouver's Douglas & McIntyre explored proposed changes to Canadian laws on copyright and pornography. He offered a devastating critique of Bill C-54, with which the federal government proposed to curb freedom of expression.

Anna Porter, who controls Key Porter Books, Seal Books and Doubleday Canada, gave a frank and funny talk on the concentration of ownership in publishing. Porter said big companies are usually "bottom-line driven," and that this does not bode well for "mid-list books" of literary merit. Malcolm Lester of Lester & Orpen Dennys (which folded in 1991) tackled free trade as it relates to publishing. He noted that, in books, Canada "already has the most open market in the world." Lester identified American laws on countervail as a serious threat which could turn all Canadian government ministers against any cultural initiatives out of a need to protect their own turf. He also hailed as a victory the exemption of cultural industries from the agreement, dismissing as "specious" and "fatuous" arguments that the exemption means nothing.

The panel on "The Future of Writing" was the most spirited and provocative of the week. Writers discussed changes in literary genres, the emergence of feminist literature and the relationship between writer and reader. Canada's Robert Kroetsch declared forcefully: "Without a great audience, there is no great art. I don't mean large but great, in the sense of openness and willingness to explore." Rodney Hall of Australia argued that literary works can be appreciated only in the context of a tradition which is always changing. And Erich Wolfgang Skwara of Austria drew applause when he said: "Literature fights the passing of time, and will always have this task."

The discussion moved from lively to heated when an audience member mentioned a local nurses' strike (now settled) and suggested that, by comparison, writers' panels were elitist and irrelevant. Calgary's Aritha van Herk gave the clearest rebuttal, arguing that writers contribute to such struggles by broadening consciousness: "We're trying to make readers think so they'll be capable of sympathizing when issues like the nurses' strike arise."

Minutes later, a surprise petition supporting the land claims of the Lubicon Cree Indians hit the floor—and received a mixed reaction. Presented by Edmonton non-fiction writer Myrna Kostash and Quebec poet Gaston Miron, the petition called on the Canadian government to begin negotiations with the Lubicon Indians using the recommendations of government appointee Davey Fulton. About 230 people were present, and 30 or 40 left while Kostash and Miron read their preamble. Panel chair Rudy Wiebe called for a show of hands and 90 percent of those remaining indicated their support before traipsing to the front to sign their names. Many of those who opposed the petition said they considered it inappropriate in the context of the festival.

Among other panel discussions, "Why We Write" and "Voices of the Wilderness" were among the most popular. The first, which could have drifted in any number of directions, surged into an exploration of the writer as outsider. Robert Kroetsch described how Canadian writers, unlike American or Soviet ones, must battle a sense of marginality and "the feeling that you don't matter." American Sam Hamill said that as poet, editor and translator, he is always in "limbo-land," though he also feels that he belongs to something greater—a tradition of social responsibility.

Even Donleavy, whose successes are conspicuous, said he has endured continual rejection and persecution. In the United States, 45 publishers rejected his bawdy classic *The Ginger Man*. Finally, he published the book in France. "Writing," he said, "is turning one's worst moments into money." Shiraishi, who was born in Vancouver and moved to Japan as a young girl, described the cruelty she experienced among her Japanese peers because she was different, and said that the experience shaped her. Jaan Kaplinski of Estonia described how he grew up during the Stalinist era in "an Orwellian atmosphere where everything was called its opposite." He said he is better received on the West Coast of the United States than in his native land, and that finally he feels "totally cosmopolitan," belonging everywhere and nowhere.

The ever-popular Pierre Berton chaired the panel on "Voices of Wilderness," setting forth the thesis that Canadians are less romantic about the wilderness than most peoples because they live closer to it. Novelist Rudy Wiebe said there exists in the Judeo-Christian tradition an irreducible ambivalence about the wilderness, adducing examples from Bunyan, Hawthorne and the Bible. And Alberta poet and non-fiction writer Sid Marty read a powerful, evocative essay about literature and the wilderness. He decried the sissified European response to the ruggedness of western

Canada, and lambasted contemporary magazines for their indifference to the environment: "Why don't they tackle wilderness issues instead of giving us beauty for the yuppies?"

For some of visiting foreign authors, highlights of the week usually included experiences outside the festival. Rodney Hall of Australia returned from a long, cold walk along the Bow River and said: "I've never seen a frozen river before. It's fantastic!" And Ireland's Donleavy, who walked the streets incessantly, said he found Calgary absolutely fascinating: "All that space, those long corridors with nobody in them, the cafes with a single person sitting inside, drinking coffee. It's Kafkaesque."

55. J.P. Donleavy: Tennis With The Ginger Man

Writers of genre or popular fiction—mysteries, romances, horror novels—frequently become rich and famous. Think of Robert B. Parker, Agatha Christie, Stephen King. But for a writer of serious fiction to achieve material success—ah, now that takes something special. J.P. Donleavy has had whatever it takes. Donleavy, born in 1926 and raised in Brooklyn by Irish-immigrant parents, lives these days on an estate in Ireland's lake country.

In a telephone interview before the Olympic Writers' Festival, Donleavy sounded charmingly modest—but not apologetic—about his success. He was modest about the walled orchard on his property, the rolling hills and parklands, the 75-head of cattle he keeps along with "the odd horse," and the palatial mansion in which he lives with his wife and two of his four children. About the nine bathrooms and the indoor swimming pool, the suite of rooms in which he works, with his secretary at the other end of the house, and who could ask where the servants stayed?

Donleavy has produced over 15 books, among them the novels A Singular Man, The Beastly Beatitudes Of Balthazar B., The Onion Eaters, The Unexpurgated Code, The Destinies Of Darcy Dancer, Gentleman, Leila, Schultz *and* Are You Listening Rabbi Low? *He has also written plays, film scripts, short stories and non-fiction books, and painted thousands of watercolors.*

All this began with The Ginger Man, *a bawdy classic published in Paris in 1955, but not available in unexpurgated editions in North America until 10 years later. Donleavy employed the third person to show his hero in action, and the first person to reveal his thoughts. This technique of shifting perspective, something of an innovation, proved remarkably adaptable, and has figured in most of Donleavy's later works.*

In fact, most of the author's hallmarks are present in that amazingly mature first novel: stream-of-consciousness, constructions using the pronoun "one," chapters that end with a line of doggerel, black humor and a hero obsessed with sex and money. Along with Tropic Of Cancer, Lady Chatterley's Lover *and* Ulysses, The Ginger Man *was one of the novels that led to the easing of American censorship laws in the early '60s.*

Donleavy said he doesn't have a favorite among his own works, although A Singular Man *"interests me a lot." That novel contained more autobiographical background than usual, "and one feels more connected with that work than with most others." Does Donleavy consider himself a humorous novelist? "Not exactly. Though one does try to use humor to say something." He writes "in deadly seriousness," and adapts his language to the book he's writing. "I try to use English in every possible way."*

Donleavy, who painted before he wrote, continues to paint. He has had many exhibitions and sold hundreds of watercolors: "I'm a pretty serious painter." Donleavy is also a fitness buff who invented a game called De Alfonce Tennis. In his book of that title, Donleavy argued that the game should be recognized as an Olympic sport. It requires special equipment but can be played on any badminton court, he told me. And it's simple enough that a proficient tennis player can learn it in 20 minutes.

Not so long ago, while interviewing Irish novelist J.P. Donleavy by telephone, I made the mistake of asking him about his book *De Alfonce Tennis: The Superlative Game Of Eccentric Champions.* "Is that book about a real game?" Donleavy insisted it was. He said he always travelled with his equipment, and perhaps I'd like to play a game when he was in town for the Olympic Writers' Festival? All we needed was a badminton court.

Now, racquet sports have never been my forte. But I like to think I'm athletic. I work out regularly and, at 61, Donleavy had 20 years on me. Secretly, I believed I could hold my own. And so I ended up facing the grey-haired author across a knee-high badminton net at Lindsay Park Athletic Complex. Where I discovered that somehow, by donning shorts, T-shirt and sneakers, the tweedy intellectual had transformed himself into an indefatigable, racquet-brandishing ball-fiend.

Earlier, in his hotel room, when he was still a sensitive, caring human being, Donleavy had explained that he conceived De Alfonce Tennis in New York City in the early '70s. There, about twice a year, he'd visit his oldest son, who'd emigrated from Ireland.

Like the author himself, this son had always been athletic, and "in America" he'd become a champion badminton player. Father and son would work out together at The New York Athletic Club, and there, in a strange miniature court, they saw club members playing a curious game called "hand tennis."

Donleavy tried it and loved it. Over the next few years, obeying the inner compulsion that has driven him to write over a dozen big books and half a dozen plays, and also to paint thousands of watercolors, Donleavy transmogrified the game—reinvented it as De Alfonce Tennis. Squash and badminton champions would surround the court to watch, and afterwards accost the players. "What's that game you're playing? My God! It's wonderful!"

Donleavy details the rules of his creation in *De Alfonce Tennis: The Superlative Game Of Eccentric Champions*. In all its glory, the game is played on a special court with racquets and soft, nerf-like balls. The court is walled, as in racquetball and squash, but players also use the ceiling and don't stand side by side, but rather face each other across a net.

"The game is a great leveller," Donleavy said—and, in this respect, it's more like racquetball than squash. De Alfonce Tennis, when played with the proper accoutrements, is also blindingly fast: "It gives you a slightly better workout than squash." And, because the ball is feathery soft, it doesn't threaten the eyes.

At Lindsay Park, Donleavy demonstrated De Alfonce Tennis at its most rudimentary. No walls, no ceilings—but he'd brought balls and racquets and set the net at the proper height (a racket plus four fingers). Then he started slamming curve balls and even a couple of "nert serves" that landed and didn't bounce—perfect aces. A certain 12-year-old Irish boy, Donleavy said across the net, regularly blasts a serve that makes an S in the air, leaving his opponents gasping.

Later, as I drove him back to the Skyline Hotel, Donleavy said there are 125 or so ranked players of De Alfonce Tennis around the world. There's even a De Alfonce Tennis Association, which boasts a bust of Donleavy the founder, on Broadway in New York.

Oh, yes. I almost forgot what happened on the court. The contest started wonderfully as I won the rally, then surprised Donleavy with a series of blistering serves. Before he knew it, the world-famous novelist was down one game to zero. Then the man started to dance, and by the time he stopped I'd won only one more game. The grey-bearded author with the dancing feet had chalked up 12 or 15—so many, anyway, that we'd stopped counting.

It'll take a better tennis player than I'll ever be to find out what Donleavy's like when he's losing. When he's winning, he's all generosity—a ball-fiend whose game is punctuated by overly generous remarks: "Good shot! Hey, you're a natural."

About halfway through the debacle, a Lindsay Park staffer stopped by to watch. Soon he was peppering Donleavy with questions. I offered him my badminton racquet and he quickly showed that he knows his way around courts far better than I do. "This game is great!" he declared. "It's fantastic. What'd you say it's called?"

56. Rodney Hall: Not Since Patrick White....

Kisses Of The Enemy, *the third of Australian Rodney Hall's novels to be published in North America, was better received in Canada than the United States. Set in the 1990s, it dramatizes the take-over of Australia by the American Central Intelligence Agency. In 1989,* Herald *reviewer*

Audrey Andrews wrote: "Canadians who fear the consequences of our free-trade agreement with the United States and our government's increasing subservience to American economic and military influences will see their worst fears extravagantly played out in this prophetic fantasy."

For Canadian book-lovers, one of the great discoveries of the Olympic Writers' Festival was Australian author Rodney Hall. Not since Patrick White, who won the 1973 Nobel Prize for literature, had a writer from Down Under stirred such excitement in North America.

Hall's 1982 novel, *Just Relations*, was hailed in *Saturday Review*, to cite a single example, as "a career-making book... the sort of performance that immediately establishes its author's place among the best writers of his time."

Hall had published five novels, two biographies, 11 books of poetry and a photographic history of Australia. He had edited six anthologies, and his work had been translated into French, Dutch, Italian and Hebrew.

Hall had won Australia's top awards in both fiction and poetry, and was the 1986 winner of the Canada-Australia Prize, which includes a month-long tour of Canada and accounted for Hall's presence at the festival—a lucky accident.

Born in England of Australian parents who returned home after the Second World War, Hall grew up mostly in Brisbane. His mother was a singer, he said over lunch, and music and literature were always part of his life.

At 16, his mother widowed, Hall left school to work at a series of menial jobs—everything from office boy to army conscript. "I served my nation by playing the trombone." The man remains a baroque musician to this day, and is founder/director of the Australian Summer School of Early Music.

In his early 20s, Hall spent two and a half years walking around Europe: Italy, Spain, France, England, Scotland, Belgium, Denmark and Yugoslavia. When he returned home in 1961, he began writing radio scripts. For the next 15 years, while he and his wife raised three daughters, these scripts provided bread and butter.

Also in 1961, Hall published a chapbook of poems called *Penniless Til Doomsday*. This work elicited a long, detailed and encouraging letter from poet and scholar Robert Graves, of which Hall said: "It was like receiving a letter from God."

Hall wrote a couple of unpublished novels—he began the first when he was 17—before he found a taker for *The Ship On The Coin* (1968). More books followed. But the author didn't attract international attention until he published his 502-page third novel, *Just Relations*, which won the 1982 Miles Franklin Award.

In Australia, Hall published *Kisses Of The Enemy*, a 625-page novel, in 1988. And on this continent, that same year, he brought out *Captivity Captive*, a literary spell-binder based on an unsolved triple murder.

Hall said he'd just finished writing *Kisses Of The Enemy* and was walking his dog when he suddenly got the idea of telling the story, set in 1898, as if someone were looking back on it from the mid-'50s. He pulled out his notebook and, before he'd closed it, had scribbled a 5,000-word opening.

Since 1974, Hall has lived with his family in a house without electricity on the south coast of New South Wales, where he does most of his writing in long hand. When interviewed, he was halfway through another mammoth novel called *The Colony Club*. Hall wasn't writing much poetry, but he said that's because the large, sprawling novels he favors allow him to incorporate everything he thinks about.

After finishing his tour of Canada, Hall visited New York City and Chicago. Then he was off to China for a three-month teaching sojourn, during which his wife joined him. After that, Hall returned to South Australia where, writing by the light of candles and oil lamps, he resumed work on *The Colony Club*.

* * *

V

Visiting Allies

If the English language is an ocean, then a literary festival is a sun-speckled regatta, with writer-sailors vying for recognition and glory. But the Sea of English also inspires solo crossings—by Americans as different as Jean Auel and Richard Ford, and by South Africans like Andre Brink. Early in 1989, while Salman Rushdie was in the headlines, and before the Soviet Union began falling apart, a delegation of Soviet writers visited Canada.

57. White Hats For The Soviets

Writers in the Soviet Union were disturbed that death threats were made against novelist Salman Rushdie, a leading Soviet writer said in Calgary. "Yes, we are concerned," poet Egor Isaev said through a translator. "And we feel at one with him because he is a writer."

Isaev, who headed a delegation of visiting Soviet writers, said the general feeling of the 10,000-member Soviet Writers' Union was that the Iranian government of Ayatollah Khomeini "is overdoing it."

But Isaev also said that writers should be sensitive to religious, national and ethnic traditions. "We do not believe in God," he said, "but we would insist on a respect toward any religious belief and not stand for mockery or ridicule."

The Soviet Writers' Union did not communicate its concern to Soviet leader Gorbachev, Isaev said, because literature is an entity unto itself. Besides, "he has enough on his shoulders."

Isaev was one of four Soviet writers welcomed to Calgary and western Canada with a reception and white-hat ceremony at Mount Royal College. The others were novelist Victor Petelin, poet Olga Fokina and translator Alexander Vaschenko.

Novelist Vasilii Belov was absent because he was invited to join the Supreme Soviet Council shortly before he left home. He joined the delegation for the second part of a two-week visit that took the writers to Edmonton, the West Kootenays, Vancouver and Victoria.

The showcase of the sojourn was a two-day conference called "Writers In Their Society" at Selkirk College in Castlegar, British Columbia. Participating Canadian writers included W.D. Valgardson, Tom Wayman and Kristjana Gunnars.

Gordon Turner, head of language and literature at Selkirk, said the Soviet visit—the first part of an east-west exchange—was conceived at the college in 1987. The occasion was a festival dedicated to Leo Tolstoy, who at the turn of the century helped finance the emigration of Doukhobours from Russia to Canada.

Today, roughly 20,000 people of Russian descent inhabit the West Kootenays around Castlegar, Nelson, Trail and Grand Forks, Turner said. And some local schools teach Russian as a second language.

Isaev, a national figure in a country of 300 million people, and already a member of the Supreme Soviet Council, answered a question about Glasnost with a pun. "For a real writer it (Glasnost) is as necessary as a gift, a talent," he said, "because real talent cannot be without a voice." Glasnost, the translator explained, means "voiceness."

Vaschenko, who speaks excellent English, has a doctorate specializing in North American Indian literature. He said that the Soviet Union and Canada have geographical similarities (size and northerliness), and also historical and literary affinities.

This cultural exchange is overdue, he said, noting that in the past decade many American critics visited the university where he teaches, but only one Canadian "and that was by accident." Yet, during the past five years, he said, books by Margaret Laurence, Margaret Atwood and W.P. Kinsella have appeared in Russian.

Vaschenko had not read an article in *Books In Canada* magazine, in which author Douglas Glover described a sojourn in the Soviet Union. But he agreed with Glover that while Glasnost enabled publishers to bring out long-suppressed material, one side-effect was to clog the channels for contemporary work.

Petelin, who is both a literary critic and an historical novelist, drew a laugh when he said that he has visited Italy, Germany and Great Britain, but this is the first time his teenage son has ever asked him to get an autograph—that of Canadian writer Farley Mowat: "Can anyone here help me?"

58. Jean Auel: Queen Of The Blockbusters

In 1990, Chicago-born Jean M. Auel published The Plains Of Passage, *the fourth of a projected six novels in her best-selling "Earth's Children" saga.* The Plains, *which continues Auel's epic tale of prehistoric humans in Ice-Age Europe, leapt straight into the number-one spot on most bestsellers lists and stayed there. Sales of the saga have now topped the 20-million mark. Auel, who pronounces her name OWL, visited Calgary in 1986.*

An unemployed, 40-year-old mother of five was getting ready for bed one night in 1977 when she got an idea for a short story. Jean Auel had never written fiction, but she sat down at her kitchen table in Portland, Oregon, and roughed out a tale.

It was about a young woman who lived during the Ice Age, and Auel realized that she didn't know enough about the period to do her story justice. Next day she visited the public library to rectify this—and the rest is publishing history.

The story Auel sat down to write that night evolved into the six-volume "Earth's Children" saga. By 1986, three novels in the series had been published, all of them spectacular bestsellers—blockbusters. Sales figures, still exploding, were not available. But numbers of copies in print provided an indication of the saga's popularity: five million copies of *The Clan Of Cave Bear*, four million of *The Valley Of Horses*, and 2.5 million of *The Mammoth Hunters*.

The "Earth's Children" saga centres on Ayla, a Cro-Magnon girl adopted by a clan of Neanderthals after her own family perishes in an earthquake. And it follows her adventures with other peoples after the original Clan expels her. The saga's success stems from the characters (people love them) and the authenticity of its background.

Auel was in Calgary to promote the Bantam paperback edition of *Mammoth Hunters*. Her own story is almost as interesting as that of the fictional Ayla. Auel married when she was 18 and had five children before she was 25. By then, her husband was holding down a job and taking night courses, and Auel found herself reading his text books—everything from Aristotle and Plato to Jean-Paul Sartre and Simone de Beauvoir. When she discovered Betty Friedan's *The Feminine Mystique*, Auel said, "I was ready. Boy, was I ready. I realized, it's okay to stretch your intellect."

Auel went back to night school to study mathematics and physics. For 12 years she attended classes at the University of Portland, and in 1976 she received her Master of Business Administration. Meanwhile, she had been working for Tektronix, a computer company where her husband also toiled. She'd started as a clerk and worked her way up to credit manager, but after receiving her MBA she quit that job to hunt for something better.

Then came the short-story idea. After reading "about 50 books," Auel decided she had enough material for a novel, and sat down to write one. She had written some 250,000 words (the average novel contains fewer than 100,000) when she spotted an advertisement for a senior credit analyst with the Bank of California. "I just had to apply," she said. "It was everything I wanted."

After a series of interviews, the bank offered Auel an even more senior position. "I would have been reporting to a vice-president. But I knew I couldn't do that job and keep on writing. Only every time I thought about not finishing my story, I'd start to cry."

Auel turned down the job—even though the bank offered to match any other proposal. She committed herself to writing and went at it 16 hours a day. By the time she'd finished telling her story, she had written 450,000 words. But then, when she re-read the manuscript, she said, "I knew it was bad. I was so full of passion for this story, I just had to tell it right."

Auel went back to the library and checked out every book she could find on writing fiction. She realized then, she said, that in her 450,000-page manuscript, she had not one but six full novels. And she started again from the beginning, concentrating on "showing rather than telling." She finished *The Clan Of Cave Bear* in 1978, sent out query letters and sample chapters and received nothing but rejection slips.

Then, in the spring of 1979, she sent it to an agent she'd met briefly at a writers' conference. In July, the agent phoned and told Auel to sit down. She had just sold *The Clan Of Cave Bear* for an advance of $130,000—the highest ever paid for a first novel. (The agent has since topped her own mark.)

When *Cave Bear* appeared in 1980, it climbed onto the bestsellers lists and stayed there for 56 weeks). Auel's husband quit his job and became her business manager.

These days, the two of them live alone—their children are in their 20s and 30s, and have produced nine grandchildren—in a house overlooking the Pacific Ocean. When she's not on the road, Auel writes all night, every night: "Minimum six hours, though I usually try for 10."

What happens when she finishes Ayla's tale? "Oh, I have 247 ideas. There are other prehistoric eras, like the Neolithic and the Bronze. And there are so many interesting historical periods. I've also thought about doing something contemporary. And then there's the future."

59. Richard Ford: Travelling Man

In 1976, when American writer Richard Ford published his first novel, *A Piece Of My Heart*, reviewers called it a southern novel. "That's why I quit writing about the south," Ford says. "I wanted to create a body of work that was not localizable—that anybody who reads English could read. I didn't want to be classified as a western writer or a southern writer."

Ford set his second novel, *The Ultimate Good Luck*, in Mexico, and his third, *The Sportswriter*, in New Jersey. Then he produced an acclaimed book of stories, *Rock Springs*, and another novel, *Wildlife*, set in Montana.

Ford was in Calgary—"my wife and I ride my motorcycle, a big Harley, up here all the time"—to talk about this 1990 book. It's a deceptively quiet novel about a Montana teenager—now an adult—who sees his parents' marriage fall apart.

But before focusing on *Wildlife*, I should note that some literary critics are hailing Ford as the Ernest Hemingway of his generation. "With a single collection," one wrote of *Rock Springs*, "Richard Ford has established himself as the leading short story writer in the United States today."

Who is this tall, slim man who turns up in well-matched slacks and corduroy jacket, looking like an English professor and speaking with a hint of southern drawl? The key facts are on record.

Born in Jackson, Mississippi, Ford was eight when his salesman father had a heart attack and he went to live with his grandparents in Little Rock, Arkansas. His father died when he was 16—a fact which, once known, resonates in some of his fiction, certainly in *Wildlife*.

Ford has been writing since 1968, when he quit law school, went home to Arkansas and told his mother he was going to write fiction. Forthright, unassuming, Ford shrugged and declared: "I don't know why I did it. I was looking at a blank wall. Then a door opened, light came out and I walked toward that. It was that fundamental."

Ford has lived all over the United States—New York City, Chicago, Princeton. In southern California, he studied with novelist E.L. Doctorow. In Ann Arbor, Michigan, he completed a doctorate in English, while his wife Kristina—they met in 1962, married in '68—finished hers in urban planning.

Ford moved to Montana in 1983 when Kristina landed a job as town planner in Missoula. Four years later they rented a house near Great Falls—they live there still, though until recently they've spent part of each year in the French Quarter in New Orleans. They were leaving Louisiana for Mississippi, Ford said, mainly because "the political climate has changed radically in the last three or four years. Alberta is conservative, but Louisiana makes it look like Walden. They've got Ku Klux Klan members running for Senate."

Ah, the travelling life. The constant is writing.

Ford's work is memorable, not just for the lean precision of its language, almost poetic; but also for its wisdom, its emotional maturity—in a word, its voice, multi-faceted as it is.

A review of *Wildlife* in *The New York Times* mentioned Ford's story "Great Falls," which is found in *Rock Springs* and has a superficially similar plot. In both works an adult recalls himself as a teenager and explores how, as a result of his mother's infidelity, his parents' marriage fell apart. The reviewer suggested that this "supremely haunting" story has a mystery and a weight the novel lacks.

"Baloney!" Ford said, having rejected the first word that came to mind. "In 'Great Falls' I was trying to find a vocabulary for disintegration." He tapped *Wildlife*: "Here, I was seeking one for affection and understanding."

Yes, we're back to what distinguishes Ford from merely competent writers, to what elevates his work far above anything a plot summary can convey: precisely this attention to nuance, to tone and cadence and attitude.

"In 'Great Falls' the narrator doesn't really get it," Ford said. He flipped open a paperback copy of the book and read the story's final passage, in which the first-person narrator, looking back, can understand his parents' disaster—they are never reconciled—only by dismissing them as "low-life."

By comparison, Ford said, *Wildlife* explores "a much more complex set of relationships." And at the end—but that wouldn't be fair. "In 'Great Falls' I settled for less. The ending was bleaker than I liked. The bleakness of the ending of 'Great Falls' pushed me into writing this book."

Ford was looking forward to seeing *Bright Angel*, a movie based on two stories in *Rock Springs* —"Great Falls" and "Children"—and for which he had written the script. He was also gearing up to write a sequel to *The Sportswriter* called *Independence Day*. It will explore real estate and fatherhood, among other things, and will open in New Jersey and move elsewhere, though Ford didn't yet know where: "Maybe south, maybe west."

60. Andre Brink: Afrikaner In Paris

The work of South African writer Andre Brink resonates with startling implications in Canada, especially in the context of French-English relations. As an Afrikaner, Brink belongs to a tiny minority that feels it existence is threatened by a continental majority. Yet Brink has repudiated the almost monolithic thinking of his own people, arguing forcefully that individual rights and not collective ones must be the cornerstone on which any just society is built. The question is, can Quebec produce an Andre Brink?

"The devastating politics of apartheid," the white South African author was telling an audience of querulous Canadians, "engulfs every hidden, private corner of my existence as an individual. Where I live, where and what I teach, my association with friends and colleagues, the choice of a school for my children, the buying of a loaf of bread—the minutiae of my life and the privacies of my love are all invaded, every moment of my waking and sleeping life, by politics and the power structures from which it emanates."

By now, three minutes into the talk, the audience of about 150 writers had fallen silent. Andre Brink, visiting Calgary at the request of the Writers' Guild of Alberta, was knocking 'em dead, his English clear and clipped and grammatical, during a panel discussion on freedom of speech and the writer. "At one point, in 1974, when I was still writing exclusively in my mother tongue, Afrikaans, seeing myself completely cut off from my readership and forced into silence—which for a writer is tantamount to death—I discovered that censorship extends far beyond any legal formulation or codification of it. Where the possibility exists that books may be banned, the actual banning is the least of one's concerns as a writer."

Brink, the first Afrikaner writer ever to have a book banned in his native land, argued that the mere possibility of banning inhibits not only publishers but printers and booksellers: "It is the climate of uncertainty and fear surrounding censorship which in the long run becomes one of the most pernicious aspects of the practice—with the end result of writers inhibiting themselves."

The celebrated author took issue with members of the public who think "that censorship affects only a handful of writers—who may be potentially obnoxious anyway—without realizing that what is at stake is their own freedom—that is, the freedom of society at large: the freedom of choice. When that is taken away from us, when that is eroded or threatened, everything that constitutes our common and individual humanity is in danger. When we consent to that, either actively or by not resisting it, it is our own humanity that is insulted."

Brink, whose 13 novels have appeared in 26 languages, was one of the first Afrikaner writers to question apartheid, and became openly committed to the anti-apartheid struggle in the early 1970s. His subsequent novels—among them *Looking On Darkness* (1974), *An Instant In The Wind* (1976), *Rumors Of Rain* (1978), *The Wall Of The Plague* (1984) and *States Of Emergency* (1988)—have earned him acclaim internationally while at home his reception has been, well, mixed.

Twice Brink has been nominated for England's prestigious Booker Prize, and he has won the Martin Luther King Memorial Prize and France's Prix Medicis Etranger. In France, his recent novels have sold about 100,000 copies, while in Sweden they've topped the 250,000 mark. In 1989, Brink's novel *A Dry White Season* was made into a movie starring Donald Sutherland and Marlon Brando.

In South Africa, Brink has won the CNA, the country's highest literary award, three times. Yet, in the early '70s, he became the first Afrikaner to have a book banned. The novel was *Looking On Darkness*, which explores a multi-racial love triangle through the eyes of a "colored" actor who awaits execution for the murder of his white lover.

Published initially in Afrikaans, *Looking On Darkness* "was received with widely diverging attitudes," Brink said in a two-hour interview. "On the one hand it was absolutely acclaimed by the younger generation of readers. But it was totally rejected by the establishment—denounced from pulpits, burned in public, attacked by cabinet ministers. And then it was banned. It became the first Afrikaans book ever to be banned, which was a totally traumatic experience, because at that stage I was writing exclusively in Afrikaans. So my whole contact with readers was dependent on that. And suddenly there I found myself without a reader, which for a writer is kind of a spiritual death."

Andre Brink was born in a small South African village. His father was a magistrate, and for more than 20 years he led what he has described (in his 1983 book *Mapmakers: Writing In A State Of Siege*) as "a tranquil, almost uneventful life in a succession of small South African villages, all of them predominantly Afrikaans, all of them extremely conservative, all of them steeped in an almost Old Testament world of Calvinist rigorism." After school, Brink attended Potchefstroom University, a small, all-white institution in the South African hinterland—"a bastion of Calvinism." Then, at the age of 24, the would-be writer went off to Paris to study comparative literature at the Sorbonne.

Brink has written eloquently, again in *Mapmakers*, about his two years in Paris (1959-1961): "The simple experience of sitting down for a meal in a student restaurant and finding blacks at the same table, came as a shock." In Calgary, Brink said: "Those years opened me up completely toward everything that was happening in Europe at the time. I went over as a convinced, totally conditioned, conservative Afrikaner." He'd long since started writing, but had worked within the tradition of Afrikaans fiction. "It was all terribly realistic: droughts, poor whites, locusts—the sort of thing you got in American literature in the '30s."

In Paris, after the initial shock, "suddenly I discovered all the cross-currents of existentialism. Camus, Sartre—everything that was happening in Europe at the time. And that influenced very much my writing, and the writing of a whole group of Afrikaners. All of us had spent a shorter or longer period in Europe at that stage. The result in practical terms was that we started writing a European, a cosmopolitan literature. We were almost, or I certainly was, ashamed of my roots at that stage. I thought that my Afrikaner experience in South Africa was so backward and insignificant and uninteresting that I would rather write about what I had seen and lived through in Europe."

Having returned home and begun his second career as a university teacher, Brink did just that—most notably in a novel called *The Ambas-*

sador, first published in Afrikaans in 1963. The book was the highlight of what Brink later came to call his Sestiger phase, when he and a handful of other young writers, working to push back the boundaries of Afrikaans literature, became known as the Sestigers or Men of the '60s.

The initial fervor waned as Brink and the other Sestigers began to realize that they had been struggling to gain freedoms taken for granted everywhere else. "That, at least, was what it seemed like in the mid-'60s," Brink has written, "because we were still wary of admitting, even to ourselves, that in a totally politicized society like South Africa, we had simply not yet gone far enough. Our very 'literariness' was beginning to turn into our own enemy."

The year 1968 was a watershed for Brink. At the end of 1967, he'd again gone to Paris, this time with the intention of settling there permanently. "I wasn't married," he said, "and had no children (he now has four), and I just had no specific reason to remain in South Africa." Brink's best friend, the poet Breyten Breytenbach, lived in the French capital, "and I love the city above all others in the world."

"Then, of course," Brink continued, almost wistful, "'68 was '68 in Paris. One of the central issues involved in the whole tumultuous student movement was the relationship between the writer, the artist in general, and the whole community. So my whole perception of literature, of writing, changed drastically. I no longer viewed culture as a sort of elitist something, but as something which ties together the whole mass of a population. And I saw the necessity for a writer to take, to assume full moral and social responsibility for his writing, instead of just doing it in a little ivory tower. At the end of that year, I returned to South Africa, and from that moment everything I wrote took on this added dimension of the social/political."

Brink arrived home, transformed by French existentialism, "it was with an exhilarating rediscovery of my South African and African roots. I discovered that was the one thing I could write about which other writers, conditioned by Europe or America or wherever, didn't know anything about."

Brink wrote *Looking On Darkness*, and its banning, which he described as "one of the most revelatory experiences of my life," compelled him to start writing in English as a way of ensuring that he reached an audience—a practice he has followed ever since. "I still write in Afrikaans as well, but everything I write now, certainly fiction, I write in both languages, Afrikaans and English."

How does this work? "It varies from book to book. With *Looking On Darkness*, it was a matter of rewriting in English. But each book really determines the way in which it wants to be written. I might do certain portions in Afrikaans and others in English. When I wrote *A Chain Of Voices* for instance"—an historical novel about a revolt of South African slaves which is structurally reminiscent of William Faulkner's *As I Lay Dying*—"I wrote some voices in Afrikaans and some voices in English, to get different distances and textures of writing."

Now Brink is writing what he described as "a double-decker thing—a contemporary story grafted onto a long historical fiction. One of these I'm writing in English, the other in Afrikaans. Which means that afterwards, one has to disentangle two separate versions. What complicates things is that it's never a matter of simple translation. It's a total rewriting, a refeeling, a rethinking of the whole experience in the other language. That makes it very complicated and a very long process. Before *Looking On Darkness*, I used to write very fast. But from that book onwards, the whole process has slowed down, leading to about one book every two years, and now one book every three or four years."

Brink's most recent novel is *States Of Emergency*. The author wrote and set it in 1985, which an epigraph describes as "a watershed year" in South Africa. "It actually started late in 1984," Brink said, "with the introduction of the new tricameral parliament, which triggered a wave of violent resistance in the country worse than anything South Africa had known before."

The tricameral parliament, he explained, "was an attempt by the white apartheid government to draw into the framework of apartheid some more or less middle-of-the-road, moderate supporters from the Indian and so-called 'colored' community, the mixed-blood community, hoping that by bribing them into the system—which is really what it came down to—the base against the large black majority could be broadened.

"This meant on one hand that blacks felt more directly excluded from power than ever before, and the resentment and resistance became more violent. But even in the white and the colored and Indian communities, anger and resentment reached critical proportions, so more and more whites also were drawn into the anti-apartheid struggle. And given the kind of leadership we had in the country right then—P.W. Botha and his almost imperial style of ruling—everything was just beginning to subside into chaos, and there really seemed moments when the situation was becoming apocalyptic."

This went on through 1986, Brink said, and changed slightly from '87 to '88. But even with the government having declared a state of emergency, and using enormous state powers to crush the resistance, Brink said, "under the surface there were tensions building up which threatened a total volcanic explosion in the country. And this was only defused by the transition of leadership from Botha to De Klerk."

Against this real-life backdrop, or rather in the midst of it, Brink wrote *States Of Emergency*, which has at its heart a South African trying to write a love story while the country around him is going up in flames. The novel is postmodern in its questioning of the nature of narrative, and also in the way "real-life" violence intrudes on the writer's art. "I've always liked experimenting with new techniques, new approaches, new possibilities of writing," Brink said. "I think one of the greatest dangers a writer faces is repetitiveness, and so perhaps it was inevitable that I should try to explore this, a direction which I first explored many years ago in the '60s, in one of my Afrikaans novels which has never been translated.

"But in a sense the peculiar form of this book was dictated by the circumstances in which I wrote. I found myself in 1985 at the end of a very dark and difficult and sterile period in my writing. For three years I hadn't written anything at all—partly for personal reasons, but mainly because the whole political situation in the country had been deteriorating so much that my practical, everyday life was drawn into the problems the country was living through, so there simply was no time for writing. And so the mosaic form of shorter incidents and passages, reflections, quotations—

that whole form was really to take advantage of the situation in which I wrote—writing about the very problems which made it almost impossible for me to write."

About the future of South Africa, Brink is cautiously optimistic. The lifting of prohibitions on organizations like the African National Congress, followed by the freeing of Nelson Mandela, led to "a kind of euphoria that swept the country," Brink said. "Everybody was just elated by the sudden new hopes that seemed to stream into the vacuum. But we are at the beginning of a very difficult and dangerous period, where this euphoria, these hopes, these promises and possibilities now have to be translated into political and social realities."

❋❋❋

VI

Winds Of Change

Over the Sea of English blow the Winds of Change. In recent years, those Winds have brought us computer technology and the New Physics. The former is changing how, where and even what we write and publish. The latter is revolutionizing the way we think and perceive the world. But let's take them one at a time.

In 1985, yours truly—what can I say?—became the first *Calgary Herald* writer to send a story from home using a personal computer. I filed a review of a 674-page tome called *The Information Technology Revolution* directly into the newspaper's mainframe computer. In that review, I quoted editor Tom Forester: "If the automobile and airplane business had developed like the computer business," he'd written, "a Rolls Royce would cost $2.75 and run for three million miles on one gallon of gas. And a Boeing 767 would cost just $500 and circle the globe in 20 minutes on five gallons of gas."

Okay, so Forester sees cars and airplanes as emerging from the same business. Never mind. By 1991, many *Herald* writers —like those at other newspapers and in other businesses around the world—were using home computers equipped with modems to transmit stories over telephone lines from their living rooms and basements. This "teleworking" has not superseded the workplace, if only because many employees enjoy going into an office and most employers like having them there. Still, as an option, the electronic cottage has arrived. And writers, obviously, are among those most affected.

What? Just journalists? Not so. The word-processor has transformed the writing and editing, not just of articles but of books. To do a "complete rewrite" in 1980, using a typewriter, an author would have needed maybe six months. Today, using a word-processor and a hard disk, he can do a better job in six weeks. And I won't even get into the world of bulletin boards and on-line magazines.

The Computer Revolution is having an even greater impact on publishing. Ever since the 15th century, when movable type was invented, publishers have been specialists with access to expensive equipment. For hundreds of years well-financed experts have designed, typeset, pasted up and printed everything published: books, magazines, newsletters, sales brochures, concert notices, menus—the list is endless.

Desktop Publishing is changing all that, as people use personal computers to produce camera-ready pages complete with graphics and fancy type faces. And they're doing it cheaply and quickly. A publisher who, using conventional design, layout and typesetting methods, would have spent $1,000 to produce a 16-page newsletter, can now create it for roughly $150. Producing it the old way took 26 hours; the desktop publisher needs only eight.

In the mid-'80s, legendary Canadian publisher Jack McClelland denounced traditional publishing as "an incredibly slow and wasteful process that uses some of the most antiquated techniques on earth." He predicted that, within five years, Desktop Publishing systems would produce the majority of books. No figures are available. Probably McClelland spoke too soon. But the message is clear.

Skeptics argue that the type in the finished book is not as sharp-looking, not as clearly defined. This is because early laser-printers created 300 dots to the inch, while the average typesetting machine slaps in 2,500. Even then, to the untrained eye the difference was almost indistinguishable. And today, state-of-the-art laser printers create 2,200 dots to the inch. Consider the book you hold in your hand. Can you read this sentence? It's 800 dots to the inch.

Desktop Publishing is here to stay.

61. The Novel Meets Artificial Intelligence

In the mid-'80s I hailed the arrival of computerized "interactive fictions." Today I see that I underestimated the significance—and popularity—of spectacular graphics. (Check out King's Quest V on a VGA monitor.) Still, I think I was onto something. And that, eventually, a synthesis could emerge, gorgeous graphics and stylish language combining to create a new kind of literary experience.

Take an old-fashioned novel, cross it with a game of Snakes and Ladders and cram the result into a Rubik's Cube. Slap the whole thing onto a floppy disk, pop it into a personal computer and push a few buttons. Presto! You're lost in an "interactive fiction," an electronic novel in which you, the reader/player, take an active role, participating in the story by typing commands at a keyboard.

According to some computer buffs, interactive fiction is revolutionizing literature. Novelist and movie-maker Michael Crichton (*Congo, The Andromeda Strain*) calls it "the future of fiction." Douglas Adams, who helped create a computerized version of his best-selling *Hitchhiker's Guide To The Galaxy*, says interactive fiction is like film in the early 1900s: "It's a real novelty medium, and only the people doing them (interactive fictions) really know how great they are."

But let's distinguish between an interactive fiction and a text adventure—a fine distinction if ever there was one. A text adventure is a computerized puzzle and fantasy-oriented game built out of language. Players go on quests, typing in simple, two-word commands to unlock doors, cast spells, slay dragons and the like.

The earliest well-known text adventure was *Zork*, brought out by Infocom in 1979. Three years later, that same software company brought out the first interactive fiction—*Deadline*. In *Deadline*, players assume the role of a detective who must solve a murder; they search rooms, question suspects and make accusations. We're talking attention to plot and language, but more significantly secondary characters who move around, seemingly of their own volition—and with whom the detective can communicate.

The difference, then, is first one of emphasis. But it's also technical. Consider the choose-your-own adventure book, which relies on branching.

If you think your hero should do such-and-such, then turn to page 98; otherwise, go to page 84. What takes electronic novels beyond these do-it-yourself adventures—beyond branching—is the so-called parser.

The parser, which developed out of research into artificial intelligence, is the interface between the player and the story. It's that part of the program that classifies a player's input into words and phrases the computer "understands"—and to which it responds.

A simple parser will respond to two-word phrases such as SHOOT GUN or KILL DRAGON. A more sophisticated one will accommodate multiple-object commands like TAKE THE GUN, THE SCALPEL AND THE SWORD. And a state-of-the-art parser for interactive fiction will allow the user to address characters: WINGED WOMAN, GIVE ME A HINT ABOUT THE CAGE.

Infocom's parsers, featured in such releases as *Hitchhiker's Guide To The Galaxy*, *Cutthroats* and *Suspended*, "understood" between 600 and 1,000 words. A company called Synapse developed a parser that has a vocabulary of 1,600 words for use in an interactive fiction called *Mindwheel* by American poet Robert Pinsky. No doubt these are already old landmarks.

Infocom, Synapse and other companies have been using teams of writers and programmers to create their interactive fictions, or else to translate them from existing novels such as *Fahrenheit 451*, *Robots Of Dawn* and *Rendezvous With Rama*.

Other software houses have been designing tools that take care of the down-and-dirty programming, and thus enable writers to create their own electronic novels. These "interactive editors" are available from such software houses as CBS, Hayden, Millennium and Codewriter.

Trouble is, the parsers in these design tools aren't as sophisticated as those used at Infocom or Synapse. So it's impossible, as yet, for a writer working alone to compete with works released by those companies.

For interactive fiction to come into its own as a literary genre, the microcomputer revolution must continue to grow, so the potential audience becomes large enough to encourage investment. Programmers must radically improve parsers so players don't become frustrated by the game's inability to speak English. And writers must have access to high-quality "interactive editors" so software publishers can't monopolize the genre.

From where I stand, it looks as if all this is happening. By the year 2,010, interactive fiction may well be a recognized literary genre. You heard it here, if not first, at least early.

62. Superstrings And Cosmic Blueprints

Mainstream fiction has discovered the New Physics. Does it matter? Tremendously—but don't take my word for it. Check out recent novels by Margaret Atwood, Janette Turner Hospital and John Fowles. The first is set in Canada, the second mostly in Australia and the United States, the third in 18th-century England. The three works are wildly different in theme, structure and technique, yet they manifest an all-important similarity—the New Physics.

One of two epigraphs to Atwood's best-selling *Cat's Eye* comes from eminent physicist Stephen Hawking. In an author's note, Atwood acknowledges her indebtedness not only to Hawking but to three other physicists. And the first sentence of her novel—"Time is not a line but a dimension, like the dimensions of space"—draws attention to the New Physics.

Hospital's *Charades* is even more committed, and indeed celebrates the New Physics in both form and content. Quantum theory provides the novel's controlling metaphor—it evolves specifically from "Heisenberg's uncertainty principle"—and generates chapter headings alluding to matter and anti-matter, to wave mechanics and probability theory. And the book's elusive heroine has an affair with a world-famous physicist, a situation that enables Hospital to touch on everything from "grand unified theories" to the microseconds leading up to the Big Bang and even parallel dimensions.

Fowles's *A Maggot* is less obviously—but no less certainly—a product of the same scientific influences. Fowles takes pains to create an uncannily authentic 18th-century reality, and then introduces into this world technologies—movies, for example—that did not appear until the 20th century, or that have not yet been created. The maggot of the title is a time machine of some sort, but Fowles offers no explanations. He insists simply that the miraculous is real, and hints strongly at one of the more radical theories derived from quantum mechanics: that of parallel universes.

Leading scientists have been telling us for over a decade that the so-called "New Physics" is revolutionizing the way we look at the world. Now, obviously, serious mainstream novelists have started proclaiming the same message.

Of course, the revolution is everywhere. In May of 1989, *National Geographic* carried an illustrated, 20-page article entitled "Searching for the Secrets of Gravity." And Hawking's last book, *A Brief History Of Time: From The Big Bang To Black Holes*, rode bestsellers lists for well over a year.

What does it all mean? Science writers have suggested that we're witnessing the birth of a new consciousness, that the New Physics is changing our understanding of ourselves and our role in the universe. Forget what you learned in school about how an atom is an indivisible particle made up of a nucleus and one or more electrons. Turns out that, at the subatomic level, matter and motion are vague and unpredictable. Particles turn up in unexpected places without reason, and appear and disappear without warning. Our universe is not a mechanical watch but a multi-dimensional hologram, and the emerging world view features not only waves and particles but uncertainty principles, black holes and grand unified theories.

With all this, Hawking's *Brief History* is a good place to start. It's distinguished not only by its authority—many scientists regard Hawking as the most brilliant theoretical physicist since Einstein—but by its readability. The physicist has eschewed difficult mathematics, deliberately confining himself to a single equation—Einstein's famous $E=mc^2$—to write a layman's primer.

Hawking traces the development of our "world picture" from Aristotle to Galileo and Newton, and then outlines the two major contributions of the 20th century, ideas that have revolutionized classical physics. First, Einstein's general theory of relativity, which looks out at the cosmos, treating the structure of space-time and the nature of gravity. Second, quantum mechanics, which treats the extraordinarily tiny and has overturned classical ideas about the nature of matter. Here we encounter Heisenberg's uncertainty principle: the more accurately you measure the position of a particle, the less accurately you can measure its speed, and vice versa.

Hawking's bestseller identified the major themes of the New Physics, and for most readers that may be enough. Others will want to know that many scientists are extending these theories and trying to unify them with results that are furiously controversial. The closer one gets to the frontier, the fiercer the fighting.

Physicist Paul Davies, best-known as author of *God And The New Physics*, is an especially lucid science writer. In *The Cosmic Blueprint*, Davies drew on a welter of recent discoveries in diverse fields to demonstrate that matter and energy have the ability to organize themselves according to common holistic principals. He showed that matter develops toward progressively higher levels of organization and suggests that a "cosmic blueprint" governs the entire universe.

In his earlier book, *Superforce*, Davies focused on how quantum physics and cosmology have altered scientific understanding of the physical world and traced attempts to weave discoveries into one Grand Unified Theory. But Davies went further than Hawking into controversial areas, noting in passing that "those who enjoy science fiction cannot fail to find in the new physics a bonanza of weird ideas." Among these is the notion that space and time really consist of 11 dimensions, not four; and that, as gravity is a geometrical function of four-dimensional space-time, so invisible dimensions manifest themselves as forces such as electromagnetism and weak and strong nuclear forces.

Another readable writer who takes chances is Michael Talbot. In *Beyond The Quantum*, he explores the idea that quantum particles are projections of a deeper, multi-dimensional reality, and argues that scientific discoveries cry out for research into paranormal phenomena.

In *The Tao Of Physics*, Fritof Capra approached all this from another direction. Capra explored the parallels between the New Physics and ancient eastern religion (Hinduism, Buddhism and Taoism). Both stress the interconnectedness of all things, argue that space and time are constructs of the mind and insist on the vital significance of the observer. For the modern physicist, Shiva's dance is the dance of subatomic matter. Capra also noted, almost incidentally, that the new interconnectedness "raises the intriguing possibility of relating subatomic physics to Jungian psychology and, perhaps, even to parapsychology."

Yet another approach surfaced in *Beyond Einstein* by Dr. Michio Kaku and Jennifer Trainer. The authors provided a coherent overview of the New Physics and then advanced one unified theory over others—that of superstrings. This is a combination of string theory, according to which matter is ultimately composed not of particles but of tiny strings that form loops and circles; and of supersymmetry, a mathematical theory large enough, apparently, to encompass all current knowledge in physics. The authors claim that Superstrings is the only grand unified theory not contradicted by any current knowledge.

From here things just get wilder.

American physicist Fred Alan Wolf won an American Book Award for his early book *Taking The Quantum Leap*. In his next, *Star Wave*, Wolf applied quantum physics to the study of human consciousness and the mind. He argued that the future shapes our lives and not the past. And he posited a particular "unified theory" involving parallel universes.

This he developed further in his latest book, *Parallel Universes*, which merrily kicks sand in the face of common sense. Wolf argues that an infinite number of worlds exist all around us, some of them closely resembling our own. He uses this idea to unite the theories of quantum physics and relativity: black holes become gateways of information between universes, alter egos pop into existence at the flip of a coin and time travellers make history.

Wolf is a good writer whose excitement is palpable, but he's also demanding. Those who lack a background in mathematics will find him difficult, if not impossible. But he points in passing to the relation between science and fiction, offering a mini-review of Ursula Le Guin's SF classic *The Lathe Of Heaven*, which he calls "one of the best science fiction books dealing with how mind enters a parallel world" through dreaming. Published in 1971, but still available in paperback, Le Guin's book takes place in 2002 and focuses on a man who moves between parallel worlds—incidentally changing them—simply by dreaming lucidly. Dr. Who fans will feel at home.

Right or wrong, Wolf is mightily suggestive. He observes that parallel-universe theory might account for UFOs—and that takes us even further afield, to *Dimensions: A Casebook Of Alien Contact* by Jacques Vallee. Vallee is the real-life model for the character of the French scientist in Steven Spielberg's classic movie *Close Encounters Of The Third Kind.*

He is an astrophysicist by training, a computer scientist by profession. Here he outlines numerous historically unexplainable incidents to explode the visitors-from-outer-space hypothesis and argue that the parallel-universe theory could in fact explain such incidents: that UFO phenomena represent evidence for dimensions beyond our conventional space-time. Vallee alludes to the religious dimension of all such "close encounters," lauding the Spielberg movie for expressing this but noting that "it has been captured in the most complete and artistic form in John Fowles's extraordinary masterpiece, *A Maggot,* published in 1986."

That brings us full circle and, not incidentally, face to face with the truism that Art has always developed in tandem with consciousness. Mainstream fiction has discovered the New Physics. It matters.

***

Cease-fire

Tomorrow's Canada

63. Postscript For A Quebec Separatist

To: *Monsieur Jean Larose*
Author of *La Petite Noirceur*

So, Monsieur Larose. You never responded to my letter. You must have seen it because I sent copies to the publisher of your book, to *Liberte* magazine, to *Le Devoir*, to novelist Yves Beauchemin—to everyone I could think of. No response. But no matter. I didn't expect one. Look! Blatantly snubbed, I punch out this postscript.

I realize that you don't care, Monsieur Larose, but I'm no longer angry. Placid stupidity, indeed. Big dumb Canada. Vulgar and primitive. I'm glad you launched that attack. If you hadn't, I never would have written this book. So thank you!

Thank you for reminding me that culture is politics, that creating literature is making war, and that every time a Quebec separatist puts pen to paper he assumes a monolithic "English Canada" into existence and a multifarious culture out of it. I needed to be reminded that a diverse literary community is flourishing in Canada. It's a community of writers and publishers and booksellers, but also of readers, a community for whom words like "referendum" and "free trade" and "Meech Lake" and "Oka" have resonance, whatever language they're written in, and however differently we respond.

Thank you for reminding me of the vigor, the vision and the vitality of contemporary Canadian literature, and that, in a myriad of ways, writers like Margaret Atwood and George Bowering and Mordecai Richler are storming barricades both at home and abroad. I needed to be reminded that Canada is part of an international community, that it's situated on the Sea of English and open to daring seafarers like Salman Rushdie and J.P. Donleavy and Richard Ford, to reckless sailors like Jerzy Kosinski and Andre Brink and, yes, Jack Kerouac!

Thank you for reminding me that here a multicultural, North American alternative is taking shape. How did John Dutton put it? "In 1970 one out of 360 Calgarians was a member of a visible minority. By 1988 that had changed to one out of six." As with Calgary, Monsieur Larose, so with Canada. But Dutton, director of the Calgary Public Library, was introducing a panel discussion called "Cultural Diversity: Visions for the '90s."

Katherine Govier, a native Albertan whose books include *Between Men* and *Before And After*, said Canadian writers who surfaced in the 1980s—many of them from other cultures—haven't received the attention they deserve: "The canon of Canadian literature is in desperate need of renovation." Govier cited Tomson Highway, Sharon Butala, Sandra Birdsell, Neil Bissoondath and Bharati Mukerjee—"even though she's left the country."

Lee Maracle, the native Indian author of *I Am A Woman*, evoked the strongest response from the predominantly female audience by talking about "the intimate agony of native women." Maracle offered some cogent examples of how language can be used as an oppressive tool. A white town has a mayor, she said, "but we have 'a chief'—and that has negative connotations. You have 'alder persons,' but we have 'village headmen.' You have 'formal attire'; we have 'full regalia.'"

Gail Scott, a Montreal writer, said that in Quebec, "everyone's a minority." Scott described herself as "completely sympathetic to the cultural aspirations of the Quebecois," and argued that "writers from a dominant culture have to be prepared to listen." At times she seemed almost to apologize for writing in English in Quebec, as when she wondered aloud whether it's possible in that province to take seriously an anglophone narrator.

Familiar themes? To a Canadian, certainly. Multiculturalism, native-white, English-French. Come what may, these themes will continue to shape life in the northern half of this continent. And so to figure in Canadian literature.

Thank you, too, Monsieur Larose, for reminding me of the victories that Albertans have won in the past decade—collective victories on the home front that have transformed the province's literary infrastructure, individual ones in the international arena by writers as different as W.P. Kinsella and Aritha van Herk and Pauline Gedge.

And the emergence of an Alberta-based national vision! If not entirely new, that vision is being articulated with unprecedented panache. I think of *Breakup: Why The West Feels Left Out Of Canada*. I think of David Kilgour's *Inside Outer Canada*. I think of publisher Mel Hurtig— Tomorrow's Canadian.

Two months after I wrote you, Monsieur Larose, I received a copy of Hurtig's five-volume *Junior Encyclopedia Of Canada*. I reviewed it enthusiastically, noting that *Junior* shows its real value when you turn to something like the crisis at Oka: "Did any American TV station broadcast more than a few words about it? Does any American encyclopedia provide a context within which to understand it? Check out *Junior*. A separate entry under Iroquois tells us that Mohawks and Francophone Quebecers have been at odds since the 1650s...."

Before I wrote about *Junior*, though, I checked my files. And turned up a story I'd written five years before, when Hurtig brought out *The Canadian Encyclopedia*.

> What an experience it is to flip through this work for the first time. It's an encyclopedia, damn it! With all the authority, weight and resonance that implies. And at the same time it's so Canadian—so jubilantly, so triumphantly our own.

> No references here to American constitutional amendments, no long essays on the historical significance of 16th-century British poets. Instead, we find elucidations of our own obscure wranglings, musings on our own forgotten heroes. These are the places we come from, the issues we hotly debate, the politicians we love to hate.

> This encyclopedia is alive! I discovered it first flip. On my way to Richler, Mordecai, I found myself repeatedly distracted, diverted. See the color photo of Michael Ondaatje! And here's an entry on Montreal's Place des Arts. What's this about Prescott, Ontario? And look! Oscar Peterson!

Talk about harbingers! While re-reading that review, Monsieur Larose, I recalled that I'd also done an article for Calgary *Sunday* magazine on the making of the encyclopedia. Hurtig was still working out of his famously dreadful office located beneath an underpass in a quasi-industrial section of Edmonton. That's where I interviewed him and discovered that the encyclopedia was a 15-year-old dream come true. That Hurtig had envisioned the work in the early 1970s and approached the Canada Council for help.

"They loved the idea," he told me. "But after we'd spent $14,000 of our own money on planning and going to meetings in Montreal and Ottawa, they said we had to do a French edition simultaneously. We got back to them with a budget for that and they said, 'Great! But we can't afford it.'"

Flash forward to 1979. Hurtig heard that the Alberta government was going to spend $75 million celebrating its 75th birthday the following year. He told those in charge: "Listen, instead of spending all this money on ourselves, why don't we give Canada the gift of a brand new Canadian encyclopedia? You put up the seed money and we'll give a set to every library and school in the country as a gift from the people of Alberta."

Eventually, the government put up $3.4 million for development and $600,000 for free sets. That was a third of what Hurtig needed. And among eastern bankers he ran into skepticism and worse. Then came betrayals and marketing mishaps. But the man persevered. He even lined up a Quebec publisher—*Les editions Alain Stanke*—and, along with the Alberta government, gave away the French-language rights, waiving all royalties.

Why do I rehearse all this, Monsieur Larose? Because Mel Hurtig is not just a man with a vision. He's a symbol, a personification. Relentless, unstoppable, a survivor of setbacks, he's a flesh-and-blood visitor from Tomorrow's Canada. Thank you for reminding me, Monsieur Larose, that Tomorrow's Canada is here today—whether Quebec knows it or not.

But I'm getting ahead of my argument.

Late in 1990, Laurier LaPierre published *1759: The Battle For Canada.* It's a controversial recreation of a key moment in Canadian history, the battle of the Plains of Abraham. The Vancouver-based ex-Quebecer, who became famous in the '60s as co-host of the TV program "This Hour Has Seven Days," spurned the historian's documentary approach to employ the techniques of the novelist.

Hence the controversy. But the significance of the book lay in its thesis: that the battle was really between France and England—two European nations—and 68,000 Canadians, who had been living in Quebec for two to four generations, were its incidental victims.

Those Canadians, LaPierre told me in Calgary, were abandoned by France, not defeated by England. LaPierre put it this way: "Ultimately the Canadians declared themselves for Canada. They chose to save the land."

You see, Monsieur Larose, why I consider LaPierre's book a good omen? It repudiates a favorite Quebec nationalist myth at a fundamental level. The so-called Conquest didn't destroy but rather created the Quebecois—certain of my ancestors among them.

And here's Michel Vastel in Calgary late in 1990, expressing second thoughts about *The Outsider: The Life Of Pierre Trudeau*, a book-length hatchet job he did on the former prime minister. "I got scared at times this summer," Vastel told me. "Scared that Trudeau just might be proven right. Maybe Quebec does have to be protected against itself."

Vastel was alluding to the Mohawk Crisis, and specifically to the stone-throwing incident at the Mercier Bridge, which revealed the dark underside of Quebec nationalism. As you know, Trudeau has always insisted that any nationalism has racist undertones, and that the best hope for the future of the world is the federal, multi-national state.

"I'm a journalist, not an historian," Vastel said, "and my book is somewhat shaped by current events. If I were writing it today, I might write some parts differently."

For Vastel, the Meech Lake debacle brought a major insight: "English Canada is not a monolithic society!" This realization puts an odd spin on the separatist thesis that Canada is essentially a compact between two founding peoples. As Vastel put it: "Quebec has no partner to discuss with."

That realization implies a huge advance over your own revealed assumptions, Monsieur Larose. But can it be read as another good omen? As a harbinger that Quebec will come to its senses? No, I think not. And if, as I believe, Quebecers are bent on rejecting the optimism of LaPierre, the second thoughts of Vastel, if they wish to turn their backs on their patrimony, on a Canada they helped create, so be it.

Surprised, Monsieur Larose?

In my original letter, I declared Quebec independence a non-starter. Now I think separation would be traumatic for all Canadians, tragic for Quebecers. But it looms like the lesser of two evils. The greater would be the deconstruction of this country, the de-nationalization of Canada.

Culturally speaking, Canada can survive without Quebec. Writing this book has convinced me of that. Whether the country can survive *with* Quebec is now the question. Canada's literary culture has flourished since the early 1960s precisely because the federal government has supported it through institutions like the CBC, the Canada Council and the Department of Communications. Any attempt to dismantle national support programs —either to satisfy Quebec, the United States or confused, New-Right Canadians—represents an attack on the essence of Canada and a threat to our continued survival.

But let's bring our war metaphor into the bosom of the family, where Quebec plays the troubled teenage brother. He and a number of siblings live in a roomy old house that their now-dead parents bought years ago with borrowed money. Times are tough and mortgage payments high. But by sticking together and pooling their resources, the siblings have been able to keep the house, which is secretly coveted by wealthier neighbors.

Trouble is, teenage brother has been having tantrums. He's got a part-time job, contributes to the family kitty and says this gives him the right to play rock music full-blast until three o'clock in the morning—and that includes week-nights. The whole family is being disrupted, its survival threatened (can't sleep, can't work). But if teenage brother doesn't get his way, he says he'll move out.

His siblings love this kid. Some of them try to talk sense to him. By living here, they tell him, you've been sheltered, protected from countless slings and arrows. And you've been paying a reduced rent. Stick with us and you can afford to attend university. You can become a doctor, a lawyer—anything you want.

But the kid, who stacks lumber in a sawmill, remains adamant. He's got to have rock music at three in the morning. "Build me a sound-proof room!" he cries. "Each of you guys can have one too!"

The more patient siblings explain that they don't need sound-proof rooms. That if they spend their money building sound-proof rooms, they won't be able to meet the mortgage payments.

"You're rejecting me!" the kid cries. "Besides, anybody who doesn't like rock music is boring. I'm out of here! I'm taking my sound system and I'm gone!"

"Hey, you want to go?" So says the sibling who loves the kid most—but the family's togetherness even more. "You're a damn fool, but go! Go! Maybe with you gone we'll get some peace around here, be able to get on with our lives."

"Okay, I'm gone," teenage brother says, "but I'm taking the car. Also the TV and the fridge and the microwave. You guys can keep the washer and dryer. That's fair. I'll drop off my laundry once a week when I come to collect my allowance...."

You'll understand, Monsieur Larose, that teenage brother is in for a rude awakening? That problems loom? No, I won't turn my back on Maritimers or Quebec Anglophones any more than I'd allow a tantrum-throwing teenager to load up the family car and drive off. Yes, we'll be discussing corridors and boundaries and the fact that, if Canada is divisible, so is Quebec.

But, hey, these matters we can resolve. Monsieur Larose, you've kept me awake one too many nights. And writing this book has been cathartic. I see now that Canada doesn't need Quebec, and I'm tired of playing The Quebec Game (a separatist stars as the bad cop, a federalist as the good one, and Canada makes a false—and costly—confession).

Of course I'm torn. But if you're leaving, Monsieur Larose, the sooner you go, the better. You've sapped enough of our energies. We're especially tired of turning the other cheek. Maybe Canadian writers will at last get the respect they deserve here at home, because finally we'll be able to celebrate ourselves without having to worry about offending you. Without having to listen to a continual stream of politically motivated denigrations.

But culture is politics, after all, and because I love the sound of it, I want to shout it once aloud: CANADA DOESN'T NEED QUEBEC! Look at our literature! Vigor, vision, vitality—we've got it all. Everything we need to thrive as an independent country. Hey, if it weren't for Quebec, the free-trade deal would never have happened.

What's that? No, our current prime minister won't be negotiating for anybody, not if Canadians have anything to say about it. Though perhaps you'd like him to speak for you? After all, he's just another good cop from Quebec. Another would-be builder of sound-proof rooms.

Anyway, our final offer is on the table. It's called Canada, Monsieur Larose. Renovations are possible, but sound-proof rooms are out. What? Not good enough? Sorry you feel that way. Put your keys on the kitchen table. Also the keys to the family car.

NOW TAKE YOUR SOUND SYSTEM AND GET OUT!

Ah, that feels good.

To you, Monsieur Larose, I bid farewell.

To my brothers and sisters, I say: Think of it! No more, "Big, dumb Canada." No more, "Canada, what a bore!" We're young! We're rich! We can build a startling tomorrow! How many peoples get a chance like this one? How many generations? Look! The hills are alive with warriors! They've taken cities. They've taken provinces. "Vulgar?" "Primitive?" *Au contraire*. They're celebrated in foreign capitals! And look! Look! The Sea of English is thronged with sailboats, with well-wishers arriving from around the world. Well-wishers who want to help us build Tomorrow's Canada.

Monsieur Larose! Good luck!

*** ***

Sources

In writing this book, the author has quoted, revised and updated articles that appeared first in the *Calgary Herald*. He has also drawn on pieces he wrote for *Books In Canada* and *Quill & Quire*. The dates below, listed by section, refer to the *Herald* unless another publication is specified.

1. July 14, 1990.
2. December 13, 1987
3. March 9, 1986
4. January 10, 1988
5. November 4, 1989
6. November 28, 1985, September 14, 1988
7. October 30, 1981, *Sunday magazine*: September 15, 1985, October 9, 1985, October 27, 1988
8. October 30, 1986
9. September 24, 1989
10. June 2, 1990
11. May 29, 1988, November 28, 1981
12. November 19, 1986
13. May 13, 1984
14. February 10, 1990
15. *Quill & Quire*: June, 1990
16. November 19, 1990, December 5, 1981, December 9, 1984, November 17, 1986, September 8, 1989
17. June 9, 1990
18. *Books In Canada*: June/July, 1987, (November 8, 1980)
19. February 24, 1989
20. March 18, 1989
21. October 31, 1989, October 2, 1983, June 12, 1988
22. June 16, 1990
23. April 21, 1990
24. *Books In Canada*: January/February, 1989
25. October 20, 1980
26. April 27, 1981
27. *Sunday magazine*: November 30, 1986
28. May 27, 1989, October 18, 1980, April 23, 1983, December 15, 1985)
29. May 16, 1981, April 3, 1982, April 5, 1986

30. April 30, 1986

31. *Quill & Quire*: Spring, 1987

32. June 11, 1985, *Books In Canada*: August/September, 1987

33. *Quill & Quire*: June 1986

34. October 27, 1985

35. *Quill & Quire*: June, 1988

36. January 21, 1989

37. May 12, 1990, April 7, 1988

38. April 15, 1989

39. September 29, 1990

40. March 10, 1990

41. July 28, 1990

42. *Quill & Quire*: Spring, 1989

43. *Quill & Quire*: March, 1991

44. March 9, 1991

45. October 10, 1987

46. October 10, 1987

47. November 5, 1985

48. October 18, 1988

49. October 23, 1988

50. October 19, 1988

51. September 27, 1989

52. September 30, 1989

53. October 7, 1989

54. *Quill & Quire*: April, 1988

55. February 3, 1988

56. February 4, 1988

57. May 12, 1989

58. November 27, 1986

59. October 27, 1990

60. *Books In Canada*: August/September, 1990

61. August 3, 1985

62. May 27, 1989

63. September 8, 1990, October 13, 1990, June 23, 1985, April 23, 1990, November 25, 1990,

Index

Printed in Canada